THE ROMAN HOUSE IN BRITAIN

THE ROMAN HOUSE IN BRITAIN

Dominic Perring

Routledge
Taylor & Francis Group

LONDON AND NEW YORK

First published 2002
by Routledge
2 Park Square, Milton Park, Abingdon, Oxon, OX14 4RN

Simultaneously published in the USA and Canada
by Routledge
270 Madison Ave, New York NY 10016

Routledge is an imprint of the Taylor & Francis Group

Transferred to Digital Printing 2009

Typeset in Garamond by Exe Valley Dataset Ltd, Exeter

British Library Cataloguing in Publication Data
A catalogue record for this book is available from the British Library

Library of Congress Cataloging in Publication Data

Perring, Dominic.
The Roman house in Britain / Dominic Perring.
p. cm.
Includes bibliographical references and index.
1. Great Britain–Antiquities, Roman. 2. Dwellings–Great Britain–History–
To 500. 3. Architecture, Domestic–Great Britain. 4. Architecture, Roman–
Great Britain. 5. Romans–Great Britain. I. Title.

DA145.P45 2002
728'.09361–dc21 2001049230

ISBN10: 0-415-22198-6 (hbk)
ISBN10: 0-415-48878-8 (pbk)

ISBN13: 978-0-415-22198-6 (hbk)
ISBN13: 978-0-415-48878-5 (pbk)

CONTENTS

FIGURES

FIGURES

PREFACE

There is something deeply fascinating about other people's houses. They offer a glimpse of other lives, of other ways of living. Archaeology affords many opportunities for such curiosity. My own research into Roman houses started over twenty years ago, when excavating sites in the City of London. I was both impressed and perplexed by the variety of the buildings that had so rapidly filled this town after the Claudian conquest of Britain. This diversity demanded description and explanation. How had such a varied architectural tradition sprung into being? And why were the houses of London so similar and yet so different to houses in other parts of the Roman world? This initial interest in London's Roman architecture formed the starting point for a doctoral thesis, which spread to include the rest of Roman Britain. Although it has been rewarding to concentrate on the detailed evidence of a particular province, I am equally interested in the world within which this architecture developed. This is a study of Roman provincial culture, with Britain as its focus.

My interests and objectives have evolved as the work has progressed. Description remains a goal. I think that it is useful to know how houses looked, how they were designed and built. So I have tried to present a detailed review of the available information. Several studies have tried to make sense of the evidence of just one kind of house: villas are a particular favourite. Other surveys have concentrated on aspects of design and decoration, such as mosaics and wall paintings. But there is still no study dedicated to the Roman house in Britain. This book is intended to fill the gap. It provides a thorough description of the Roman domestic architecture of this frontier province, to set in contrast with more general surveys of houses in Italy and the empire at large.

But this is not just a textbook of description. The purpose of description is to progress towards understanding. How were these buildings used? What ideas inspired their design? What can they tell us about the changing nature of society? In the first instance this has meant attempting to identify the uses to which the different parts of the Romano-British house were put. This has not been easy and some of my suggestions may not survive the test of time, but I have tried to find the dining rooms and bedrooms hidden within house plans. In this process of trying to rediscover how Romano-British houses were used I have become convinced that this can only be done through reference to the contemporary sources that describe the architecture of other provinces and regions. Most recent research has tended to seek explanation for the peculiarities of Romano-British architecture in local tradition. This has helped focus attention on the ways in which Roman culture may have been differently interpreted in this ill-documented province. But the approach has also marginalised important sources of contextual evidence found in the writings of ancient authors and the evidence of Mediterranean architectural traditions. In my view this has encouraged a view of Romano-British culture that understates its subordination to ideas common to an aristocratic class throughout the empire. My emphasis here, therefore, is on the imported and urban traditions that witness the influence of empire on province. In order to review the role of Rome in the creation of Britain's first urban society this book gives more weight to the evidence of literary sources than is currently fashionable.

The architecture is a critical source of evidence if we are to understand the ways in which British society responded to the rule of Rome. I argue that Roman architecture gained currency in Britain because of its relevance to new political structures that were erected in the wake of conquest, although I am less certain that this reflects any fundamental shift in the economic basis of social power. Here I explain that the first Roman houses in Britain were architectural imports, influenced by military fashion. But the period *c.* AD 70 to AD 150 witnessed a rapid stylistic development that resulted in a range of local interpretations of Romano-Hellenistic architectural style. Each town and each region in the province developed its own version of the Roman house. Patrons, architects and craftsmen combined to make original contributions to how Roman life should be lived. These identities belonged to discrete and different communities. From this evidence we can build arguments about how power was obtained and manifested, and about how elite society was formed and developed over more than three centuries.

Houses expressed authority, and this book attempts to reveal some of the ideological conceits that may have structured their design. Roman houses were also places of ritual and ceremony. This was one of the reasons why they were sometimes so richly decorated with paintings and mosaics. Ritual is a difficult subject for archaeological study, since it is uncomfortably easy to build speculative interpretations that cannot be supported by the data. This too is an area where there are ancient sources that can be plundered for information with rewarding results, although it remains the case that such sources were not concerned with Britain but Roman culture at large. One suggestion advanced here, that Gnostic belief may have had an influence on the development of Christian worship, has some interesting implications that go far beyond the subject matter of this book. Somewhat reluctantly I have tried to curtail my departures into these extraneous matters in order to retain focus on the subject in hand. Regardless of the identification of the particular belief systems represented in the architecture, a strong case can be built to suggest that parts of some houses were designed against the need of cult practice. This domestic architecture in turn appears to have exercised a vital influence on the development of church architecture.

In sum, therefore, this is a book with two goals. It offers a description of the fabric and form of an important class of Romano-British artefact: the house. It also presents some arguments about how these artefacts were used and what this tells us about the ideas and circumstances of the people who used them.

Acknowledgements

Countless friends and colleagues have helped me in the intermittent studies that led to the writing of this book. Richard Reece first introduced me to many of the ideas with which I have struggled here, and I owe him an enormous intellectual debt. John Schofield and Steve Roskams offered unstinting support during my studies of Roman London, and John Wacher and Andrew Wallace-Hadrill pointed me in useful directions during the first years of my doctoral research at Leciester University. David Mattingly, Sarah Scott, Tom Blagg and Ray Laurence suggested useful improvements to the thesis that eventually emerged. Subsequent pub arguments with Mark Whyman and other friends at the University of York have helped me escape the limitations of that work and given my thoughts final shape. Along the way Hugh Chapman, Mick Jones, Mike McCarthy, Alan McWhirr, Ralph Merrifield, Nick Pearson, Ken Quarlman, Peter Rowsome and Brian Yule were all kind enough to keep me abreast of aspects of their own research. My greatest debts are to family and friends who have suffered the consequences of my selfish distraction with this project. I am unable to properly thank all those who have helped in this regard, but can single-out Tim Williams who is a supporting force in all that I do.

Illustrations presented here are reproduced courtesy of the Society of Antiquaries of London (figs 6, 44, 49, 51 and 66), English Heritage (fig. 33), the Museum of London (figs 12, 29, 34–6, 38, 42–3, 45, 47 and 50), the Trustees of the British Museum (fig. 46), the Colchester Archaeological Trust (figs 37 and 41), Mike McCarthy Carlisle Archaeology Ltd (figs 30, 31, 32 and 40), the Yorkshire Museum (fig. 64), the Society for the Promotion of Roman Studies (figs 14 and 15), Corinium Musem (fig. 18), and Yale University Press (fig. 3). Other line drawings were prepared with considerable help from Stefania Perring.

Errors are bound to remain. In some cases these will be the consequence of my stubborn rejection of wiser council, and in others the result of the unchecked introduction of ill-considered revisions. I am already aware of one problem that cannot easily be corrected. My use of ancient sources has generally relied on published translations from Latin and Greek originals. I made extensive use of the parallel texts in the Loeb Classical Library but also found useful material in source books and other secondary sources (especially Gardner and Wiedemann 1991). I have additionally exploited on-line libraries available through the world wide web (such as the Gnostic Society Library). Unfortunately I failed to take adequate note of the source of the translations and editions consulted, and cannot therefore give proper credit on such matters where this is due.

1

INTRODUCTION

Rome made aggressive use of buildings. Few societies have so richly documented their social arrangements, their beliefs and their vanities in architectural form. The lavishly decorated Roman house with its hierarchical use of space, its command of the contemporary landscape and its complex use of classical form was rich with meaning. The first purpose of this chapter is to consider why architecture was so important to Rome. Why were houses so vocal and what kind of messages were intended?

Space in the Roman world was closely measured, mapped and regulated. The ordering of space was necessarily hierarchical and the Roman landscape was regimented by a series of potent boundaries: dividing sacred from profane, urban from rural, and domestic from public. The considered drawing of boundaries was not only practically necessary, but was accorded ritual significance deriving from archaic Roman and Etruscan practice. This fixation with spatial order can be seen in many ways. It found expression in the grid-plans of new urban foundations. It was represented in the centuriation of territories attached to colonial settlements, where landscapes were measured out in a chequer-board of regular plots. It was manifest in the use of imposing town walls and frontier works to mark boundaries. It was reflected in the close adherence to street and property boundaries that characterised formal Roman settlements, and it was a principal concern of Roman law and cadastral documentation.

The city was itself a ritual enclosure, within which sacred laws enabled the government of civic affairs. The concept of boundary and the sanctity of the *urbs* were powerful instruments in shaping social behaviour. Rykwert has drawn attention to the potency of the town boundary and the way in which entering through the gates of a city could be seen as a religious act (1976: 137–9). Such boundaries needed to be marked, and hence the importance attached to gates, doorways and arches in the Roman world. Concepts of procession, entry and penetration were integral to the social and spatial order established within Roman cities, and the built environment presented a variety of contrived settings in which rituals of passage and induction could

1

take place. This can be seen in the religious and triumphal processions of Rome, where celebrants navigated a ritual landscape in a series of liminal leaps. Such concepts were readily imported into the house: in so many regards an idealised and rationalised form of urban space.

The aristocratic house stood at the heart of a controlled landscape. Land was both the reward of power and the means by which it could be sustained. Monuments declared rights of possession. Walls, gates, signs and paths established physical controls over space. Boundaries were marked to facilitate the division of land, the resolution of property disputes and the assessment of taxation liability. Although these features can be described in purely practical terms, they also reflected an essential concern with man's place in the natural landscape. Every boundary imposed human order on an uncertain world. Every house was a carefully contrived landmark.

One of the most constant refrains in Roman architecture was that of nature shaped, subdued and dominated. This was in part a poetic exaltation of civilised man's supremacy over wilderness and disorder, a theme close to the heart of many Latin authors and a philosophical justification for Rome's imperial mission. But it also reflected a sensible awareness of the fragility of prosperity. Famine was a constant threat; and the ability to produce and store surplus both legitimated temporal power and bought allegiance. The landscape of design celebrated the privileged access to the wealth on which the *pax Romana* was built. Granaries and barns were given monumental emphasis to better boast the rewards of harvest. Images and inscriptions invoked the gods of abundance and good fortune whose favours were courted. Fountains and animated fishponds were carefully placed to catch the eye, and promised life and renewal. Mosaics and paintings vividly illustrated man's control of nature, through images of the hunt and of beasts tamed in the amphitheatre or at the hands of the gods. Surplus was not just a gift of Roman engineering, but of Roman peace and of Roman gods. Allegory, history and myth made allusive reference to these powerful arguments.

The proof of surplus was also paraded in lordly largess, and this was made most conspicuously evident at the dinner table. Lofty dining rooms were as much a symbol of wealth as lofty granaries. This architecture of plenty was eloquent propaganda for the status quo. The exposition and articulation of worldly influence was therefore a central feature of the Roman house. Buildings incorporated numerous references, some symbolic others explicit, which testified to rank and status. The importance of architecture in social affairs is richly documented in the written sources. To take just one example the letters of Pliny, writing about Italy in the first century AD, include frequent detailed descriptions of his property, the very purpose of which was to advertise his cultural and economic status (Bodel 1997).

Houses did not simply declare wealth and importance through ostentation. One of the main purposes of the many-roomed private mansion was to provide settings for the controlled social encounters from which political and economic life was built. Houses were vehicles for the exercise of patronage. Their architecture exploited a hierarchy of cultural references that spoke differently to different audiences. Elite society subscribed to a complex range of beliefs and values. The palaces of the rich and powerful communicated an ideological message, in which the owner's status and learning was a key motif. Roman mythology, history and religion were exploited to this end in murals and mosaics. These images enhanced status by vaunting learning, taste and sophistication. The first-century Roman author Petronius offers a waspish satire of such pretension in his description of dinner with Trimalchio, and the houses of Pompeii provide numerous vivid examples of the reality on which this was based (Wallace-Hadrill 1994, Clarke 1991).

Roman order involved maintaining a balance, a harmony, between forces. Such harmony was both expressed and promoted by order, and the Roman house was designed not just for mortal use, but with a view to the place of man in the order of things. Divine forces were present in the affairs of men and were catered for in the design of domestic space. Domestic space was sacred and potent. Roman world order found reflection in architectural order. Leone, in a groundbreaking study of Georgian architectural refinement in eighteenth century Virginia (1984), argued that the rules of classical design generated an environment that was meant to appear fixed and inevitable. The premise is that ideology takes social relations and makes them appear resident in nature or history, giving them a veneer of permanence that protects them from challenge. Aristocratic society is perhaps most concerned with the virtues of order at times of greater stress and insecurity.

Architecture and meaning

Houses dominated the Roman social landscape even more than they dominated the physical one. They were seats of power and stages for the performance of domestic ritual. Contemporary sources help us understand how some such houses might have been used, but the evidence is highly partial and not always reliable. In Britain we only have the evidence of the buildings themselves. This evidence is not always easy to read, and scholars have reached conflicting conclusions about its significance. The argument developed in this book is that Romano-British houses served broadly similar functions to houses in other provinces of the empire, and that they witness both the cultural hegemony of Rome and the heterogeneous and changing nature of Roman identities. However the evidence is read, it is clear that message was intended. It should therefore be possible to reconstruct social arrangements from the evidence of the house plans.

In the design of houses, as with any other artefact, meaning can involve a complex series of references, ranging from the self-explanatory to the impenetrably obscure. Space has curious properties. Not only can it be measured and drawn, with plans and elevations to represent architectural conceits and the bounded realms of geometric entity, but it is also experienced. Voyages through space are described temporally as well as spatially, and they create different layers of understanding. The house is an event and a journey, as much as it is an artefact and a monument. Post-modern thinking has brought these issues to the fore, and encouraged diverse approaches to our reading of landscape and site. Writers such as Henri Lefebvre (1991) and Edward Soja (1996) have given impetus to a research community intent on reconceptualising space. Most current studies recognise that space is temporal and that buildings present ideological arguments.

Each society must develop a common and coherent language of building design, since houses need to be used and understood by a variety of players through a range of daily performances. The social use of space depends on shared knowledge and common practice, although such systems of understanding are often stratified and segmented. Ritual and routine articulate domestic and political life. Roman hegemony drew on beliefs and understandings built from a Hellenistic cultural language shared by much of the empire. These affiliations facilitated the construction of the complex relationships of obligation and dependency through which power was channelled and government effected. The root source of power was property, and the architecture of property was a critical component of the shared knowledge that bound Roman elite society.

Representations of space derived from this shared knowledge witness conformity with the Roman order. Lefebvre has argued (1991) that the spatial practices of society, the routines and rituals of daily life, result in conceptualisations of space made manifest in architectural practice. These architectural ideas in turn generate the space experienced, where social relationships are articulated through systems of symbols and signs. Lefebvre believes that each mode of production (ancient, feudal and capitalist) had its own spatial order, and that shifts from one system to another necessarily involved the creation of new types of space. Changing ideologies reflect and reinforce changes in the structure of social and economic power, and these place different demands on architecture.

Nothing more clearly marked the passage of Roman rule in Britain than the introduction, manipulation and subsequent rejection of the architectural fashions described in this book. The architecture that we describe as Roman was the product of a particular understanding of space. Such architecture carried ideological meaning and contributed to both the creation and replication of a power that was qualitatively and quantitatively different to that which came before and after. The archaeological evidence of consumption and display leaves little doubt that elite society was better able to extract surplus and accumulate wealth under Rome than previously. This is not, however, to say that shifts in architectural design simply mirror transformations in the economic modes of production or the basis of social power. It is possible to argue that the choices that made architecture Roman as opposed to British reflected changes in the manifestation of power rather than its economic basis. In other words, power might always have been based on the ownership of land and the command of rents and taxes but that the way in which power was represented in the landscape was reconfigured with the changes in allegiance provoked by Rome. Choices made about political affiliation and elite cultural identity are made in the context of the nature of social control over modes of production, but the correlation is not direct. The architecture described in this book witnesses the disruption of traditional systems of expressing power and the construction of new expressions of identity. These transformations may indeed have been the consequence of a changing approach to the command of economic surplus and may also have served as a catalyst to such change, but this was not necessarily so.

Houses are exciting things to study because they sit at this boundary between cultural and economic, between personal and collective, between real and imagined. These machines of wood and brick were fashioned for the smooth ordering of domestic affairs within a prevailing social orthodoxy. Genius was not unbound. Various factors influenced the design of these houses, and contributed to the articulation of their morphological and decorative language. Some of these factors are fundamental: such as the constraints imposed by site and setting, by the climate and by the laws of physics. Resource availability also had an important impact, both in terms of access to building materials and labour, although such limitations can generally be overcome through the accumulation of wealth. In most circumstances cultural factors were more important in the design choices that were made. Household and family structure has been a favoured topic in some of the more recent studies of Roman housing (e.g. Hingley 1990 and J.T. Smith 1997). Houses incorporate traditional, ritual and otherwise socially embedded design fashions. Such traditions can be established remarkably swiftly in order to establish a required level of cultural precedent. Within agreed norms, peer group and rank competition can drive a dynamic imitative fashion. Above all houses represent systems of belief. If functional concerns were paramount, then houses would look the same the world over. The things that make houses similar and dissimilar are the ideas – the rules, assumptions and fashions – that govern social behaviour.

Space and symbol can be read differently by different groups. Uses are not fixed, and space can mean different things at different times of the day to different users. Buildings are not only shaped by society but impose constraints on subsequent social actions. Different forms of behaviour are made more or less appropriate by the suitability of the surroundings. It therefore follows that the spatial arrangements of a house can shed light on contemporary perceptions of social organisation. Architectural fashion, in particular in the field of interior design, contributes to definitions of social and cultural identity. There is a tension in the evolution of such fashion. The need to conform to the expectations and norms of a peer group can be offset by desire to imitate fashions of greater social cachet, and will also be influenced by the degree to which individual identity can be expressed within the externally established parameters. Houses are usually the products of many hands, and their design may involve negotiation between disparate interests: those of architect, builder, client, owner, tenant, neighbouring landowners and the community at large. Houses are often transformed by different generations of tenants, and can have different meanings to different people at different times. The bolder an original architectural statement, the more likely it is to change in impact and meaning as circumstances change. The process of redundancy can be as telling as the process of creation.

The recovery of meaning is further complicated by the limits of archaeological inference. In order to extract a rewarding degree of sense from the houses of Roman Britain it is necessary to make certain assumptions about the language that is being used. These assumptions can be tested through continued application, and proved in the face of alternative interpretative models, but should not be mistaken for an objective reality.

The nature of the evidence from Roman Britain

Rome held sway in Britain for nearly four hundred years, and much happened during this time. Britannia was an invention of Rome and the province a mosaic of different peoples and places. So although there are elements of unity and continuity that make it possible to treat Britain as a coherent subject of study, it is important to realise that we are not dealing with a single set of values and understandings. Different parts of Britain had different experiences of Rome and these changed through time. Everywhere the institutions and apparatus of fourth-century rule differed fundamentally to those that had supported the initial conquest. This diversity was expressed in the architecture.

The subjection of Britain was undertaken in stages. After the invasion ordered by the emperor Claudius in AD 43 the legions moved north and west in a series of campaigns. The Romanisation of the southeastern part of the island was soon underway, although the revolt of Boudicca in AD 60 interrupted progress. Further conquest was delayed until the accession of the emperor Vespasian in AD 69. The Flavian period (AD 69–96) was characterised by busy military activity in the north and by programmes of civilian construction in the south. The northernmost campaigns, undertaken in the 80s, took conquest to the Scottish highlands before a retreat to more-or-less fixed frontiers resulting in the construction of Hadrian's wall in the early second century. Many parts of northern Britain remained dominated by the presence of the army, down to the abandonment of the beleaguered isle in the early fifth century. In the south a civil administration developed, based on a series of towns. The plantation of veteran colonies at Colchester, Lincoln, Gloucester and York gave impetus to the process of urbanisation. Others towns provided administrative centres for local communities based on pre-existing tribal divisions.

In its early days Rome conceived of its empire as a subject federation of self-governing city states, most of which paid tribute in exchange for peace and security. A provincial governor took overall responsibility for the administration of justice and held a monopoly of force, but otherwise Roman rule relied on the active participation of local landowners to serve as magistrates and raise taxes. This curial class obtained its status from the ownership of land, and was reinforced in its position of power through association with Rome and access to the benefits of imperial patronage. No significant administrative or economic distinction was drawn between town and country. Wealth derived from the produce of country, but political power and social status were usually reinforced through urban institutions. An important landowner needed somewhere to live at the heart of his country estates, as well as a place near to the courts and clubs of town. These elite residences are the villas and town houses with which this book is most closely concerned (fig. 1).

It seems somewhat churlish to complain that Romano-British houses survive only as ruins, it could hardly be otherwise! There are, however, ruins and ruins, and one of the key problems to confront in this study is the scarcity of complete plans, especially from dated urban contexts. The lack of detailed stratigraphic accounts of the development of town houses is in part a reflection of the absence of any modern, large-scale, excavation of such structures. Most recent investigations have been driven by the requirements of rescue excavation. Since it is rare in the extreme for a modern building plot to coincide with an ancient one those buildings excavated within the constraints of rescue archaeology have been recorded as fragments only. There are thousands of these building fragments, frequently well studied and tightly dated, but their value is limited by their incomplete nature.

The more complete plans available for study derive from earlier programmes of research that took place on green-field sites, such as the abandoned towns of Silchester (*Calleva Atrebatum*, near Reading), *Verulamium* (by St Albans) and Caerwent (*Venta Silurum*) in Monmouthshire, or on deserted villa sites. The bias of the evidence is towards the more monumental buildings that were easier to recognise and more attractive to study. Research techniques were comparatively primitive when many of these sites were dug, and the published reports lack detail. Most of the houses identified in these programmes of work cannot be dated reliably, and evidence for timber and earth constructions was often missed. It is also unusual to have detailed information on earlier sequences since only the latest buildings were fully exposed. There is a further problem to address in

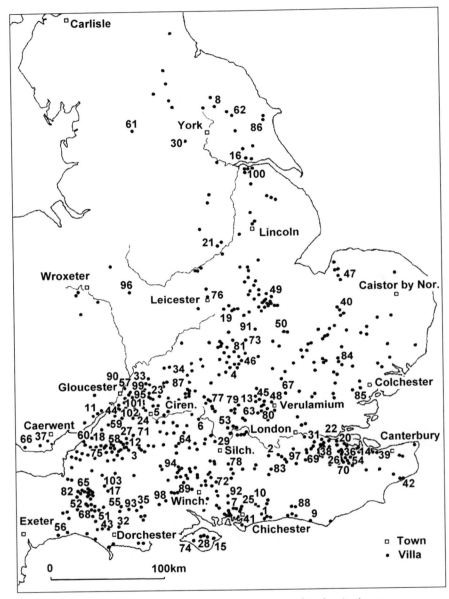

Figure 1 Villas and towns in Roman Britain, showing sites referred to in the text.

the interpretation of these later Roman buildings: because of the comparative longevity of their use the surviving remains will usually incorporate many phases of reconstruction and redecoration. The published evidence does not show how much the buildings had been altered during their use. It is usually the case that where we have good evidence for building plan we have poor evidence for building sequence.

Even where more complete building plans have been recovered it is unusual for the walls to have survived to a sufficient height throughout the building to provide a complete set of doorways. Of all the Roman buildings excavated in Britain, only one, the Roman villa at Newport on the Isle of Wight (fig. 67), appears to present a plan complete in all relevant detail at ground floor level. Even here it is not possible to establish whether

---

Key to Figure 1

1. Angmering
2. Ashtead Common
3. Atworth
4. Bancroft
5. Barnsley Park
6. Barton Court Farm
7. Batten Hanger (Elsted)
8. Beadlam
9. Beddingham, Preston Court
10. Bignor
11. Boughspring, Tidenham
12. Box
13. Boxmoor
14. Boxted
15. Brading
16. Brantingham
17. Bratton Seymour
18. Brislington
19. Brixworth
20. Burham
21. Carsington
22. Chalk
23. Chedworth
24. Cherington
25. Chilgrove
26. Cobham Park
27. Colerne
28. Combley
29. Cox Green
30. Dalton Parlours
31. Darenth
32. Dewlish
33. Ditches (Woodmancote)

34. Ditchley
35. Downton
36. Eccles
37. Ely
38. Farningham
39. Faversham
40. Feltwell
41. Fishbourne
42. Folkestone
43. Frampton
44. Frocester Court
45. Gadebridge Park
46. Gayhurst
47. Gayton Thorpe
48. Gorhambury
49. Great Casterton
50. Great Staughton
51. Halstock
52. Ham Hill
53. Hambledon
54. Hartlip
55. Hinton St Mary
56. Holcombe
57. Hucclecote
58. Keynsham
59. Kingscote
60. Kingsweston
61. Kirk Sink
62. Langton
63. Latimer
64. Littlecote Park
65. Littleton
66. Llantwit Major
67. Lockleys, Welwyn
68. Lufton

69. Lullingstone
70. Maidstone
71. Marshfield
72. Meonstoke
73. Mileoak
74. Newport
75. Newton St Loe
76. Norfolk Street
77. North Leigh
78. North Warnborough
79. Northchurch
80. Park Street
81. Piddington
82. Pitney
83. Rapsley, Ewhurst
84. Ridgwell
85. Rivenhall
86. Rudston
87. Shakenoak
88. Southwick
89. Sparsholt
90. Spoonley Wood
91. Stanwick (Redlands Farm)
92. Stroud, Petersfield
93. Tarrant Hinton
94. Thruxton
95. Turkdean
96. Wall
97. Walton on the hill
98. West Park, Rockbourne
99. Whittington Court
100. Winterton
101. Witcombe
102. Woodchester
103. Wraxall

or not the building had an upper floor. Fifty or so other buildings present plans which require only a modest amount of reconstruction in order to give a similar level of detail, but this remains a small and partial sample.

It is not possible to propose realistic estimates of the number of Roman houses built in Britain. A recent survey of rural Britain listed some 2,250 Roman period buildings, most of which were of a high status character (Scott 1993). It is likely that a list of building fragments found in Roman towns and roadside settlements would be of similar length. This sample, although numerically large, forms a small and unrepresentative sample of the original population. Only a small minority of the provincial population would have lived in towns; and it has been estimated that even in southern Britain villas did not form more than 15 per cent of the total number of settlements (Hingley 1989: 4).

But the bias of the evidence lends itself to the interests of this study. More complex structures involve more complex and more socially revealing uses of space. There is more chance of understanding some part of a building's meaning where there is a larger architectural vocabulary. Here we are more concerned with the nature of elite society, than with the circumstances of the rural poor.

Ways of describing space

Various approaches to the study of space have been adopted in archaeological studies, especially since Clarke's pioneering, if flawed, work on the study of the prehistoric settlement at Glastonbury (Clarke 1972). As with any typological study, the base requirement of spatial analysis is to develop a descriptive language that permits the identification of common patterns from a confused body of information. In the study of houses spatial information can be reduced to two primary ingredients: units of space, such as rooms and gardens, and the pathways that articulate those spaces. Descriptions of buildings must work from a description of units of space, and find ways of expressing how those spaces are linked. From these ingredients descriptive hierarchies can be established in which patterns are identified, from which the social and economic uses of the buildings might be understood.

For the purposes of this study, this means giving most of our attention to the different types of rooms that have been found in Romano-British houses. Some rooms contain several discrete spaces of separate character. Early Christian iconography, such as the church mosaics and reliquaries of north Italy, suggests that curtains and wall hangings were frequently used to divide and frame space. Unfortunately the evidence described here is not of a quality to permit analysis of these more subtle distinctions.

The following characteristics seem to be most useful in describing Romano-British houses, and contribute to the identification of room function and status:

10

1   Size and proportion (width: length measurements and surface area)
2   Decoration (pavement and wall finishes)
3   Heating (hypocausts and hearths)
4   Fittings (apses, ovens, etc.)
5   Accessibility (distance from the main building entrance/public spaces, and ease of accessibility from other rooms within the building)
6   Permeability (number and width of doorways/openings)
7   Association (relationship to adjacent areas and spaces).

The measurement of these aspects of design introduces many variables and the consequent complexity can frustrate description. There is wide diversity, both in the layout and decoration of individual rooms and in the building plans.

Ordinarily an architect describes space by function, and this is a proper objective of this study. This demands that assumptions be made about the activities that took place. The problems of such an approach are legion (see Allison 1993). In proposing typologies predicated on the assumption that different functions attached to different spaces, it is important to remember that there would have been flexibility in the use of domestic space. An illustration is found in the letters of Pliny (*Letters*: 2,17), who refers to a room that could serve either as a large bedroom (*cubiculum*) or as a moderate-sized dining room (*cenatio*). The characteristics of this room were such that either use was possible. Roman furniture was portable and room use could easily be transformed.

In palatial houses rooms can be set aside for highly specialised functions, and the presence of these may in turn reduce the functional range of adjacent chambers. The specialisation of space and the creation of redundancy can be used to demonstrate wealth and status, and does not always need functional explanation (Riggsby 1997: 54). On the other hand, cramped properties may see several activities compressed into a single space. There was considerable scope for the aggregation and segregation of activities. These considerations frustrate the search for common patterns.

The analysis of finds distributions appears to offer an alternative means of describing spatial variation. The potential of such studies is considerable in contexts where there is a close association between objects and the places where they are found. Recent studies of artefact distribution at Pompeii have done much to illustrate the value that such studies can have in adding to our understanding of patterns of occupation within buildings, not least by challenging our preconceptions (Allison 1993). Hoffman (1995) also has used variations in the distribution of features and finds within barrack blocks to define different areas of functional activity within Romano-British forts. This has shown a concentration of higher status finds in areas with higher status architectural features.

A detailed study has been made of the evidence of artefact distribution within the aisled Roman building found at Lodge Farm, North Warnborough (Hants). Complex models of social arrangements have been built on the evidence of the 'artefactual signature' of this building (Hingley 1989: 43–5 following Applebaum 1972). These approaches are undoubtedly worth pursuing but are fraught with difficulty because of the many assumptions that must be made in order to exploit the evidence (see Smith 1997: 37 for a critique). Most artefacts end up in middens and rubbish pits, and are not left to lie on the floors where they were used. Old rubbish set in the foundations of new floors tells us little about how those floors were used. Where rubbish is allowed to accumulate this suggests some form of abandonment, and the activities of such phases are likely to be atypical. It is, of course, useful for the purposes of this study to know which areas were kept clean, and which received rubbish, but in most cases meaning cannot be taken much beyond this level. The evidence of the finds is more evidently worth pursuing where assemblages are likely to have been abandoned at their place of use. In particular, fire destruction horizons repay attention. Even in these instances care needs to be exercised in ascribing meaning to the finds.

In recent studies more attention has been given to the pathways that linked different rooms, than to the ways in which the rooms were used. This reflects the influence of the work of Hillier and Hanson (1984) who developed various methods for representing and measuring space. These are concerned with describing the relationships between elementary spaces in the formation of more complex structures, and have gained considerable popularity in archaeological studies (e.g. Foster 1989, Laurence 1994a: 115–16). The ideas advanced by Hillier and Hanson are over-dependent on ideal-types, present over-simplified accounts of the processes by which spatial complexity is generated, and cannot provide an all-embracing theory of settlement morphology (Leach 1978). They have, however, significantly expanded the descriptive language available. One of the most useful techniques that Hillier and Hanson describe ('gamma analysis') involves the analysis of flow diagrams within buildings ('justified permeability maps'). These diagrams illustrate pathways between rooms and spaces ('cells'), and their analysis provides a measure of how easily any given room could be reached from elsewhere within the house ('relative asymmetry'). Such analysis can reveal patterns of relationships that are not immediately evident from plans, and this can reflect on the ways in which the houses were used. The study by Grahame (1997) of the House of the Faun at Pompeii is a splendid example of what can be achieved through the intelligent use of this approach. Physical constraints also have a critical influence on building layout. In particular narrow urban plots are likely to demand greater internal permeability because of the problems of arranging external lateral access (Brown 1990: 99). Unfortunately flow diagrams can only be reconstructed for a small minority of Romano-British houses because of the limitations of the evidence (fig. 60).

In this volume buildings are described in three ways: by the general characteristics of building morphology (Chapter 4), by the ways in which they were built and decorated (Chapters 5 to 7) and by the range of activities they were designed to house (Chapters 8 to 11). This evidence is drawn on to discuss the social practices and domestic arrangements that characterised Romano-British elite society. In reviewing possible meanings it is first necessary to look to the ancient world at large in order to identify similarities and contrasts that might cast light on the Romano-British evidence. Our main interest here is in tracing the extent to which the classical world provides a valid model for the interpretation of Romano-British houses. This is the purpose of Chapter 2. This concentrates on the evidence of Roman Italy, but also explores a range of other architectural traditions that might have influenced Romano-British fashion.

2

HOUSING IN THE ANCIENT WORLD

Romano-British houses took inspiration from the Mediterranean world. These foreign ideas may have been transformed in the process of transmission, but they remained a powerful influence in all aspects of Romano-British design. Baths, wall paintings, tile roofs, mosaics, colonnades and a host of other architectural features arrived in Britain in the wake of the Roman conquest. The purpose of this chapter is to set the British evidence in this wider context. By exploring the origins of classical house types, we can describe those features of elite architecture that emerged from the Hellenistic east to influence Roman provincial fashion. The aim is to show that Roman architecture was not just of Rome, but part of a broader Romano-Hellenistic culture that shared certain common approaches and concepts.

Notwithstanding the vital mediatory influence of Etruscan and Italian architecture, Rome's was a regional variant of Hellenistic culture (Kuttner 1993). The traditions of palatial architecture involving complex hierarchies of spatial arrangements and interior design were introduced to Europe from the eastern end of the Mediterranean. Elements of the design of Bronze Age palaces were repeated in the houses of the wealthy throughout antiquity. One of the most significant building types of the Greek Bronze Age was the megaron, a hall entered through a porch flanked by columns. This building form established several of the principles that continued to influence Greek, Hellenistic and Roman building design: in particular the importance of a formal facade and a hierarchical use of space to guide the visitor to principal reception areas. Features that can be traced back to the Bronze Age include courtyard layouts, the widespread use of wall paintings and the provision of private bathrooms.

Asian architectural traditions, from which the Greek ones were essentially derived, were extensively drawn upon. Intriguingly a sixth-century BC palace building at the Aeolic city of Larisa, essentially a megaron in imitation of a Persian form of palace known as a *bit hilani*, presented a facade of a porch with a colonnade linking two square corner towers containing stairs (Lawrence 1973: 239). This has an uncanny, if largely coincidental,

14

resemblance to the winged-corridor villa that was the dominant building type in Roman Britain some thousand years later. These oriental traditions played an important part in the evolution of the courtyard house, the archetypal house in cities around the Mediterranean throughout antiquity, and continued to exert a strong influence on building design along the eastern and southern littoral of the Mediterranean long after the fall of Rome.

Examples of this Greek domestic architecture have been studied in the planned fifth-century town of Olynthus. The street blocks here were divided into a series of adjoining courtyard houses; each about 20 m square and built with mud brick walls set over stone footings (Robinson 1946). Typically these houses contained six or seven rooms set behind a veranda arranged around two sides of a courtyard. There was no axial symmetry to the layout of these buildings, in which the entrance to the courtyard was flanked by a small porter's lodge. The main dining room or *Andron* was located at one corner of the house, where light could be taken from more than one side. Classical sources have been used to suggest that such houses were separated into men's and women's quarters (*andronitis* and *gunaikonitis*), although this is difficult to identify from the archaeological evidence (Jameson 1990: 104, Nevett 1994).

The courtyard house proved a remarkably resilient building type, and changed little over a period of some thousand years, notwithstanding wide-ranging changes in many spheres of life. Several features drawn from the domestic architecture of this period were to exercise an influence that can eventually be traced into the houses of Roman Britain. The most important of these were the veranda overlooking the courtyard, and the emphasis placed on a corner dining room.

The *atrium*-peristyle house

For much of its history ancient Rome favoured a different style of domestic architecture: the *atrium*-peristyle house. No houses of this type were built in Britain, but their study offers clues as to the ways in which domestic space was conceived in the Roman world at large, as well as an illustration of the adaptation of Hellenistic forms to create a distinctive regional architecture.

There is presently too little in the way of good archaeological data to confidently describe the origins and evolution of Roman house forms (but see Wallace-Hadrill 1997: 221). It seems likely, however, that Etruscan and Italian departures from regional traditions of Iron Age building design were inspired by Hellenic models imported to Italy by way of the Greek settlements in south Italy. This took place in the orientalising period of the eighth and seventh centuries BC (Boethius 1978: 75–94). The replacement of circular timber structures with rectangular structures built first in timber and then with stone footings, as at Veii (Ward-Perkins 1959), finds close parallel in Britain's own orientalising period after the Roman conquest.

By the end of the seventh century large courtyard buildings appear on some sites in central Italy. The villa-like complex at Murlo near Siena is an important example (Holloway 1994: 55–9). This high status tile-roofed building covered an area approximately 60 m square, with ranges of rooms reached from a portico built around three sides of the central courtyard. In Rome itself the main period of change dates to the late seventh and early sixth centuries, at a time when the city is supposed to have been under Etruscan rule. Previously houses here consisted of oval and sub-timber huts of the type found on the Palatine hill (Puglisi 1951). Subsequently ashlar-walled and tile-roofed buildings were increasingly in evidence. Excavation of the Regia in the Roman Forum has revealed a sequence of two- and three-roomed structures set behind a portico within a courtyard: a house type identified on several other sites of this period (Holloway 1994: 63, Brown 1974–5: 15–36).

The *atrium*-peristyle house probably developed in central Italy at about this time, and recent excavations alongside Rome's via Sacra have revealed an example of the form dating to the sixth century BC (Carandini 1990). There is no direct parallel for this building type from the eastern Mediterranean or North Africa, although the open spaces of the courtyard buildings from this region may be more similar in character and function to the *atrium* than has been supposed (Allison 1993: 6–7, Wallace-Hadrill 1997). Two strands of evidence are generally brought to bear in the description this class of structure. Many hundreds of such buildings, buried by the eruption of Vesuvius in AD 79, have been excavated at the sites of Pompeii and Herculaneum. This archaeological evidence is supplemented by the writings of Vitruvius *c.* AD 25 (*On Architecture*). The evidence from these sources is not wholly consistent, and this has caused problems where the documentary information is used uncritically. None the less a particular regional variant of a Roman and Italian tradition of domestic architecture can be described.

These buildings were dominated by a single large covered forecourt (*atrium*), which was rarely entirely roofed-over and often contained a central basin for water catchment (*impluvium*). The *atrium* provided access to a series of smaller rooms around its margins. Early texts suggest that it was the focus of many household activities, including cooking and weaving, and was where the household shrine was located. The *atrium* can therefore be described as a type of hall. Later republican buildings were additionally equipped with a large open garden surrounded by a colonnade towards the rear of the building. This was the peristyle. The introduction of the colonnaded garden is considered to have been inspired by Greek practice, and at Pompeii to date to the period after *c.* 180 BC (Boethius 1978: 187). Three stages of architectural evolution can be proposed (Dickmann 1997). Prior to the introduction of the peristyle the *atrium* served as the principal focus of the house in much the same fashion as the central courtyards of contemporary Hellenistic houses. Subsequently the Pompeian peristyle was treated as an additional facility: a courtyard added to the rear of the house and chiefly suitable for the promenade (*ambulatio*). By the end of the second century BC, however, the peristyle was more likely to be surrounded by the main rooms of the house, and had become an integral part of the reception and circulation space that distinguished higher status houses. Dickmann convincingly argues that the peristyle was more important as an area for perambulation than as a corridor giving access to private rooms.

Notwithstanding problems in the interpretation of room function, and the evidence for widespread divergence from the ideal type, the principal elements of the Vitruvian house can be recognised in many Pompeiian buildings. The House of the Faun at Pompeii is perhaps the most famous example (fig. 2). Such houses offered an ordered progression from the street, where entrance was gained through a narrow passage sometimes described as the *fauces*, or 'throat' of the building (although this term may be inappropriate, Leach 1997: 53). This led into the covered forecourt (*atrium*) sometimes flanked by one or two wings (*alae*). A reception room (*tablinum*) was frequently placed centrally opposite the entrance, and divided the forecourt from the garden beyond. The main rooms of the house surrounded the garden. Forecourt and garden provided light and focus for the surrounding reception rooms, and allowed for free circulation through the house. At the time of the eruption at Pompeii the forecourt and adjacent reception rooms (including the *tablinum*), seemed to have lost in importance to the peristyle garden and surrounding rooms. The evolution of this building type in Italy after AD 79 is less well documented. Although the Severan (early third century), marble plan of Rome (the *Formae Urbis Romanae*), illustrates several buildings of *atrium*-peristyle form, many of these would have been survivals from earlier periods (Rodríguez-Almeida 1981).

The arrangement and decoration of these Pompeiian houses was designed

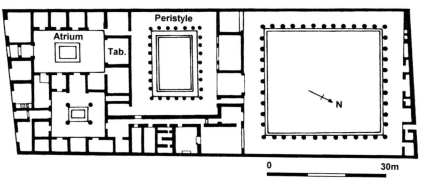

Figure 2 An *atrium*-peristyle house: the House of the Faun at Pompeii (after Sear 1982).

to emphasise the importance of certain vistas, and a series of focal points providing framed views can be found in many buildings. Garden features and wall paintings had particular use in this regard. Light entering the house from both forecourt and garden drew attention to such views, the most commonly significant one of which was obtained from the entrance. A similar emphasis on aspect and vista was central to the design of Romano-British houses.

The wealth of information recovered from Pompeii and Herculaneum must properly inform any general study of Roman housing, but the limitations of such evidence are legion. It is in particular unfortunate that the spatial and temporal range of the available information is so narrow. One of the most interesting aspects of the archaeological study of houses is the prospect it offers to study social change. The evidence for change at Pompeii and Herculaneum can only be interpreted with difficulty and cannot be taken beyond AD 79.

A body of documentary evidence supplements the archaeological study of these type-sites. Sources include the writings of Vitruvius, Pliny, Petrarch and Juvenal. These texts are literary constructs and were not intended to provide factual evidence on house design (Bergmann 1995: 408). There are therefore problems in relating such evidence to the less perfect but more representative sample of housing revealed by archaeology.

The social activities that took place in this type of house are well documented. Roman literature makes frequent reference to the entertainment of clients and friends. A contrast can be drawn with Greek practice in which the house seems to have had less significance as a means of demonstrating social position (Wallace-Hadrill 1988: 55). Several functions attached to the Roman house. These included receiving clients at the morning greeting (*salutatio*), when supplicants visited their patron to conduct business and request favours. These activities employed public halls and audience chambers (*atrium*, *tablinum* and *oecus*). The evening supper party was the most important social event organised in most houses and dining rooms (such as the *triclinium*) were crucial. Entertainments and readings, as well as mealtime rituals such as the mixing and preparing of wine (*symposium*), could accompany the meal. Houses also witnessed a variety of religious rites, both in cult practice and in the more mundane observances demanded by the sprits of the house (*lares*). More intimate meetings and gatherings could take place in private chambers, bedrooms and baths.

The Roman house was designed around these different social activities, and involved a public approach to domestic space. Wallace-Hadrill (1988: 59) has emphasised the significance that was attached to the grant of privileged access to more intimate spaces and activities within the house, and has described the demands that this made of the ways in which houses were designed. A useful parallel is drawn with *ancien régime* France, with its prescribed hierarchy of house types. Wallace-Hadrill recognises two principal axes of distinction between the types of domestic space referred to by Vitruvius: allowing the identification of contrasts between grand and humble, and private and public (an *atrium* is considered grand and public, a dining room grand and private, a corridor humble and public, etc.). A structured approach to these distinctions allowed for an ascent in privilege as the more honoured visitor progressed towards the most intimate parts of the house.

The *insulae* of Imperial Rome

A separate tradition of Roman domestic architecture resulted in the construction of the multi-storied apartment blocks of Rome and its principal port at Ostia. This form of housing, commonly referred to as *insula* houses, was made possible by improvements in the use of cement construction and vaulting, and developed in response to urban crowding. At Ostia multi-storied houses were essentially a second-century phenomenon, but at Rome they had been common from late republican times and it is here that the type first developed (Ward-Perkins 1981:145–6). There has been some speculation as to when and how this happened, with particular reference to the extent to which the design of atrium houses influenced their genesis (Packer 1971).

A key feature of apartment housing was that light was obtained not from courtyards and openings within the building, but from large windows onto the street. Principal rooms were often located at the corners of buildings to best exploit such lighting, and commonly rooms were built around three sides of a central room, the fourth side of which faced the street. Although some such rooms could have functioned in a similar fashion to the traditional *atrium*, they were often little more than corridors linking more important rooms at either end. The design of these buildings was perhaps influenced by earlier, low status, houses. This argument was developed by Packer in his description of Ostian building types, who identified a class of simple *atrium* house (Packer 1971, type IIc) in which the entrance forecourts had been fully roofed over (a *testudinate atrium*). Smaller Pompeiian houses, 'row-houses', have subsequently been the subject of studies by Hoffman (1980) and Nappo (1997). It appears that in their earlier phases these houses, terraced rows of which were being built in the late third to early second centuries BC, were initially laid out with an open courtyard. Only in later phases, and as a consequence of increased building density, were these spaces eventually enclosed as upper stories were built. It not certain that these earlier developments influenced the architecture of Ostia, but it is safe to assume that the pressures to build upwards encouraged the roofing-over of forecourts and that this contributed to the reduced emphasis given to such space. It seems likely, however, that even where the dictates of space had robbed architects of a central courtyard this missing space still exercised an influence over the internal layout of the house. A parallel can be drawn with the development of the medieval hall. Here, too, a space that in early buildings had served as the main focal and gathering point for household affairs became little more than a circulation area, as functions devolved to increasingly specialised surrounding rooms.

Apartment houses would not always have allowed for the full range of social uses that were found in *atrium*-peristyle houses. There was less scope for a hierarchical procession of space, and distinctions between private and public space were necessarily less subtle. It is, in any case, clear that many apartment houses were of lower social status. These buildings were rarely provided with water supply or private sewerage, and were usually left unheated. In most phases the ground floor flats had no kitchens or separate latrines. Flats on the upper stories were more poorly decorated than ground floor ones. The higher one ascended the poorer the perceived quality of the accommodation. Juvenal, a Roman satirist whose surviving works were penned in the first century AD, had choice words on the unattractiveness of life in and around such houses (*Satires* 3: 268–77). Most Romans, however, had no choice but to live in such accommodation. According to contemporary lists there were some 46,000 apartment blocks to 1,790 town houses in fourth-century Rome, although it has been estimated that the town houses occupied one third of the residential space and their households would have been disproportionately large (MacMullen 1974: 168).

The residents of the apartment blocks had social aspirations and these houses usually included reception areas. Mosaic floors and painted walls were designed to impress visitors and guests. In this regard Rome and Pompeii present a similar picture. Despite Vitruvius' belief that the man of average wealth had little call to offer hospitality (*On Architecture* 6: 5.1–2), it is clear that reception activities were important to most city dwellers.

Courtyard houses

There was little need to build apartment blocks in Ostia after the population of the city went into decline. New properties in the later town were, once again, laid out over only one or two floors. These third- and fourth-century buildings usefully illustrate the later Roman style of town house. The *atrium* with a central *impluvium* had disappeared from use, and although some smaller houses remained of similar design to the apartment houses, the better buildings were courtyard houses influenced by earlier Mediterranean traditions. These houses were entered by way of a vestibule or corridor that gave access to a central courtyard, from which major rooms were easily reached. These later houses were more likely to be provided with one or sometimes two larger and more magnificent reception rooms, with an open aspect to the peristyle or courtyard. The House of the Fortuna Annonaria illustrates the type, and shows how much emphasis was placed on the main reception room (fig. 3). This room may have replaced the function of the

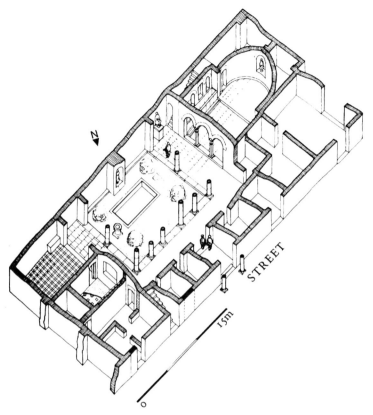

Figure 3 The House of the Fortuna Annonaria at Ostia as remodelled in the fourth century. Drawing by J.B. Ward Perkins (1981). Copyright Yale University Press.

tablinum, allowing also for the abandonment of the *atrium* as an architectural feature (Wallace-Hadrill 1988: 90).

Although only now in widespread use, this approach to the design of houses had clear roots in Roman architecture of the first century. Some Pompeiian houses, notably the House of the Menander, had unusually large reception rooms associated with peristyles. The emperor Domitian's palace on Rome's Palatine hill was provided with grand audience rooms opening onto a central court. The taste and patronage of the imperial household had a major impact on cultural and artistic development in the Roman world and the preferences of the imperial family influenced fashion in domestic architecture.

Roman houses were far less ordered than is sometimes assumed. Most buildings were irregular in plan and showed considerable variation in detail.

This was not just the case with smaller town houses tucked awkwardly into the available urban space, but is also a characteristic of larger houses. Many later Roman houses were characterised by a complex series of courtyards, peristyles, corridors and reception rooms. For example the main reception rooms of the fifth-century House of the Fountains in Beirut were reached *via* four separate peristyle courts (Perring 1999a). The approach to domestic space in these Byzantine houses finds close parallel in the contemporary approaches to urban design (MacDonald 1986). The routes through houses and towns were established not by symmetrical planning but by a procession of impressively designed public spaces. Although most evidently a feature of the east, this processional approach was also a characteristic feature of late antique palatial housing in the west.

The design of Nero's *domus aurea* can perhaps be seen to have had an influence: this palace consisted of a group of interlocked blocks, each with strong internal logic but combining in complicated and asymmetrical patterns. Hadrian's villa at Tivoli is another example. Although this building complex was designed around a number of key vistas with highly symmetrical elements, the overall plan of the complex lacks evident coherence. The point that needs to be made here is that Roman houses were not laid out with rigid symmetry, but were designed to comprise a hierarchy of reception areas linked by porticoes and corridors. Similar approaches to domestic space, if on a more modest scale, can be reconstructed from the Romano-British evidence.

Villas

The term villa has been subject to many definitions (Percival 1976: 14–15), but is used here to describe country houses designed to display high status through the use of architectural motifs of Graeco-Roman inspiration. It is not unreasonable to hope that most buildings that meet this definition would have been considered villas by their owners, if not always recognised as such by more snobbish guests.

There was a close relationship between villa and urban architecture, and although the rural landscape of Italy and Greece had long been populated by small farmsteads, villa development was essentially a product of the introduction of urban values into the countryside. The social and economic life of the Roman elite depended on an involvement in both town and country affairs, and it was not possible to function at higher social levels without owning property in both. This need for a country residence was more evidently a feature of Italian urban society than it had been in the earlier Hellenistic world. In the Greek-speaking east, villas were generally a Roman introduction of late date (Rossiter 1989).

A descriptive typology of the Italian (essentially Campanian) villa was proposed by Rostovtzeff (1957) on the basis of the evidence of the Pompeiian sites, supplemented by the writings of Varro and Columella, and is followed in most contemporary studies. Some villas were exclusively places for luxurious living and entertaining, especially those in suburban or maritime locations. More commonly the villa was also a place of agricultural activity where sophisticated reception and living quarters of a country house (the *pars urbana*) were set alongside a working farm (the *pars rusticae*). In some cases the farm buildings stood alone, and although of impressive scale were not attached to a luxurious residence. For these the Rostovtzeff model, supported by the evidence of classical sources, presumes the presence of a large, slave-run estate.

These different circumstances generated a wide variety of building form. The suburban and maritime villas, such as Oplontis, the Villa of the Mysteries outside Pompeii or Hadrian's villa at Tivoli, are amongst the most palatial of Roman houses (fig. 4). As the most costly, luxurious and extensive of Roman establishments, clearly given over to entertaining on a large scale,

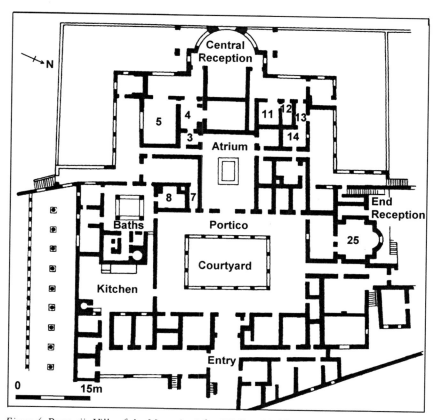

Figure 4 Pompeii, Villa of the Mysteries (after Wallace-Haddrill 1988).

these would have been built following latest fashion, and it has been argued that such houses would have influenced developments in urban architecture (D'Arms 1970, Zanker 1979).

The writings of Pliny and other Roman authors make it clear that it was common for members of the elite to own a multiplicity of villas. The scattered nature of landholding in Italy (Siculus Flaccus: 152), added emphasis to the need for bailiffs and slave labour (or sharecropping) to work these estates. The land register of the *Ligures Baebiani*, a town near Circello in Italy, describes some 300 properties, where thirty-seven owners held more than one property, and one owned 26 properties (MacMullen 1974: 5). The transmission of architectural ideas would have owed much to these complex patterns of ownership.

In several important respects villas were similar in design to contemporary town houses. Those of the late republic and early empire were frequently built around a central circulation and reception space identical in its main characteristics to the urban *atrium*-peristyle of the period, as in the villas at Settefinestre, Boscoreale and elsewhere (Carandini and Ricci 1985). The porticoes and peristyles were given greater prominence and importance in such buildings in the period after the social war (late republic), and it was after this period that most of the grander villas were built. Many of these early villas did not survive the second century and in the later Roman period greater emphasis was given to the group of principal reception rooms opening onto the peristyle or courtyard, as at Piazza Armerina (fig. 54, Wilson 1983).

There were, however, many significant differences between the layout of town houses and villas in Roman Italy. Villas were designed to provide views out onto the surrounding countryside as was rarely possible in town, and this was reflected in their aspect and facade. Loggias, verandas and colonnades were built around the house, the plan of which was adapted to present well-lit corner rooms. Space was not a constraint, and villas could benefit from the addition of long projecting wings, and a variety of outhouses and separate units. This was especially the case with the maritime villas, where the sea view was highly valued; a preference made evident not only in the choice of villa sites in early imperial Italy, but also in a range of Byzantine texts (Hemsoll 1990: 14–15, Saliou 1994: 238–47). Town houses were more likely to draw light into the buildings from secure and secluded inner courtyards, with the perimeter area occupied by the shops and workshops that made best use of the street frontages. Such plots offered little scope for growth and extension. In addition to the storage and working areas needed on those villas that served as farms (the majority), and the accommodation required for a larger household and workforce, villas were also more likely to be provided with baths. In the city it remained fashionable to frequent large public baths, but these were not available in the countryside.

These differences of circumstance account for most of the differences that can be identified between the arrangements of urban and rural buildings. There is nothing to suggest that social life and domestic households differed significantly between town and country.

Gallo-Roman domestic architecture

Roman culture reached Britain by way of Gaul, and it is the Gallic interpretation of Rome that might be expected to have had the greatest influence on developments in this province. The southern parts of Gaul had been much influenced by Greece prior to the Roman conquest, most notably as a consequence of the foundation of a Greek colony at Marseilles. The southern Gauls were also incorporated into the Roman world at a comparatively early date, after the establishment of the Roman colony at *Narbo Martius*, Narbonne, in 118 BC. Provence was consequently more clearly part of the classical world than was Gallia Belgica. It was only under Augustus, little more than a generation prior to the conquest of Britain, that the process of Romanisation was set firmly under way in the more remote parts of Gaul (Wightman 1985: 77).

The evidence for the penetration of Greek ideas beyond the immediate Marseilles hinterland and into pre-Roman Gaul is illustrated by the diffusion of the fashion for first mud brick and subsequently masonry construction (de Chazelles et al. 1985). The technique of building houses with walls of air-dried bricks had origins in the middle-east and was probably introduced to Italy and Gaul by Greek colonists, although houses near Rome had been built with cob walls from at least the eighth century BC (Bietti Sestieri et al. 1990). Throughout the Mediterranean parts of Spain, Italy and Gaul houses built of mud bricks over stone footings are first evident in the seventh/sixth century BC (e.g. André 1976: 95–128). The Etruscans were building mud brick houses at Metaponto in the seventh century BC, probably following developments in Magna Graecia.

The most notable penetration of these Greek-influenced techniques into northern Europe is represented by the mud brick walled hillfort at Heuneburg, on the upper reaches of the Danube (Kimmig 1983). Some house plans of classical form, such as the stone-built peristyle house in Ensérune (Herault), are also found in hilltop settlements of the late second century BC (Gallet de Santerre 1978). Hellenistic peristyle houses, dating from the first century BC, have been identified in a number of towns (Goudineau 1979: 239–48), but are more likely to be a consequence of the early progress of Romanisation rather than a continuity of Massiliot influence (Blagg 1990c: 203). Outside of Provence the earliest evidence for the development of domestic architecture in the classical tradition dates to the period immediately after the Roman conquest. Courtyard houses, and peristyle houses with *impluvia*, are found into the Flavian period, as at Autun and Beauvais (Blanchard-Lemée et al. 1986, Frézouls 1982: 168). The late first-century BC houses of Lyons provide some of the best evidence for the urban architectural fashions of this period and influenced subsequent architectural developments in both Gaul and Britain (Desbat 1985). Types of building common in the south of Gaul are not widely found in the north. This may reflect both the later progress of Romanisation and the lack of a previous classical tradition in the region. The early phases of domestic construction in towns were dominated by constructions in timber and clay, and the poor survival of such structures has made it difficult to describe full building plans. A distinction can be drawn between the narrow strip buildings that were used as commercial properties and larger town houses with courtyards and mosaic pavements.

The peristyle was an important feature in villas in the southern parts of Gaul. Montmaurin (Haute Garrone) is perhaps the most spectacular example (Fouet 1969). In the earliest phase of this villa, which showed the influence of the Roman *atrium*-peristyle house, a central peristyle was given greatest emphasis. Later a magnificent curved portico was added to the southeast facade. It is likely that the portico became a setting for the promenade (*ambulatio*) and replaced some functions of the enclosed peristyle. Roman styles of villa architecture made little impact on the countryside of non-Mediterranean Gaul until the second half of the first century AD (G. Woolf 1998: 152). Several regional styles were subsequently adopted. In the northeast the villas were often built around a large central hall, but the most widely diffused style of house placed most architectural emphasis on a portico flanked by two small pavilions along one side of the building (fig.25). Houses of this type are generally known as winged-corridor villas. The villa at Anthée, one of a series of large estates in the Somme valley, illustrates a slightly different approach (Agache 1975). Here the main house was surrounded by a series of lesser houses and buildings flanking an elongated trapezoidal forecourt. These establishments are of interest both for their unusual emphasis on axial symmetry and for the way in which they incorporated several houses, potentially providing accommodation for several households.

It cannot be assumed that Britain followed the example of Rome's Mediterranean provinces. Other sources relevant to arrangements in Britain demand attention. Post-built aisled long houses were common in Scandinavia, Germany and Holland prior to and during the Roman period. Such buildings were also present in settlements within the empire's borders, as at Rijswijk between the first and third centuries AD (Bloemers 1985: 140). Recent research has suggested a southern boundary to the distribution of this northwest European *Wohnställer* running through central Belgium (Roymans 1995: 50–1). In terms of the durability of the fashion and the extended area of its influence, this was the regional equivalent to the courtyard house (James *et al.* 1984). Typically the long houses were up to 24–28 m long (80–90 ft.) but no more than 6–9.2 m wide (20–30 ft.). These narrow timber buildings generally had living quarters at one end, with stalls for animals at the other. The living quarters usually consisted of a large rectangular hall with a central hearth, and were often separated from the rest of the house by a cross passage. The animals were quartered in stalls set in the aisles of the building, which was divided longitudinally by a central passage. Wattle and daub walls and earth floors were common, and there was little evident attention to decorative order. The buildings were sometimes round-cornered. Some impression of the social and domestic arrangements represented by these buildings can be obtained from Norse sagas and early English sources. The hall could be a key location for gatherings and provided a focal point for social life. It was the product of a particular type of social arrangement, in which nuclear families are thought to have been subordinate to kinship groups. Attempts have been made to identify hall-based extended families in some Romano-British settlements (e.g. Hingley 1990). Although aisled buildings were popular on many Romano-British sites and these included large workrooms and halls, these buildings were of very different form to the northern European long house and did not normally include the characteristic cross-passage or any stalls for livestock. There is no good reason to believe that the long house had any direct influence on domestic architecture in Roman Britain.

The innovations of the Roman period saw the introduction of very different forms of building to those that had previously been found in the region, representing a strikingly different attitude to the purpose of architecture and the use of space. It will be argued further below (p. 212) that such attitudes reflected the changed social and economic circumstances promoted by the Roman administration and adopted by an increasingly cosmopolitan elite class. Two sources of evidence are key to this understanding. The development of building techniques illustrates the ways in which new architectural ideas and approaches were developed within Roman Britain, whilst the uses to which houses were put testifies to the Hellenised cultural and social attitudes of their inhabitants. We will address these issues separately. Chapter 3 concentrates on the evidence of changing architectural fashion, and does this by way of a narrative account. Much of the structural detail on which this is based is explored in more detail in the succeeding chapters.

3

A HISTORY OF ROMANO-BRITISH HOUSES

Iron Age houses in Britain

The dominant building form in Iron Age Britain was the circular house. Contrary to popular belief these were not crude huts. These imposing structures were typically about 6 m in diameter, built from round-sectioned posts set into the ground at irregular intervals (Cunliffe 1978: 174–8). The posts supported the roof, but the eaves were taken beyond the ring that they formed to an insubstantial wall near where the eaves reached the ground. The space inside these buildings was therefore separated into a high-roofed central area and a lower area between the ring of posts and the outer wall. There is little other evidence for any internal divisions of space. In later houses posts were generally larger and more regularly spaced, and substantial porches were used to provide imposing entrances.

It is generally assumed that the large central area, where the hearths were most frequently placed, was likely to have been more public: a circulation space suitable also for communal and reception activities, whilst the fringes of such rooms were more suited for storage, sleeping and privacy. This simple ordering of space is made much of by Hingley, who sees evidence amongst the aisled buildings of Roman Britain for similar approaches and believes that there was a strong element of continuity from Iron Age to Romano-British types (Hingley 1990: 132–3). This understates the import-ance of changes in attitudes to space evident in internal arrangements and in approaches to the representation of power found in the different architectural forms. But where circular spaces were simply replaced by rectangular ones it is plausible that social practices remained unchanged. This is likely to have been the case where it can be demonstrated that details of interior design and use were constant despite the change in form, but the evidence for such continuity is questionable.

Most settlements included several hut sites. In Clarke's study of the Glastonbury lake village, evidence was adduced for the use of a repeated module, with house-groups consisting of two large round huts (perhaps occupied by males) and a single smaller hut (possibly used by families), with associated working and storage areas (Clarke 1972). Altogether about seven of these compounds were identified, each of which was thought to have housed around twenty people. This attempt to reconstruct the evidence for past communities from spatial information has been challenged. The evidence that Clarke was using was unreliable, and recent improvements in our understanding of these buildings have failed to support his thesis (Barrett 1987). It remains the case, however, that Iron Age huts were grouped into compounds. Direct comparison of the household arrangements represented by late Iron Age buildings with those of the Roman period are difficult because complex spatial hierarchies can be achieved through the aggregation of huts in patterns that cannot be identified from the archaeo-logical evidence. Each hut could house a hierarchy of activities without leaving clear evidence of the fact, and these buildings could in turn have functioned in a similar fashion to rooms or suites of rooms in Romano-British houses (Rivet 1964: 108). A much quoted example is that of the transformation from native to Roman styles of housing at Park Street in Hertfordshire, where two Iron Age houses were replaced by a small villa with six rooms. The villa offered two to three times the amount of space, but could have housed a similar set of social arrangements.

Some pre-Roman houses in southeast Britain were built to a rectangular rather than circular plan. Rectangular houses were a late innovation, largely restricted to Hertfordshire and Essex (fig. 5). These buildings were similar in style to the pre-Roman houses of the adjacent parts of continental Europe, which were also rectangular timber buildings with wattle and daub walls, and few internal partitions. It seems likely that this fashion was associated

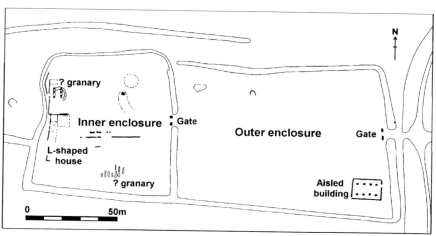

Figure 5 The pre-Roman villa complex and enclosures at Gorhambury near St Albans (after Neal 1990).

with a range of other changes in southeast Britain that reflected growing cross-channel contact, perhaps even immigration from Gaul (Haselgrove 1984). At Park Street sub-rectangular timber houses had been burnt down (perhaps in the Boudiccan revolt of AD 60) only to be replaced by circular huts with wattle and daub walls. The rectangular houses had been built with wattle and daub walls set on sleeper beams with puddled chalk and clay floors. One of the other sites where such buildings have been studied in detail is at Skeleton Green, also in Hertfordshire (Partridge 1981: 37–40). Here the post-built houses had wattle and daub walls, and were probably floored with planks and roofed with thatch. Timber ground beams may have been used in some instances. Some doorways were emphasised by porches, but no complex internal arrangements of space were identified. Most of the buildings were single roomed, although one structure was divided into two. Four of these structures appeared to form a group linked by pathways, and similar arrangements can tentatively be identified at other sites (Black 1987: 20–1). The introduction of rectangular structures changed the character of the domestic space, and involved the use of a different range of building techniques.

The arrival of Rome

Rome arrived in a Britain that was changing. Elite society, at least in the south and east of the country, was already experimenting with ideas influenced by contact with Gaul and Rome. In architectural terms this can be seen in the construction of rectangular houses in place of round ones. Aisled buildings, a type of structure that was to become a familiar component of the Romano-British landscape, were also introduced to high status sites shortly prior to the Roman conquest. These architectural changes were comparatively inconsequential in the light of what was to happen after the conquest, but many other sources of evidence suggest that this was a period of increasing social differentiation (Millett 1990b: 29). Powerful men in late Iron Age Britain sustained their reputations and followings through a lavish expenditure on feasting and in the paraphernalia of warfare. But this language of power was not yet Roman. Rome had different ideas about how power was expressed and replicated. In provincial society, power was seen to derive from the ownership of property and not from the fortunes of war. As we have already seen (p. 2), Roman dominion was made manifest in the landscape and expressed in architecture.

The army was a primary agent in introducing Roman architecture to Britain and the patronage of Rome's commanders and quartermasters provided an early model of Roman life. The earliest known Roman structures in the province are from military contexts, as at Richborough and Hod Hill. The fort was a partial mirror of urban society, complete with public buildings and a hierarchy of housing that borrowed on civilian forms and motifs. Once established it was a focus of social relations extending far beyond the camp walls. The economic impact of the army and the indirect contribution it made to the urban impulse is well documented. Veterans exercised a particular influence: as immigrant settlers, as mediators between civilian and military life, and as investors in local business (Poulter 1987). Many of the architectural elements that were subsequently developed to display status in the private houses of Roman Britain were first seen in the houses of the army.

The extent to which the army was directly involved in building the earliest Romano-British towns is more disputed. Several of Britain's first towns were established as planted veteran settlements. Within these *coloniae* the early civilian buildings followed the plans of the legionary barracks that had preceded them and some military buildings were retained for civilian use (Hurst 1999, Crummy 1988, Webster 1988: 137). This was a convenient and inexpensive solution to the need to develop an urban infrastructure, but these planted settlements were the exception and not the norm. It has also been suggested that the army might have lent its support to civilian construction programmes elsewhere in the province. It has been argued that a row of shops in early Roman Verulamium might have been the product of such assistance (Frere 1972: 12). This hypothesis relies on the superficial resemblance of the plans of these shops to contemporary barrack-blocks, but fails to convince. The striking similarities between timber-framed constructions at the earlier fort of Valkenburg on the Rhine and the first civilian Romano-British timber-framed constructions is a more certain indication that the skilled carpenters employed in building Britain's first Roman houses had learnt their trade in the army. This does not, however, prove a direct military involvement since many of the artisans and traders to crowd the newly established towns of Roman Britain were likely to have been discharged veterans.

Notwithstanding these military influences, Blagg's work on the use of decorative stonework (1980, 1984 and 1991) suggests that the army had little direct involvement in early programmes of civilian building, which in any case took place at a time when army engineers were distracted by the needs of military campaigns. It is similarly difficult to credit military craftsmen with the later first-century wall paintings and mosaic pavements found in towns and villas. These show the hand of immigrant craftsmen and artists. There are sound reasons for believing that the army exercised an important influence on the ways in which Britain adopted Romano-Hellenistic culture, and this is a theme that we will return to in Chapter 13, but this was infrequently the consequence of a military involvement in civilian construction.

The first Roman-style buildings (*c.* AD 50–60) were built of timber and earth. Even the higher status houses of this period had wattle and daub walls, earth floors and thatch roofs; whilst window glass was rarely used. It is not difficult to explain the early popularity of these materials. They lend themselves to fast and economical construction and do not depend on the industrialised production of building materials or on the development of complicated systems of production and supply. Such buildings are also easy to adapt to changing circumstances. In the commonest structural type, the roof load seems to have been taken by earth-fast principal posts driven into the ground (these and other structural details are described in more detail in Chapter 5). Timber framing was an architectural sophistication, and ground beams were employed in the better buildings. Numerous sites witness a development from earth-fast to timber-framed construction during the first century. A similar shift in fashion is evident within the first half century or so of the Roman conquest in Gaul, and is considered to represent the adoption of Roman, as opposed to native, construction techniques (Bloemers 1985: 134). Roman builders were not averse, however, to using the simpler earth-fast post construction techniques. Because of this it is not possible to draw a clear distinction between construction styles introduced in the pre-conquest phase and those more directly a consequence of the Roman presence (Black 1987: 20–3).

The use of painted wall plaster and mortar floors marks out higher status structures. These include the early building complex at Fishbourne and pre-Flavian houses in London (Perring 1991b: 11). The first evidence for sophisticated interior decoration is represented by Claudian wall plaster associated with window glass and roof tiles found at Verulamium and Colchester (Frere 1983: 105, Crummy 1984: 40–2). But these are rare finds, and nine out of ten houses in Neronian London were undecorated. This reflects the hastily assembled nature of the new Romano-British urban communities. The private house, like the town itself, was not yet a significant place in the competition for status (Blagg 1990a). This may in part reflect the absence of an established urban aristocracy. Power in the towns remained in the hands of agents of Rome and the short-term values of fort and supply depot prevailed.

Flavian architectural developments

The first evidence for conspicuous expenditure on domestic architecture dates *c.* AD 65–75 and is found in the design of early villas in the southeast of the province. A select group of villas on the south coast has justly been given emphasis in reviews of the architecture of this period (Todd 1978, Blagg 1990c). The villa at Fishbourne is the best known (fig. 6), but contemporary buildings that competed in quality are known or suspected at Angmering, Southwick, Eastwick and Pulborough (all in Sussex). The earliest palatial house at Fishbourne had been laid out with wide corridors around a central courtyard and was provided with stone baths. This house was decorated with mosaic and opus sectile floors, painted walls and

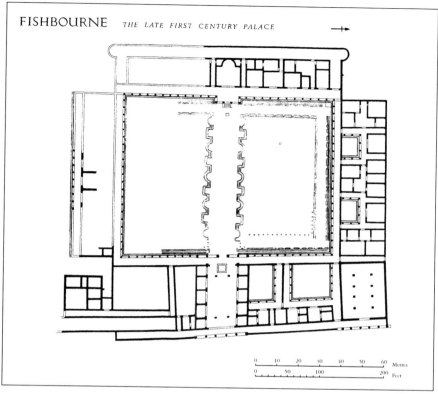

Figure 6 The late first-century (Period II) courtyard villa at Fishbourne (Cunliffe 1971a). Reproduced by kind permission of the Society of Antiquaries of London.

ornamental stonework. Immigrant craftsmen were undoubtedly employed on this project. The emphasis placed on the central courtyard at these early Sussex sites was not otherwise a common feature of early villas in Britain. Todd (1978) concluded that the early ostentation of these houses and the Roman character of their coastal location and decoration, suggests mercantile and immigrant influence in their development. The alternative suggestion (Cunliffe 1971a) that the Fishbourne villa was built as a palace for the British client-king Cogidubnus remains resistant to proof, despite suggestive epigraphic evidence. Millett (1990b: 96–7) has, however, drawn attention to the evidence of mid to late first-century villas built within late pre-Roman Iron Age aristocratic estates. Several such houses were built within enclosures associated with important oppida complexes. Fishbourne itself was possibly one of these, because of its relationship to Chichester. Others are found at Ditches (Bagendon), Gorhambury (Verulamium) and possibly also Ditchley and Shakenoak (Silchester). The close association of these villas

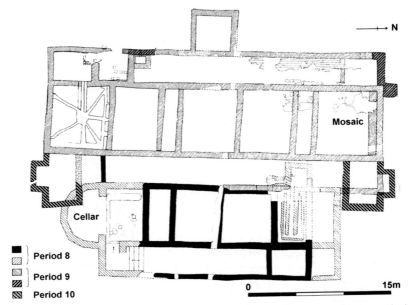

Figure 7 The Roman villa at Gorhambury. The walls of the earliest stone villa are marked in black (Period 8). After an early phase of improvement this house included a cellar beneath an apsidal-ended room at one end of the main range and a heated room (with a channelled hypocaust laid out in a simple labyrinthine pattern) at the other. The villa was entirely rebuilt in the mid to late second century (Period 9) and an end room in this later building contained a union-jack hypocaust (after Neal 1990).

with pre-Roman aristocratic estates, and their proximity to emergent urban centres, supports the suggestion that these Roman style houses were built for a native aristocracy using the architecture to define its position within the new social-order (figs 5 and 7).

With the exception of the palatial villas along the south coast, reception facilities within the first Romano-British villas were given but modest emphasis. The typical house consisted of a single row of rooms forming a long and narrow block, usually about 25–30 m long and containing five or six rooms (fig. 24a). Several houses of this type are known from around Verulamium. From the outset these included a range of architectural features that were subsequently to characterise Roman houses in Britain. These included the use of a portico or corridor along one side of the house, heated baths, and a slightly more imposing room at one end of the house that is likely to have been a dining room. In this earliest phase of Roman architecture these features were more modestly proportioned and discretely decorated than was later the fashion. These early row-houses established a style of housing that remained in use in Britain throughout the Roman period. The contrast that can be drawn between these houses and the palatial coastal villas suggests that there was little direct overlap between the societies represented by these two regional groups of housing.

Even in the smallest and most modest villas the importance of the portico was soon evident. Many houses that had been built without this facility in the first phase of villa construction were extended or rebuilt to include it, and very few of the houses built after AD 100 omitted it. It offers one of the clearest architectural manifestations of the diffusion of Roman concepts of status display. The baths built in the period after AD 65 give a similar picture of architectural change, as do the large apsidal-ended reception rooms found at the centre of villas at Fishbourne and Southwick before the end of the first century. These architectural advances show that Roman practices of dining and bathing had been adopted. The first use of Roman domestic architecture to display status was more marked in the country-side than it was in town. Developments in villa design were broadly contemporaneous with related changes in the architecture of public build-ings in the first Romano-British towns. The earliest public baths and apsidal basilicas were a product of late Neronian and Flavian building programmes. More appears to have been invested in sustaining rural power than in competing for urban status and, where money was being spent in the towns, it was in the public rather than the private sphere (Blagg 1990c).

London was something of an exception, since several Flavian town houses here were lavishly decorated (Perring 1991b: 40–1). This almost certainly reflects the close links between this town and the imperial administration. Like the better villas of the time the best town houses in London were built with earth walls set over masonry foundations. Unfortunately most of the excavated fragments are so small that few plans can be reconstructed. The crowded nature of the early city reduced the scope for exploiting gardens and vistas in the rural fashion. A house built at Watling Court c. AD 70–80 contained a large mosaic-paved central reception room. An apse-ended mosaic-floored reception room from a clay walled structure built c. AD 100 provides further evidence for the early provision of reception rooms of complex design in Roman London.

Colchester and Verulamium are the other urban sites where one might expect to find early evidence for an investment in urban property. Although the majority of early buildings excavated in these settlements were timber structures of indeterminate form and modest appearance there are some signs that the Flavian period saw an advance in the complexity and quality of urban housing. This is illustrated both by the occasional addition of porticoes and reception rooms and by improvements in the quality of construction and decoration. One of the earliest examples of this was found in a Neronian or early Flavian house excavated at the Balkerne Lane site in Colchester. This building incorporated a decorated corridor leading to a larger end-room (Crummy 1984: 119). The location of this house in Colchester's western suburb, set some distance back from but overlooking a principal Roman road, suggests that this might better be considered a suburban villa than a town house. Two early town houses at Verulamium were built with flint wall footings and *opus signinum* (cement) floors. These houses were also laid out with main corridors leading to large reception rooms at the end of the block. The Wheelers (1936) suggested a date of *c*. AD 70 for these houses, although Frere (1983: 10) considers an early second century date more probable. Excavations in Winchester uncovered a more securely dated example of a timber-framed Flavian town house with its main rooms laid out in a row behind a south-facing portico (Zant 1993: 31–4). Two pre-Flavian timber-framed houses from Dorchester may also have been built with porticoes, although these rooms may have been no more than service corridors (Woodward *et al.*, 1993: Buildings 477 and 5502). The principal feature of all these buildings was the presence of a corridor or portico along one side of the house, leading usually to a reception room at one end. The towns of Britain adopted this architectural form in the period AD 65–90, a little while after such houses had already made their appearance in the surrounding countryside. Although some Flavian town houses, especially in London, could be expensively decorated, the towns remained dominated by a utilitarian style of housing. The shops, workshops and mean apartments known from London, Colchester and Verulamium were unlikely places for the display of status through architectural extravagance.

The emergence of mature building types

The first masonry structures associated with private houses were the free-standing baths attached to villas like those at Angmering and Eccles. These had probably been built by *c*. AD 65 (Black 1987: 87–9). Concrete was otherwise restricted to the foundations of half-timbered or earth-walled constructions. Such structures date from the period AD 65–75, as in the villa at Mileoak (Green and Draper 1978). The late Neronian or early Flavian 'proto-palace' at Fishbourne included masonry elements, especially in the construction of the baths, but daub from destruction debris shows that the building had been half-timbered (Cunliffe 1971a: 67). It seems likely that most late first-century villas were either earth-walled or timber-framed, although frequently only the masonry footings survived for modern discovery.

The use of stone represented a significant choice, requiring an investment in mechanisms for the exploitation of suitable quarries, systems of pro-curement and supply, and a suitable level of technical familiarity with masonry construction. Because of the poor survival of elements of super-structure it is difficult to accurately chart the introduction of full masonry construction. The Period 2 villa at Fishbourne had neatly built walls of stone and probably dates *c*. AD 75/85 (Black 1987: 84–6 prefers a date closer to the end of the century). The villa at Eccles in Kent may also have had a stone superstructure, although the published reports leave this uncertain. In most other cases villas were not built in stone until the early second century. The villa at Wall in Staffordshire illustrates a common pattern of architectural improvement. Here a wattle and daub timber building was replaced in the Flavian period by a timber building with painted walls and glazed windows. This was in turn replaced in the early second century by a structure of similar sophistication but with stone foundations (Goodburn 1976: 328).

The introduction of stone construction to London is well documented. No masonry structures are known from the first phase of settlement here, although earth-walled storehouses adjacent to the forum were set over concrete footings. Soon after the Boudiccan revolt, probably in AD 63, a series of stone warehouses was built beside the waterfront (Brigham and Watson 1996). The stone and brick basilica was probably built in the early 70s, and several other masonry public buildings of this period are surmised (Perring 1991b: 23ff.). By the end of the century a large apsidal-ended building constructed of stone and tile had been built over a waterfront site facing the Roman city from the south bank of the Thames (Yule 1989: 33–5). The function of this building is disputed, but a strong case can be made for it to have been a suburban villa built for a public official. Stone was introduced piece-meal on lesser domestic sites, first in foundations, then for cellars and bathhouses and finally in the upper parts of the house. Flavian houses with stone foundations have been recorded at several locations. At Gateway House and Watling Court stone walls from at least two houses survived over one metre tall beneath fire debris of *c.* AD 125. Such houses were more common following the rebuilding of the city after the fire. Some private baths were also built at this time. Timber and clay-walled buildings were widely replaced in the late second and early third centuries by large stone-founded structures with mosaic pavements and hypocaust floors.

Other Romano-British cities were slower to adopt masonry construction, even where stone was more easily available. Late first-century masonry foundations, which had probably supported timber-framed structures, have been recorded at several sites (Frere and Williams 1948, Zant 1993: 44–5, Wheeler and Wheeler 1936: 140). Generally, however, timber-framed houses were not replaced by more substantial stone-founded ones until after *c.* AD 120 and this change was more usually a feature of the period between AD 150 and 250 (fig. 8). The character and chronology of change suggests that the choice to build in stone was as much a matter of fashion as of economics. The use of stone initially evidenced the status of the site, with palatial houses at Fishbourne and in London the first to adopt a construction technique previously restricted to public buildings. Some of the better villas were soon to follow this fashion, as was also the case in other parts of London. Other towns were slower to adopt these changes. By the end of the third century, however, it was unusual not to find most town houses built with stone foundations. This was even the case for shops and workshops in suburbs and

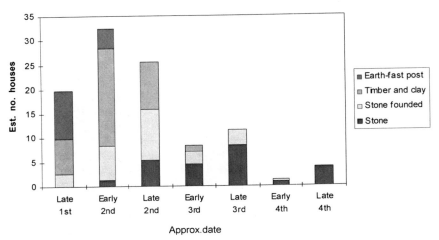

Figure 8 Changing types of wall construction used in the houses of Verulamium as reported on by Frere (1983). This particular sample understates the importance of property development in the early fourth century.

roadside settlements. Stone buildings were less easy to adapt and change, and suggested a more permanent approach to domestic arrangements. These more durable constructions also facilitated the use of buildings as a means of storing and disposing of wealth (Gregson 1982).

A similar architectural progression has been observed in other northwest provinces, where the first Romanised houses were often built of timber and were sometimes replaced by earth-walled constructions. Stone building was usually restricted to public constructions, and only became widely used in domestic context many decades after the Roman conquest. Urban sequences of this nature are commonly recorded in Gaul, where in Belgica the main shift towards masonry construction took place in the mid first century. Similar sequences have also been recorded in Milan (Perring 1991a: 105ff.).

With the advent of a popular tradition of masonry walling, the use of clay-walled construction went into decline. Amongst the latest high status Romano-British structures known to have been built with clay block or adobe walls were the Period I villa at Bignor, *c.* 190–200, and the Dover Painted House of *c.* 180/200 (Frere 1982, Philp 1989). Mud and stud continued in use in both Colchester and London, but in lesser circumstances. This change in emphasis has encouraged the view that building with clay walls was essentially a failed experiment (Williams 1971a: 176). This is a cruel verdict since earth-walled construction had been employed in many of the best Romano-British houses for several generations. Indeed some of the very best first-century houses were built with clay walls. There are several good reasons why such buildings declined in popularity with Romano-British architects. Although the use of unfired brick allowed for more rapid construction, earth walls can be expensive to maintain. Once stone became more readily available, as the requirements of public building established mechanisms for its exploitation, the advantages of building in clay were diminished. Access to brickearth quarries within cities declined as the built-area expanded, and destructive fires prevented the recycling of the clay used in earlier walls. Such factors may have contributed to the shift towards masonry construction that followed the Hadrianic fire in London and the Antonine fire in Verulamium.

The use of masonry was the most evident of several ways in which building quality was improved in the course of the second century. Floor mosaics and wall veneers of continental marbles were also more common than previously (Pritchard 1986: 186). Hypocaust floors, which in the first century were restricted to baths and villas of rare quality, were also built in domestic contexts in early second-century London (fig. 50). Second-century town houses made more extravagant use of the available urban space. The use of more expensive building materials, and in particular of masonry footings, was linked to the introduction of more complex plans. Villas had been designed with a view to exploiting the gardens and open spaces from their first introduction to Britain. Considerable attention has been given to the fact that similar plans were not introduced into towns in Roman Britain until later, and that Roman-style architecture was more advanced in villas until the middle of the second century (Walthew 1975: 189). Notwith-standing the evidence of some of the precocious examples described above, the earliest common use of porticoes in towns dates to the early second century. Several sites in Colchester illustrate this pattern. At Culver Street irregular Flavian buildings were replaced after AD 100–25 by a series of houses with masonry foundations that were designed with extensive corridor-porticoes (Crummy 1992: 31–2). Another early timber-framed corridor-house is Building 69 from the Middlesborough site at Colchester, which is also likely to have been built early in the second century. In Canterbury the buildings excavated in the Marlowe Car Park illustrate a similar sequence: here the houses with masonry foundations and corridor-porticoes were a feature of reconstruction dated AD 100/110–25 (Blockley et al. 1995).

The earliest winged town houses date c. AD 125–50 (Crummy 1984: 131–2, Milne 1985: 139–40, Frere 1983: 247). There seems little doubt that these plans were inspired by developments which had taken place in villa architecture a generation previously (described in more detail in Chapter 4), although the early second-century addition of reception facilities behind commercial properties may also have had an influence. These houses have been described as rural homes adapted for the city (Grimal and Woloch 1983: 91). Town was not averse to following the lead of country in such matters. Villas in the Roman west were always likely to be more more advanced in matters of fashion and design than contemporary town houses (Clarke 1991: 23, Zanker 1979, Hemsoll 1990: 13).

Initially the best town houses were not winged houses, but were instead laid out around an internal courtyard or peristyle. In London part of an early second-century courtyard house was found in Lothbury and the contemporary buildings at Gateway House seem likely to have incorporated a central courtyard (Frere 1991: 266, Shepherd 1986). Early second-century peristyle and courtyard houses have also been recorded at Colchester and Leicester (Crummy 1992: 96–108, Wacher 1995: 352–6). Such houses remained few and far between, and may have taken inspiration from the courtyard houses found in Roman forts.

The introduction of large dining rooms at the back of the house was a characteristic of the early second century. The first common provision of end reception rooms dates to the period AD 125–50. A shift in emphasis away from central reception rooms reflects a change in the nature of status display. Something slightly similar had taken place in Italy in the late republic, when rooms arranged around the peristyle were given decorative emphasis at the expense of the *atrium* and *tablinum*. This revised architectural design enhanced the processional nature of the domestic setting. Furthermore it suggests that the dinner parties and other ceremonies conducted in these rooms had become more central to the display of status than the activities which took place in the audience hall (evidence for this will be presented in Chapter 9). Notwithstanding these changes the audience room remained an important feature in many villa houses. This may reflect on the ways in which villas were designed to provide a range of functions that in towns were provided in the public fora. New types of porch were also introduced in the second century. These were also used to contribute to a more complex hierarchy of processional space. Another design change of the early to mid second century involved the integration of baths into private domestic space. Previously baths were usually built as free-standing buildings of easy public access.

From the period AD 75–125 onwards most town houses and villas were equipped with expensive reception facilities. The social life of the province relied on the patronage exercised at the supper table and in the baths, and this was common to all urban parts of Roman Britain. These social require-ments had a direct impact on Romano-British architecture and the period AD 125–50 witnessed a series of significant changes in architectural fashion which were fundamental to the shape of the later Romano-British house. These changes represented the culmination of a longer period of architectural innovation within the province and may also reflect on the changing social practices of the period. This second century witnessed significant changes in attitude to the locus of social life. In particular the growth of interest in individual salvation may have promoted new approaches to the use of domestic space, perhaps at the cost of the rituals of public solidarity that had previously characterised urban life. Private baths, porticoes and dining rooms were now much more important in the routines and rituals of elite society.

Many of the handsomely decorated town houses of the second and third centuries stood on sites previously occupied by properties engaged in some form of commercial activity. This might witness no more than the social upgrading of a particular part of settlement were it not for the fact that the commercial properties were not replaced elsewhere. At Colchester, Verulamium and London more buildings were in occupation and more industrial hearths and ovens in use in the late first century than in any equivalent period. London underwent a significant reduction in building density in the period between AD 150 and 200 (Marsden and West 1992). There is no reason to believe that a depopulation of London was accompanied by a phase of decay and dereliction, indeed the clearance of redundant shops suggests the opposite. London was an extreme case, but other towns also saw change. Verulamium lost much of its early commercial vigour, with the urban landscape transformed from a crowded agglomeration of timber buildings into a garden city dotted with handsome town houses. There were fewer shops and workshops, and such buildings occupied a much smaller proportion of the urban area. Similarly late Roman Cirencester became a city of richly decorated houses where those employed in menial tasks are likely to have lived in the houses of the rich (McWhirr 1988: 83). Changes of a similar character, although sometimes of much later date, were evident in most other towns in Britain. Some villas also show evidence of decline and abandonment at this time (Neal *et al.* 1990: 94) although the problems of the period were most marked in the towns. Many towns were transformed, with a reduced emphasis on functional, productive and commercial space. Strip buildings and workshops never entirely disappeared, but fewer such buildings were needed to service the urban population of the principal towns. This loss of commercial vigour may have encouraged landed classes to dedicate more time and money to their urban properties (Perring 1991c). Large urban plots could now be formed without any significant loss of rents. This neglect of commercial requirements may have permitted the development of the more complex house plans typical of later Romano-British towns.

Houses of late antiquity

The main forms of Romano-British house had been established by the end of the second century. In this period the villa habit penetrated deeper into the British countryside (Gregson 1982). Most late second-century villas were medium-sized winged-corridor villas, and some earlier houses were also improved by the addition of corridors and wings. There is some suggestion that smaller estates were swallowed up by larger ones from the mid third century, but in general the pattern of building evolution was unchanged from earlier periods. The fourth-century villas at both Feltwell and Barton Court Farm were built in a style indistinguishable from the villas of the late first and early second centuries (Gurney 1986, Miles 1984). Most building alterations of the late third and early fourth centuries involved adding baths, corridors and wings to houses where these had not previously been present. The construction of numerous smaller houses in this period contributed to a progressive reduction in the average house size. It can be suggested that the popularisation of Roman architectural idiom represented by this trend resulted in some dilution of the social prestige which derived from the possession of a villa (Millett 1990b: 186). The greater emphasis subsequently placed on interior decoration and on the provision of magnificent reception rooms, as illustrated by the evidence of mosaic pavements and the construction of ever-larger reception rooms, was perhaps an elite response to the challenge.

The early fourth century was the great period of Romano-British figurative art, with impressive mythological and other scenes executed in mosaics and frescoes.

Some of these mosaics included religious designs and themes. This evidence is reviewed in more detail in Chapter 7, but there are grounds for suggesting that some rooms were occasionally used as places of worship. The widespread interest in mystery religions is likely to have placed considerable demands on the private house as a place of ceremonial gathering. Such needs might have reinforced, if not sometimes inspired, the emphasis given in the houses of this period to processional architecture and extravagant interior design.

Although average villa size was reduced, a few very large establishments were built in the fourth century. The courtyard villas at Bignor, North Leigh and Woodchester were splendidly impressive expressions of the heights of wealth and power that could be attained. The situation in some respects mirrored that of the first century, when rare villas of unusual magnificence such as Fishbourne stood apart from the normal run of country houses. Branigan has argued (1976) that the fourth-century emergence of luxurious villas may have been due to the immigration of wealthy Gauls. But there is no proof that this was the case and the architecture of most of these houses fits comfortably within the Romano-British tradition, even if their scale was unusual. The villa at Woodchester was something of an exception. This unusual building illustrated the close influence of design ideas that may have been imported from Trier, as suggested by the mosaic pavements here (Ling 1997: 268). These pavements may also have provided the model for the regional diffusion of mosaics that illustrated the demi-god Orpheus enchanting wild animals with his music (Scott 2000: 131–44). These connections with the imperial city of Trier and the possible role of the house in influencing aristocratic taste within the region lend support to the suggestion that this may have been the palatial house of a high-ranking imperial official.

Social display through architectural elaboration was most evident in the private house and the best houses were in the countryside. This was perhaps possible because power was personal to a small elite, and with the decline in the importance of municipal government the tribal aristocracies had been able to distance themselves from town life. The foundations of power appear to have become increasingly divorced from communal display and invested in private individuals (Millett 1990b: 196). These social changes were reflected in new administrative and taxation structures. Diocletian's reforms brought about greater dependence on taxes in kind, such as the *annona*, and these were more easily collected and stored at villas and local centres (Black 1987).

The increased investment in interior design and enlarged reception facilities in the late third and early fourth centuries may also have had social implications. This was not a question of giving architectural dimension to contemporary prosperity; this prosperity was being described in very particular ways. Many of the large aisled buildings of this period were given exaggerated architectural emphasis. This was perhaps a way of drawing attention to the abundance represented by the storage of agricultural surplus. Some of the mosaic pavements of the period made a similar point, although these may also have contained somewhat more complex ideological messages (see below p. 133). Elite power was rooted in the promise of prosperity. Roman architecture was always concerned with this theme, and ritual in the Roman house had always been closely concerned with fertility and fortune (see Chapter 11). Fourth-century Britain may have had good cause to celebrate its agricultural productivity. Much has been made of the grain shipments from Britain that the emperor-to-be Julian dispatched to supply the army on the Rhine (Ammianus Marcellinus 18,2,3). There is, however, something almost over-anxious about the emphasis placed on brash expressions of rural plenty. Whilst this may have been an architectural response to internal social tensions caused by increased wealth, this is not entirely satisfactory as an explanation. It is alternatively possible that the Romano-British countryside retained bitter memories of recent famines past, and that the architectural propaganda was in the vein of the 'good times restored' announced on the coin of the period. The design preferences of the fourth century may have been as much a reaction to past concerns as a reflection of contemporary social stresses. It may also have been something of a last hurrah, since this massive investment in the decoration of grand porticoes, baths and dining rooms was not sustained.

Fourth-century town houses were not as impressive as contemporary villas, and this might suggest that the gentry were mainly attached to their country estates, making only seasonal use of town houses (Esmonde-Cleary 1989: 108–9). The Wheelers identified a 'Constantinian renaissance' at Verulamium (Faulkner 1997: illus. 3) and, although Frere's work (1983) suggests that the term may be something of an exaggeration, there are many other sites which also show investment in sophisticated urban property in the years around AD 300. These new buildings were not significantly different in scale or design from their third-century predecessors, indeed it is difficult to find any significant evolution of building form and type after the middle of the second century other than that explicable by the changing circumstances of individual sites. Much of the architectural conservatism found in the towns of this period may reflect on the fact that the earlier programmes of masonry construction meant that the urban housing stock was largely inherited from previous generations.

Although masonry was preferred for high status buildings, timber walling was not wholly rejected. Villas with timber-framed wattle and daub walls were built in the late third and early fourth centuries at Gayhurst, Great Casterton, Bratton Seymour and Latimer. At Colchester wattle and daub buildings remained common even in late periods (Crummy 1984: 23). A few timber and clay-walled shops and workshops were also standing in third-century London, especially on the edges of the town and on public sites. At Verulamium a corridor house was built with timber-framed walls in the mid third century (Frere 1983: 176–7). Indeed it is possible that towards the end of the fourth century, timber building was returning to fashion (e.g. Niblett 1993: 89, Faulkner 1997, Heighway and Garrod 1980: 78, Rankov 1982: 329–30). Several late Roman timber structures were set over public buildings, the sites of which may have remained public property (Blockley and Day 1979: 270, Barker 1975: 106–117, Mackreth 1987: 139). This process finds parallel outside Britain, and there was a marked shift towards timber building in areas where brick had previously been preferred.

The end of the Roman house in Britain

Faulkner (2000) has described an early third-century peak in house use and a decline thereafter, with the construction programmes of the early fourth century representing but a short-lived revival. There is a risk that Faulkner understates the level of activity represented by the more ephemeral remains of timber and earth-walled constructions, and his figures may therefore be biased towards periods of busier masonry construction (fig. 8). But the mid to late fourth century undoubtedly witnessed a marked decline in the number of villas and town houses in occupation. Several significant changes can be seen to have taken place in the period AD 360/380. Not only were some elite properties abandoned at this time, but a more widespread change in the character of reception activity is also suggested by a variety of architectural features. This was evident in the blocking-off of front corridors into rooms at villas such as Frocester and Spoonley Wood, and former living rooms either went out of use or were converted to new uses at various sites. Ovens associated with corn drying were inserted in the corridors and reception rooms of some town houses. This indicates that the use of such spaces had changed. It is also perhaps significant that some very late town houses dispensed altogether with the portico: examples include the latest version of House 14,3B at Verulamium and the fourth-century building from Dorchester on Thames (Frere 1964). The practices represented by such spaces were becoming archaic in smaller houses in later Roman Britain. The declining importance of the portico-corridor suggests that this form of processional architecture was no longer a key part of social display. The evidence of the mosaics supports this picture of change. For some reason villa owners were no longer great patrons of figurative mosaics.

Up until the middle of the fourth century the trend had been towards an ever-greater emphasis on processional architecture emphasised by porticoes, reception rooms and mosaics. The changes that happened in the final decades of that century therefore represent a marked turn-around in social practice. So what can have happened to reverse some of the earlier architectural tendencies? The historically attested Barbarian conspiracy of AD 367 has long been held to blame for many of Britain's late fourth-century woes (Frere 1987: 339–45). This was a sustained outbreak of violence against elite society, in which raiding barbarians combined with disaffected subjects within the province. Archaeologists have rightly been cautious about associating evidence for abandonment and change with the particular events of this turbulent year. Dating is insufficiently precise, and in any case the changes were of a more protracted nature. It can, however, be argued that the unrest came at a turning point in both the economic fortunes and social attitudes that sustained Roman power. This is essentially the position of Frend (1992) who suggests that the longer-term effects of the disturbances undermined the development of the institutions of Christianity. He develops this thesis in order to account for the subsequent failure of Britain to follow the other provinces of the west and preserve an episcopal Church.

The architecture of the previous half-century might illustrate a degree of social stress. The property-owning elite had become increasingly preoccupied with ideologies and architectures that presented their status as inevitable, necessary and beneficial. The buildings and mosaics described a power, knowledge and wealth that elevated the aristocracy beyond challenge. The need to make such exaggerated architectural claims seems to betray insecurity rather than confidence. If such tensions had been present within the systems that supported social power, then the disorders of AD 367 can be seen as both part of the cycle of response to stress and a trigger for its resolution. There is, however, one further factor to be taken into consideration in this speculation. Some of the evidence for Christianity in Roman Britain might possibly have derived from Gnostic worship rather than orthodox belief. Detail in support of this hypothesis will be introduced in Chapter 7. Whether or not the case is proven, the possibility suggests some alternative ways of reconstructing the social history of the final half-century of Roman rule in Britain.

Gnosticism was a mystery religion of the educated few, very different in its social context to the metropolitan Nicene orthodoxy adopted as the religion of state by the emperor Theodosius in AD 380. The patronage and administrative functions of the Christianity promoted from Rome gave towns a social role. It supported urban populations, and generated economic activity (Harries 1992: 90). This church redirected rural surplus into the cities and developed the ceremonies and rituals that gave focus to urban life. In sum, such Christianity made power urban, and by the same token it held in check an aristocratic tendency to retreat to the countryside. By contrast the Gnostics rejected the rigid structures of bishops and clergy (Pagels 1979: 106), and relied exclusively on the 'wisdom of the brotherhood ... the spiritual fellowship of those united in communion' (*Apocalypse of Peter*). Their beliefs and structures were positively antithetical to the institutional church, and they had no need of either cities or prelates. If Gnosticism had obtained a hold on a significant faction of elite society in Britain, then this may have contributed to the under-development of urban institutions that elsewhere flourished. The diminished status of municipal bishoprics in Britain would have been the outcome. It is interesting to note that the cities that sent bishops to the Council of Arles in AD 314 – York, London and perhaps Lincoln (Thomas 1981: 197) – were those most closely aligned to the official imperial project and least in thrall to local rural aristocracies.

The proposition here is not that differences of religious belief were exclusively responsible for these contrasting approaches to the location of power within the settlement hierarchy. It is more plausible that Romano-British landowners had gravitated towards ideologies that accommodated their existing prejudices, and that this reinforced tendencies that in other provinces were reversed by the growing power of the orthodox Church. If this conjectural model were to apply, then the changes of the late fourth century can be explained without the need to place over-much emphasis on the Barbarian conspiracy. Architecture developed around Gnostic-Christian social practices would have become redundant when the religion was suppressed, a process that was largely compressed into the period *c.* AD 365–80. The ideological realignments required by Roman authority might explain both the redundancy and reconfiguration of domestic space witnessed at this time.

Whatever the merits of these different arguments the undeniable fact is that elite expenditure on reception facilities declined in the closing stages of the fourth century. This was evident in both town and country. Towards the end of the fourth century Verulamium may have contained no more than twenty or thirty houses, most of them residences of the rich. At Caerwent and Silchester there were no more than fifteen or so large fourth-century houses. Todd sees this as reflecting the presence of a stable but limited number of powerful families running the late civic government (Todd 1989). If so, power was perhaps even more narrowly based than had previously been the case.

The use of Roman forms of social display and architectural power barely survived into the fifth century. Some sites continued in occupation, and there is no doubt that both towns and villas retained an important symbolic significance within the landscape, but the Romano-British house did not survive as a viable architectural form. Social competition in post-Roman Britain was differently structured and most aspects of classical display were rejected. The historian Zosimus provides a political context for such changes in his description of the events that culminated in the severing of links between Britain and Rome in AD 410. But in many places the retreat from Roman architectural form had preceded these happenings. It seems suspiciously probable that changes earlier in the fourth century had affected the social fabric of Britain. It is possible to suggest, although with little chance of producing evidence in proof, that divisions consequent on the suppression of pagan and heretical views contributed to the disaffection that culminated in Britain's expulsion of Roman officials.

The subsequent history of architectural fashion in Britain owed little to Rome, except as a consequence of the much later episodes of reintroduction and reinvention of classical and ecclesiastical forms. The English house of the early Saxon period appears to have represented a complete break from the Roman past. This type of building was usually shorter and smaller than either the continental long house or the Romano-British aisled building, and the roof was supported by wall-posts rather than by aisle posts. These buildings were also characterised by side entrances and the presence of a small subdivision at one end. The origins of this 'Chalton-type' house, and the reasons for the comparative scarcity of the Continental-style aisled long house, have been much-debated (Dixon 1982, Hamerow 1994). Some scholars have sought Romano-British influences in these houses, but these are difficult to demonstrate. It is possible that the preference for a side entrance and separate end room was influenced by earlier Roman taste, in particular in the arrangement of strip buildings, but the evidence is unconvincing. Parallels for the English evidence can instead be found in Germanic contexts (such as the Dutch site at Wijster), and the emergence of Anglo-Saxon variations to the Continental norm can be explained through reference to social changes consequent on the migrations themselves. The Romano-British house was a parenthetical departure: as little influenced by what went before, as it was to influence what came after.

4

TYPES OF HOUSE

The purpose of this chapter is to provide a summary description of the main types of houses found in Roman Britain. This is not as easy as it might seem, since every building was crafted against individual circumstance. But amidst many expressions of unique identity it is also possible to recognise some common approaches to the use of space. Before reviewing the ways in which one house differed from another it is first useful to explore these areas of shared intent.

At the risk of over-simplification, two essential approaches to spatial order in the Romano-British house can be defined. There were areas designed to accommodate the layered encounters of social ritual and ceremony, such as the decorated dining rooms and porticoes. The design of these spaces involved an architecture of movement and signal. These parts of the house can be contrasted with undifferentiated space: the halls and workrooms of utilitarian aspect. Such halls appear to have been the common currency of industrial and agricultural buildings, whilst elite residences are likely to have been dominated by stratified space.

The consideration given to the planning of the principal room had a fundamental influence on the overall design and layout of the remainder of the house. In the first place, a fashion for high-roofed and capacious dining halls encouraged architects to set such rooms within a separate wing. Second, these rooms needed appropriate lighting, and an open aspect with a southeasterly exposure was achieved wherever possible. Third, and perhaps most importantly, the main room was placed at the distant end of the domestic establishment. Visitors were guided to the gatherings held here along formal pathways. Porticoes and corridors played an essential role in this articulation of space.

Larger houses contained two or three separate ranges, and the exaggerated distinctions that could be drawn between these described gradations in status. Public rooms, such as baths and barns, gave way to residential suites. Beyond these were the reception quarters. Different suites may have belonged to different times of the day, or suggested distinctions of status and privacy, but the most imposing rooms usually lay at the far end of the house. This

48

was certainly the case in town, where the most handsome rooms were usually placed furthest from the street entrance and were reached by a sequence of corridors and peristyles. It is harder to show that the same ideas applied in the countryside. Villa gardens and courtyards did not need to be protected from the public street and these open spaces could be reconfigured around a public facade. But even here elements of the same approach can be identified. The main rooms were most commonly set at the far end of one wing. Front and back in town became left and right in the country, but the spatial arguments were similarly inspired. Asymmetry was not only a feature of the internal layout of the house, but also an aspect of the relationship between building and landscape. Houses were monuments and their facades were designed to impress, but the views obtained from within the house were more important than the views obtained of the house.

A house from Roman Silchester can be used to illustrate these guiding principles in elite architecture (figs 9 and 60). This L-shaped building had two main ranges. The front-range was built gable-end to the street and included most of the domestic accommodation, whilst the principal

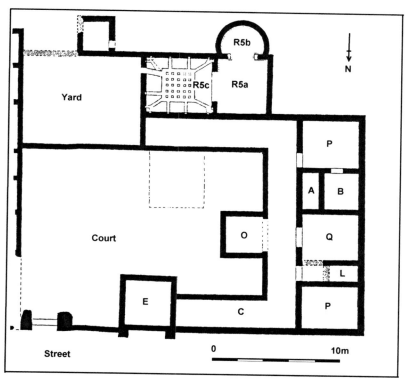

Figure 9 Silchester, House 8,1 (after Fox and St John Hope 1894). For letter codes see fig. 53.

reception rooms were placed in a separate wing to the rear. The house was reached by means of an elaborate entrance (E), in which an imposing porch took guests directly onto a passageway that circumnavigated an enclosed yard (C). This was almost certainly a portico built in similar fashion to a medieval cloister, with an open arcade or colonnade facing the courtyard on one side and a wall punctuated by doors to the rooms of the house on the other. After a short walk the first rooms were encountered. A central chamber (Q) flanked by two three-roomed suites dominated this front-range. The suite furthest from the street was the larger and better decorated of the two. Were these the living rooms of the head of the house? A large porch (O) opposite the central chamber mediated between house and the yard beyond. The portico proceeded to the rear wing. Here three chambers were united to form a large dining complex. On one side of the main hall (R5a) was an apse-ended room where the host and principal guests may have reclined to dine (R5b); on another was a heated chamber suitable for winter use (R5c). The design of the main wing, with its central reception room flanked by three-roomed suites was repeated in high status houses throughout Roman Britain. The L-shaped layout, the emphasis placed on the portico and the setting of the main reception rooms in the rear wing were also familiar features. At the same time, however, the design of this house was unmistakably influenced by local fashion. The entrance porch was of a type only normally found in Silchester.

So far we have established some common points of reference in our exploration of the Romano-British house. The remainder of this chapter is concerned with the features that have been used to describe different typologies. Many factors account for the morphological variety. Perhaps the most important was the social and economic role of the property. The richer and more powerful patron used space differently to his industrious but more anonymous clients. The houses of the rich and powerful contained impressive reception rooms and extensive living quarters. Three types of such house are described here. In the forts military commanders were given quarters that befitted their status and allowed a dignified social life. Because space was at a considerable premium in the army camps compressed forms of housing were developed for all but the most senior officers. Some similar constraints applied in the early Romano-British towns, but there were more marked contrasts between the crowded street frontages and the space that could be found at the back of the plot. Town houses turned their backs to the street and were built overlooking walled gardens and yards. Different circumstances applied in the countryside. Villa architecture could be more open in aspect and more monumental in appearance.

The scale of the establishment had a major impact on house design. More space permitted a higher specialisation of room function. Larger properties were created by the use of separate wings and ranges. A simple hierarchy can be established by describing houses built over one, two or more ranges:

hence L-shaped houses and U-shaped houses. The design of town houses, more so than villas, was also likely to betray strong regional influence. For instance a house style developed at Caerwent gave emphasis to a large forecourt through which the building was entered (figs 11b and 17e). In contrast the houses of Roman Silchester were likely to be entered through an imposing porch connected to the rest of the house by a long portico or corridor. These approaches generated distinctly local types of house plan.

Most houses were built as working establishments, servicing the needs of agricultural production, manufacture and commerce. Whereas palaces were designed with social needs foremost, more humble properties were likely to be dominated by their economic functions. A large hall was the central feature of many such houses. This provided working and storage space in industrial and agricultural buildings, but could also have been used for communal activities. Large central rooms were found in most round houses, aisled buildings and strip buildings. These three types of house may have been used in similar ways, although differences in their context, chronology and evolution can usefully be described. The decision as to whether to build within a hall, an aisled basilica or a circular building appears, however, to reflect a cultural and social choice. We will commence our review of house types by describing these more utilitarian structures.

Round houses

We have already described how most Britons lived in circular buildings at the time of the Roman invasion (see Chapter 3). Such building traditions persisted on smaller farmsteads in the post-conquest period. Small circular timber structures also made an appearance in the suburbs that sprang-up outside the first Roman towns. This was a short-lived phenomenon, probably consequent on the presence of Britons attracted to the margins of the new towns during the first phase of their urban growth, although it is a moot point as to whether this was regulated or unregulated settlement. The former seems the more likely. Rectangular buildings in Roman style soon replaced these low status buildings.

Although rectangular buildings dominated the Romano-British country-side from the second century onwards, circular houses were still being built into the fourth century in some regions. This was notably the case in the Fens where Iron Age building traditions survived in rural areas (Todd 1973, Keevill and Booth 1997). Many round houses built after the middle of the second century were designed with stone footings supporting earth-walled or timber superstructures. Circular houses of this later period were favoured in the Midlands and their distribution matches the likely area of influence of the Corieltauvi tribe (Keevill and Booth 1997). Although essentially a rural phenomenon similar buildings were also found in some 'small towns' in the same region, where the tradition survived down to the fourth century

(Burnham and Wacher 1990: 17). Circular buildings have also been found on sites on Hadrian's Wall, most strikingly at Vindolanda where as many as thirty such buildings may have been built in the third century (Bidwell 1985: 28–31). It has been argued that these were houses accommodating a civilian work force under military control. Whatever the reason for their construction they illustrate the use of such round houses in a very Roman context.

The use of circular structures does not necessarily represent an unbroken tradition of use from the pre-Roman period. In parts of Oxfordshire and Gloucestershire circular structures with masonry foundations were built on high status late Roman sites, in a region where rectangular timber structures had previously been preferred (Keevill and Booth 1997). So this late fashion appears to represent an architectural innovation of the Roman period. Some of these structures may have been used as shrines, but they are also found used as outbuildings on villa compounds. An example of this was found in the excavation of the villa at Redlands Farm, Stanwick, where stone structures up to 14.5 m in diameter had been built as outhouses and served a range of industrial and residential functions (Keevill and Booth 1997).

Some similar buildings were designed to permit wheeled access, as is demonstrated by the wheel-ruts that crossed the 4.1 m wide threshold to an outhouse of the Roman villa at Winterton in Lincolnshire (Stead 1976). By contrast the porch into a circular building at Shakenoak suggests that this was more likely to have been used as a dwelling (Brodribb *et al.* 1968–78). Hearths have also been found in several buildings. Like the aisled buildings, the later Roman circular houses were built over substantial stone foundations (often more than 600 mm wide) and were likely to have been high roofed. These circular structures appear to have been used in similar ways to the aisled buildings, and the reasons why one type of building was sometimes preferred over the other is not clear. Closer analysis of the choices made about the location of such houses, built on a closer understanding of how they may have been perceived within the broader landscape setting, might provide clues. It might also be the case that some structural forms were more closely associated with certain types of storage and industrial use than others.

Roman round houses were generally built using different construction techniques to those preferred before the conquest. This included the greater use of stone footings and the use of squared timbers in contexts where round-sectioned ones had previously been used, as in the second-century structures at Kirk Sink, Gargrave in West Yorkshire (Goodburn 1976: 317–18). These later circular houses were also more likely to have been found as outbuildings rather than as principal residences. Given these significant differences in both structural form and nature of use, it can be concluded that these structures were a product of the Roman period rather than a relic of some earlier architectural tradition.

Aisled buildings

Rectangular aisled buildings are found on many Romano-British sites, and the architectural type may have been developed within the province (Hadman 1978). An aisled building from Lixhe in Belgium provides a late parallel for the Romano-British evidence (Van Ossel 1992: 291), but most aisled structures from continental sites were of different form. Romano-British aisled houses represented a local development of a building type that first appeared in the pre-conquest Romanising phases of high status sites in southeast Britain. This is illustrated by an early example of this type of building found in pre-Roman contexts at the Gorhambury villa near St Albans (fig. 5, Neal *et al.* 1990). An aisled hall with stone pier-bases was also built as part of the Flavian villa at Fishbourne (fig. 6). In both cases the buildings had served as ancillary structures to elite residences.

Richard Hingley has shown (1990: 136) that aisled houses shared several features with circular ones, notably the use of central posts, axial entrances and central hearths. Both types of house were also designed with lofty internal spaces and an imposing external aspect. They did not, however, supplant round houses. Aisled buildings were most popular in the Fens, which was also the area where round houses continued longest in use.

Typically these buildings were about twice as long as they were wide, although a significant number were of longer and narrower form, with the nave equal in width to the two aisles. Two basic types have been defined: simple undivided aisled houses comprising a single open room and a developed type with a distinct suite of rooms at one end. Many simpler aisled buildings were evidently put to agricultural use (Morris 1979). The lack of evidence for stalls, dung or drainage indicates that they were probably not cattle byres. The wide entrances commonly found in such buildings suggest that they may have been used as barns and workshops. Industrial uses are well attested by both finds and features, especially by the frequent provision of ovens and hearths. Two interpretative models are current. Richmond (1969: 65) treated the aisled house as part of the *villa rustica*, housing the estate workers and providing facilities for agricultural storage and processing, with the owner resident elsewhere. In contrast Applebaum (1972) prefers to see these buildings as the homes of extended families. These arguments will be explored in more detail in Chapter 12.

Regional groupings of aisled buildings have been noted in Hampshire and in the Fens (D.J. Smith 1978: 126, Wild 1974). In Hampshire these free-standing buildings commonly included reception features and were usually set at right angles to a main house within a walled enclosure, an arrangement largely restricted to this region (fig. 10). The first aisled building at Sparsholt, which was probably built in the second century, preceded the construction of the main winged-corridor house and contained a bath block at one end. Although apparently the earliest structure within the compound,

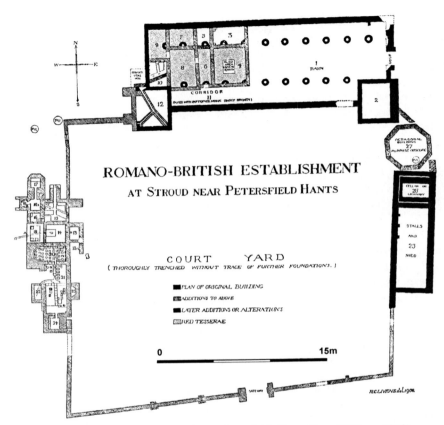

Figure 10 The aisled building at Stroud near Petersfield, Hants (from Williams 1908).

the aisled building took a secondary position (i.e. not the principal site with a southeast aspect facing the entrance). The winged-corridor house that was subsequently built on the favoured site was never provided with a bath suite of its own. Here as elsewhere it seems probable that reception rooms placed in the aisled building were for the common use of inhabitants within both structures. Public and working areas exploited the loftier structure of the aisled building, with the private rooms and suites in the main house.

Aisled buildings were important monuments in the Romano-British landscape, as was shown by their elaborate and imposing design (see Chapter 6). Villa estates were where agricultural wealth was stored. It is probable that many aisled buildings were used as barns and granaries. The emphasis given to scale and height emphasised the role of villa estates in producing and storing agricultural wealth. There are perhaps some parallels to be drawn here with the role of the medieval tithe barn. The manifestation of abundance spoke powerfully of the benefits accruing from the existing social order. The importance of such surplus has been emphasised by Purcell who observes that storerooms in the Roman tradition were intended to impress (1995: 169). This provides a possible explanation for the scale of investment made in the construction of both villa houses (as places of elite residence) and aisled buildings (as places of wealth storage). An exaggerated emphasis on the architecture of storage might have attended estates where the owners were less regularly resident and were therefore less able to define and reinforce their position through social activity. If this were the case then it might also be possible to argue that regions where aisled buildings were dominant were those most likely to be characterised by absentee landlords.

Aisled buildings also provided domestic and workshop accommodation in small towns (Burnham and Wacher 1990: 20) and have been found attached to some late Romano-British town houses. If these buildings were used as barns then their presence marks out the urban farms from which lands surrounding the town had been cultivated. An aisled building attached to the House of the Menander at Pompeii offers a close parallel for this arrangement.

Strip buildings

Suburban and other street-side settlements were characterised by rows of large rectangular buildings set gable-end to the main roads. These structures were commonly 8–9 m wide by 20–28 m long. They were typically crowded together to take full use of the available street frontage, with eavesdrips between the buildings rarely more than one metre across. The ideal type had a shop at the front, a large workroom in the main part of the building and living quarters to the rear.

Following the work of Boethius (1960: 137), strip buildings have been considered to have an Italian origin and be a feature of urban sites throughout the empire (Stambaugh 1988: 174). They were actually a rarity in Roman Italy. Admittedly shops in Ostia and Herculaneum have many of the design characteristics of these buildings, but they do not share the same building form. The normal pattern of development in the Mediterranean provinces involved blocks of houses including several shops and houses divided by a network of party walls. These were very different to the free-standing rectangular buildings described here. The preference for a complete physical separation of the shops and houses was a later and provincial fashion. strip buildings were, however, common in extra-mural and roadside sites in Gallia Belgica and especially in the civilian settlements (*canabae*) attached to forts along the Rhine. The form of the building type introduced to Britain owed much to architectural developments in this region. Excavations at Grobbendonk (De Boe 1986) have revealed a structural progression from simple rectangular timber Claudian buildings showing distinct similarities to agricultural structures of the period. Several of these houses were built with two-aisles in a type common in the region, with more complex house types evident in the later first and second centuries. These later types included masonry elements and a more complex division of internal space.

Strip buildings may represent an adaptation of a rural building type to provide workshop and commercial space. This process probably first occurred in the piecemeal development of sites along the Roman frontier, where there was less incentive for landlords to invest in the construction of rows of houses more typical of the Roman Mediterranean. It seems likely that strip buildings were only common in the northwest provinces where winged-corridor villas were preferred and *atrium*-peristyle houses were uncommon. There is a crisp fault line between these architectural regions.

In Britain buildings of this type were built in street-side locations almost as soon as the streets themselves had been laid out. Examples destroyed in the revolt of AD 60–61 are known from sites in London and Colchester. It seems likely that rows of several strip buildings could be found within a single property. Groups of such buildings appear to have been built and rebuilt in coordinated building programmes at both Lincoln and Heronbridge. At Caerwent groups of strip buildings were subsequently remodelled to form single houses.

The simplest structures consisted of a single large hall (fig.11a). There are numerous examples of such buildings from civilian settlements outside and succeeding forts in the northern part of the province (e.g. Bishop and Dore 1988: figs 3 and 5). These were generally smaller than other strip buildings, with internal areas of 75–115 m square, and in some instances may have been workshops or stables attached to neighbouring residences. Characteristic features include hearths, drains and flagged floors. A simple development of the form involved partitioning off a single rectangular room at the back of the building to allow for some separation of working and living quarters (fig. 11b).

Workshops were usually entered directly from the street. Large ovens were sometimes built on the right-hand side of these workshops, roughly half-way along the building, next to a doorway from an adjacent alleyway. This side entrance gave access to the reception rooms at the back without the need to pass along the length of the workshop and ventilated the oven. Larger workrooms were not infrequently subdivided by timber partitions during the later phases of a building's use, often to create two or three working areas.

Rear living rooms were formed by partitions in the back of the house. This was usually an original design feature, but could also be the result of later alteration. On smaller plots, where space was at a premium, the private quarters were found in separate rear extensions. Such additions were common in London (fig. 12). More elaborate building techniques were sometimes employed in the construction of these rear extensions. A slight Claudio-Neronian wattle and daub house in Colchester was improved by a rear

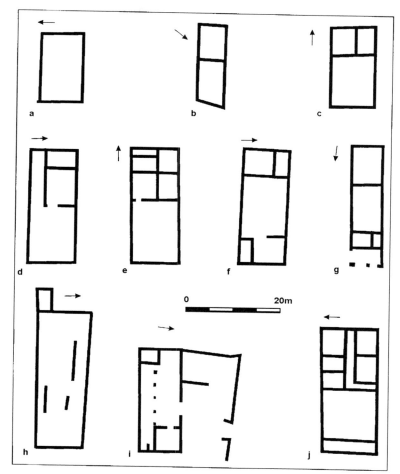

Figure 11 Hall-type strip buildings. a: single-roomed, Silchester 22, B1 (St John Hope 1902). b: two-roomed, Verulamium 1,2 (Wheeler and Wheeler 1936). c: with a two-roomed suite to the rear, Silchester 9,B4 (Fox 1895). d: with a three-roomed suite to the rear, Caerwent 24N (Ashby *et al.* 1911). e: with an extended suite to the rear, Silchester 9, B3 (Fox 1895). f: with shops to the front, Hibbaldstow 3 (Smith 1987). g: with a street-side portico, Caerwent 16S (Ashby *et al.* 1911). h: with internal screen corridors, Lincoln St. Marks 2 (Jones 1981). i: with yards, Caerwent 13N (Ashby 1906). j: hall and row buildings, Heronbridge 1 (Mason 1989).

extension built with post-in-trench walls (Crummy 1984: 107–8). In London an earth-walled rear block containing three reception rooms was built to the rear of a wattle and daub house at Newgate Street (fig. 12, Building J, rooms v–vii), and at One Poultry a third-century masonry extension was added behind a wooden building (Burch *et al.* 1997). In all cases the better-built

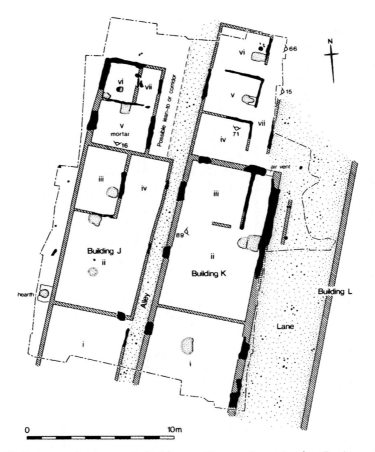

Figure 12 Early second-century strip buildings at Newgate Street, London (Perring and
Roskams 1991). Copyright Museum of London.

rooms formed a reception suite at the back of the house, where the additional
investment had allowed the construction of imposing dining rooms. The
most common arrangement involved one larger better-decorated room, sometimes with mortar floors and painted walls, and an adjacent narrow service
room (fig. 11c). These rooms were reached directly from the workshop although
sometimes a corridor was added across the width of the building, separating
the working area from the rear reception suite and allowing independent
access from the street. This arrangement is similar to that found in first-
century centurions' houses from which inspiration may have been drawn. In
more complex buildings a third room was added behind the larger reception
room (fig. 11d). Three-roomed suites of this nature are well represented at
Caerwent and mirror the reception quarters found in villas and town houses.

Only rarely were more than three rooms provided in this part of the building (fig. 11e). In a few cases the reception quarters here included a small heated room. The plunge bath attached to a heated room set behind a strip building at One Poultry in London shows this to have been a private bath. Rows of rooms found behind the larger workrooms sometimes provided a more ambitious level of accommodation (fig. 11j, St John Hope 1906: 151, Mason 1989).

At some sites along Ermine Street in Lincolnshire were aisled strip buildings (fig. 11f and g). Examples include a structure with aisles formed by large circular posts at Hibaldstow (Smith 1987: fig. 13). Further south, at Lincoln, a half-timbered strip building with timber aisles was rebuilt in stone in the late third century (fig. 11i, Jones 1981: 94–8). Glass found in a similar building at Sapperton suggests that this may have had clerestory lighting (Oetgen 1987).

Not all strip buildings followed the basic pattern of a hall with smaller living rooms behind. The main variation, best represented by buildings excavated at Caerwent, involved inserting one or two smaller rooms at the front of the workshop (fig. 11f). These may have been shops. There is no direct evidence that this was the case but strip buildings in continental Europe were often laid out with shop-counters open to the street (e.g. Kolling 1972: 238–57). More complex arrangements involved the addition of covered porticoes along the street frontage (fig. 11g. Ashby et al. 1911: 427–30, Bushe-Fox 1913).

Corridors or porticoes providing access to the rear reception rooms were rare in hall buildings, although this arrangement was found in a strip building in the civilian settlement outside the fort at Castleford (Abramson 1999: 128). This small rectangular hall, measuring no more than 9 m by 4 m, saw two phases of alteration before its replacement towards the end of the first century. The final alterations involved the addition of a 1.5 m wide corridor along the side of the structure. An early third-century building at Chelmsford was also built with a similar feature (Drury 1975). In several instances, however, it seems likely that the timber partitions within the building screened off passages from a front entrance to the rear reception rooms (fig. 11h). This was perhaps the purpose of partitions added in the strip buildings excavated at Lincoln St Marks (Jones 1981: 94–8).

All of the types described above include a large central workroom. There were, however, some strip buildings that never contained a main room, but had been divided into series of roughly equally proportioned rooms arranged in a single row. Early examples include a three-roomed house at One Poultry (fig. 13a). Longer row-houses were built behind London's early forum. Six narrow strip buildings, up to 30 m long, were found here (Milne 1992: 73–7). These were divided into a series of small square rooms, each with a hearth placed centrally against one side wall and entered separately from its own yard (fig. 13b). The buildings were given over to cramped accommodation with no

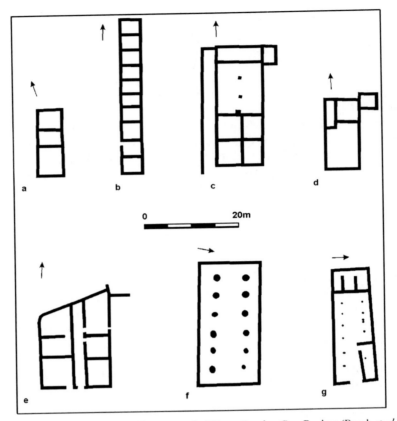

Figure 13 Strip buildings. a: small row-type buildings, London One Poultry (Burch *et al.* 1997). b: long row-type buildings, London Leadenhall Ct. (Milne and Wardle 1995). c: corridor and hall buildings, Silchester 5,B1 (St John Hope 1906). d: buildings with a projecting rear wing, Silchester19,B1 (Fox and St John Hope 1899). e: central corridor buildings, Vindolanda 'Anima Mea' house (Birley 1977). f: aisled buildings with open hall, Sapperton 2 (Simmons 1985). g: aisled buildings with rooms to rear, Hibbaldstow 4 (Smith 1987).

main workrooms. It seems likely that these were rows of rooms for rent. The Vindolanda 'Anima Mea' house, where a central corridor divided two independent series of rooms, may have been a development on the type (fig. 13e, Birley 1977: 70). Some buildings of this row type were provided with a side portico or corridor (fig. 13c). These features were found in buildings with other architectural features suggesting that they were intended to receive guests. Exceptionally living rooms were added not to the rear of the building but on one side of the house, an approach principally illustrated by examples from Silchester (fig. 13d). The introduction of rear reception rooms of this type may have contributed to the evolution of winged and L-shaped town houses.

Military houses

The first explicitly Roman houses in Britain were those built for the officers and soldiers that arrived in the wake of the invasion of AD 43. The houses of Roman Britain drew inspiration from these early military prototypes. Recent studies have tended to over emphasise the distinctions that can be drawn between military and civilian. It is therefore worth emphasising that serving soldiers were frequently billeted in the towns and posting stations, where imperial business demanded their presence, and that large civilian communities could live within the bounds of the army's camps.

The design of houses inside the earliest forts followed a pattern established prior to the conquest of Britain. Close parallels can be found along the Rhine frontier. For instance the exceptionally preserved first-century fort at Valkenburg provides an illustration of the methods of timber-framed construction that were widely adopted in Romano-British towns (Glasbergen 1972). Three types of housing provided for most military needs. There were barrack blocks for ordinary soldiers, large but compact 'corridor' buildings for centurions, and grand courtyard houses for senior officers. The soldiers lived in mess units known as *contubernia*. These groups, normally of eight men, shared two-room apartments, in which a large common room was set behind an antechamber used as a service room and store. Barrack blocks were formed of rows of such two-roomed apartments. Throughout the first and second centuries AD centurions were usually accommodated in separate houses built at the end of these blocks (Hoffman 1995). These officers were well paid, often came from families of social rank and could be accompanied by both families and slaves. This status was reflected in the scale and layout of their houses (fig. 14). Rectangular centurions' houses usually measured about 20–4 m long by 10–12 m wide and could contain between nine and twelve rooms, excluding corridors. Plans were not standardised; even adjacent houses within the same fort were different. Each house appears to have been designed to meet the particular requirements of its occupant. Certain arrangements were, however, commonly repeated. Like the Pompeiian row-houses described in Chapter 2 these buildings followed the pattern of courtyard houses, but where the courtyard itself had been reduced to a small light-well or omitted altogether because of pressures of space. The rooms in these centurions' houses were laid out in three broad groups, corresponding to the wings set around three sides of the courtyard. Rooms at the front of the house were likely to contain hearths and drains, and constituted a service wing of workrooms and stores. In the most common type of house a central longitudinal corridor linked these front rooms with the more important ones to the rear of the house, and divided the rooms in the central part of the building. On one side of the corridor lay smaller chambers, perhaps including the sleeping quarters. Opposite these was an area that in some houses was used as a yard and in others included further stores. This space

Figure 14 Centurions' quarters from the Flavian camp at Inchtuthil (Pitts and St Joseph 1985).

and the adjacent corridor were essentially a reduced version of the peristyle courtyard. Peristyle courtyards were commonly found in centurions' houses built in the half-century prior to the conquest of Britain but this feature had lost its architectural importance in the course of the first century. The most important rooms lay at the back of the house, sometimes separated from the rest of the house by a transverse corridor. These rear chambers included a main reception room, marked out by better quality floors or wall paintings (Hoffmann 1995: 130). In several buildings the adjacent area included one or more narrow chambers that might have included kitchens and latrines.

Examples of centurions' houses of this type have been found in excavations at Gloucester and Colchester and in the abandoned Flavian fort on the north bank of the Tay at Inchtuthil (Hurst 1999, Crummy 1988, Pitts and St Joseph 1985: 156). Interestingly, a Flavian building in London was identical in plan and design to these houses, lending support to the suggestion that the western part of London may have been laid out as a military enclave (fig. 16d, Millett 1994: 434). There were variations on this 'corridor type' of house. In some buildings the central corridor was dispensed with altogether, and the rooms just set in interconnecting rows. These 'row- type' centurions' houses have been found in the fortress at Colchester.

Senior officials were often housed in larger courtyard buildings. Early examples built in timber include the tribunes' houses from the fort at Inchtuthil (fig. 15). Ranges of rooms were set out around the four sides of a central peristyle court. Tribune's House I is a good example of the type and offers an early illustration of several of the features that were to become

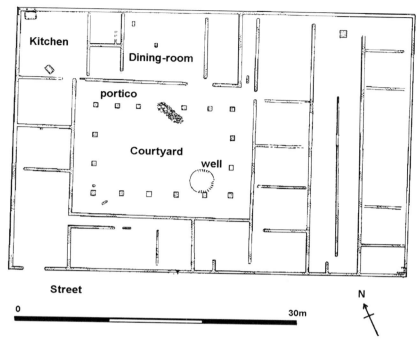

Figure 15 A tribune's courtyard house from the Flavian fort at Inchtuthil (Pitts and St Joseph 1985).

common in the high status houses of Roman Britain. Most notably the main reception room was found towards the rear of the house, and was marked by its special relationship with the peristyle court. A double-width gap had been left between the columns of the portico here, and a stone foundation supported a garden feature that could be seen from the principal room. The arrangement of the adjacent rooms in this reception wing recalls that of several later Romano-British villas.

Later examples of courtyard houses in Romano-British forts include the Commandant's house at Housesteads and the fourth-century courtyard house at South Shields (A Johnson 1983, Hodgson 1996). The house at South Shields was built around four sides of an elongated central courtyard. The narrow entrance wing contained the baths. A long range of rooms perpendicular to the entrance consisted of two suites of interconnected living rooms. At the back of the courtyard stood the reception wing, equipped with a hot room and a dining room with couches. The other long wing contained a kitchen and stable. Notwithstanding the clear Mediterranean parallels, this arrangement of space was consistent with Romano-British architectural taste of the period.

Town houses

The distinction drawn here between strip buildings and town houses is an arbitrary one. All houses were liable to include both working areas and reception quarters. Town life was, however, characterised by a class of elite housing inspired by the needs of social rather than economic use. These properties ranged considerably in scale and pretension: from small row-houses to palatial courtyard buildings. In the following review of the morphological characteristics of such structures we start with the smaller and simpler buildings.

From the end of the first century most town houses were built with a portico or corridor. There are a few buildings where this feature was not present, most of which were small houses with no more than two or three interconnected rooms (fig. 16). The central rooms in some such smaller buildings were given emphasis by a small porch. Normally, however, even small two- or three-roomed houses were given passageways that took visitors to a reception room at the back of the house (fig. 17). In some cases this space was partitioned off at its ends, to form an entry chamber beside the street and a small room at the far end. These rooms occupied the place of the corner pavilions found in the winged-corridor facade.

Although essentially a rural building form, winged-corridor houses have also been found in some towns. The type consisted of a rectangular block with a portico along one side, given emphasis by corner pavilions at each

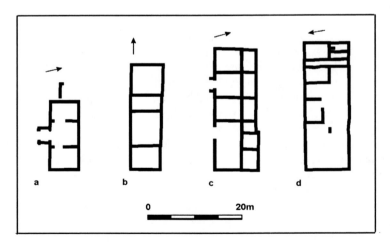

Figure 16 Row-type town houses. a: small houses with an entrance porch, Dorchester, Colliton Park (Drew and Selby 1937). b: small houses with a rear reception room, Silchester 17,4 (Fox and St John Hope 1898). c: Caerwent 'yard' house, Caerwent 23N (Ashby *et al.* 1911). d: corridor house, Watling Court F (Perring and Roskams 1991).

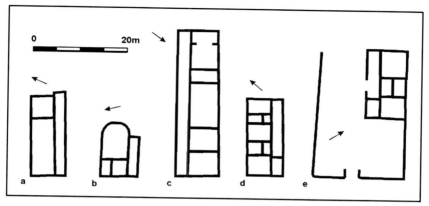

Figure 17 Row-type town houses with porticoes or corridors. a: small houses, Verulamium 3,1 (first phase) (Wheeler and Wheeler 1936). b: corridor houses with rear receptions rooms, Caerwent 24N (first phase) (Ashby *et al.* 1911). c: corridor houses with enlarged rear reception suites, Verulamium 4,2. d: complex pseudo-winged houses, Verulamium 6,1 (Wheeler and Wheeler 1936). e: Caerwent 'yard' houses, Caerwent 14S (Ashby *et al.* 1911).

end. In most towns this facade could not be seen in such a way that its symmetry could be appreciated. The urban use of winged-corridor facades may therefore have only taken place where there was an unusual amount of open space. The best examples of the type date to the fourth century, at a time when urban population densities were in decline (figs 18 and 57b).

An L-shaped plan was commonly achieved through the addition of a rear wing containing one or more reception rooms. From the middle of the second century onwards this was the most common type of Romano-British town house. The simplest of these buildings consisted of a core of three or four rooms to which a single room, sometimes a heated reception room, had been added at one corner. This rear reception room was usually reached along a portico or corridor built along one side of the house, although this feature was omitted in a few instances (fig.19a). In some buildings a large work-hall was set against street frontage: an arrangement best represented at Silchester (fig. 19c). The commonest type of L-shaped house incorporated a main suite of rooms in a wing set perpendicular to the street. A portico or corridor alongside this block ran from the street to a rear wing containing the principal reception rooms (fig. 19e–i). The influence of strip buildings is reflected in the way that the principal range was built with its gable-end towards the street and the reception rooms were set in a separate wing at the back. At Dorchester, in what may have been a particularly local fashion, the two main wings of the house were sometimes treated as entirely separate structures (fig. 20).

Complex arrangements of rooms over three disjointed wings have been

Figure 18 A fourth-century winged-corridor town house at Beeches Road, Cirencester. The entrance porch (foreground left), gave access to a short portico leading towards heated end reception rooms (right). Photograph reproduced courtesy of Corinium Museum, Cirencester. Copyright Cotswold District Council.

found at Silchester and Verulamium. These houses shared a preference for extensive porticoes but did not usually provide much more accommodation than the L-shaped buildings described above. The additional wing was mainly used to augment the working space alongside the street. In the more symmetrically arranged houses the wings were laid out with a portico around three sides of a rectangular garden or courtyard. These houses usually included a similar range of room types to that found in smaller houses but were more profligate in their use of space. A house found at Verulamium presents a good example (fig. 21). The extensive reception suite to the rear of the house contained as many as six separate heated rooms. This was separated from the main range of the house by a large room that probably served as a kitchen, beyond which lay two or perhaps three suites of smaller rooms. The entrance range, although poorly preserved, is perhaps most likely to have housed working and storage space.

One of the earliest civilian courtyard houses in Britain was built in Colchester prior to the revolt of AD 60. This appears to have had three ranges of rooms set around a central courtyard although the plan is incomplete and these elements may not have all been part of the same house (Crummy 1984: 36). This building remains a unique example, and courtyard

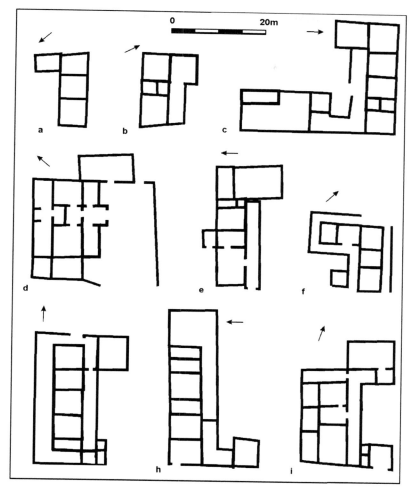

Figure 19 L-shaped town houses. a: row-type houses with no corridor and a one-room extension, Verulamium 14, 3B (Frere 1983). b: row-houses with a standard suite of
living rooms, corridor and one-room extension, Verulamium 14,3A. c: row-houses
with a front wing Silchester 18,1 (Fox and St John Hope 1898). d: row-houses
with a front wing and Caerwent yard, Caerwent 6S (Ashby *et al.* 1903). e: row-
houses with rear reception wings, Silchester 7,4 (Fox and St John Hope 1894). f:
ditto with porch entrance, Verulamium 4,1 (Wheeler and Wheeler 1936). g:
Winchester 23,1 (Zant 1993). h: Silchester 7,3 (Fox and St John Hope 1894). i:
standard type – where the rear wing consisted of one or two main reception rooms,
Silchester 9,3 (Fox 1895).

houses were not otherwise built on civilian sites until after the middle of the
second century. Irregular types, with rooms set around two or three sides of
the courtyard, included row, L-shaped and U-shaped houses. In these

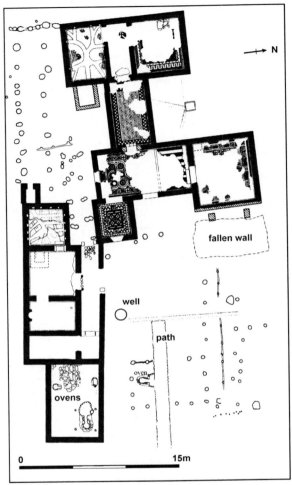

Figure 20 Building I at Colliton Park, Dorchester, an L-shaped town house with disarticulated wings (after Drew and Selby 1937).

buildings a portico or garden wall had been added to enclose the central courtyard (fig. 22a, c and d). Courtyard houses could also be formed of two parallel ranges perpendicular to the street linked to front and back by entrance corridors and garden walls (fig. 22b).

A particular type of house is represented by an elongated courtyard (fig. 23a). In these houses a main range of rooms was set perpendicular to the street, with a further range of principal reception rooms to the rear. A lesser group of service rooms was set alongside the street, whilst the fourth side of the courtyard was enclosed by irregular groups of small rooms and garden

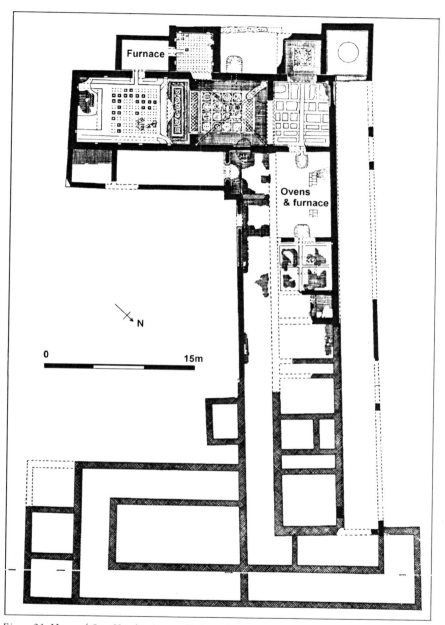

Figure 21 House 4,8 at Verulamium, a U-shaped town house (after Wheeler and Wheeler 1936).

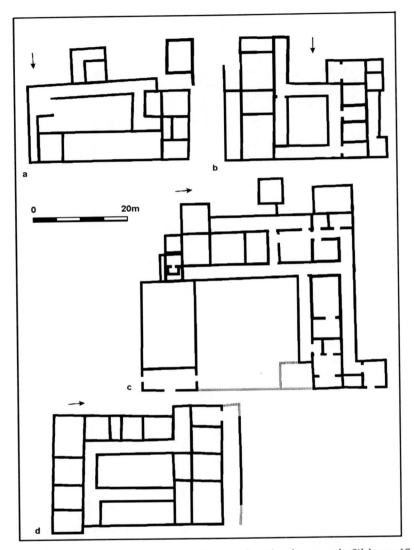

Figure 22 Courtyard houses. a: L-shaped buildings with enclosed courtyards, Silchester 17,1
(Fox and St John Hope 1898). b: two-range houses, Silchester 6,1 (St John Hope
1906). c: L-shaped buildings and workhall, Silchester 19,2 (Fox and St John Hope
1899). d: with principle ranges of rooms on three sides of a peristyle courtyard,
Colchester Lion Walk 20 (Crummy 1984).

walls. The unusual characteristic of this house type was the length of the
main range, which could also include a principal reception room with
flanking suites of more private rooms. The rear reception wing was made

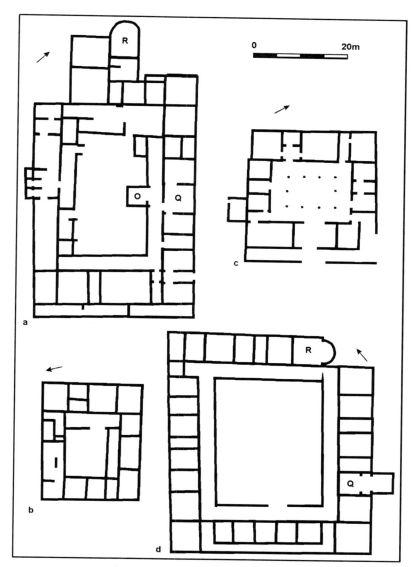

Figure 23 Courtyard houses. a: elongated, Caerwent 2S (Ashby *et al.* 1902). b: without full
peristyle, Caerwent 7N (Ashby *et al.* 1904). c: with peristyle, Caerwent 3S (Ashby
et al. 1901). d: Verulamium 3,2 (Wheeler and Wheeler 1936).

more elaborate in these houses and could include an apse-ended room. This
type of building has been found in both Wroxeter and Caerwent, where its
unusual size has resulted in the suggestion that it may have been an inn or
mansio (Wacher 1995: 382).

Symmetrical courtyard houses, with ranges enclosing all four sides, were a rarity confined in large part to the later period and the western part of the province. Most known examples of this type of house occur in the *coloniae*, although the sample is a small one (Hodgson 1996: 147). Two basic types can be described: houses with rooms on all four sides of the central courtyard but in which the peristyle was not taken all the way around (fig. 23b), and houses where the peristyle neatly defined a central garden. A house found in Gloucester (House 1.18) is the earliest yet to be closely dated and was probably built in the mid second century (Hurst 1999). A good illustration of the type is found in House 3S from Caerwent (fig. 23c, Ashby *et al.* 1901: 301–9). The rear wing of this building included a central reception room connected to a principal suite of rooms to the left with a two-roomed group to the right. As was usually the case the rooms against the street frontage were low status and may have included stores, stables and workrooms. The remains of House 25,1 at Cirencester are also worthy of note: here three sides of a third-century or later courtyard building were found with a peristyle of columns supported on a stylobate (McWhirr 1986: 222–6). Most peristyle houses showed the influence of Romano-British architectural styles and were elaborate versions of local types rather than wholly imported forms.

One large courtyard house, House 3,2 at Verulamium, was of such regular form and unusual size that it can be treated as a separate class of building (fig. 23d). Thirty-two rooms were neatly arranged around a near-square peristyle (Wheeler and Wheeler 1936: 94–6). The symmetry and order of the building is such that it must have functioned differently to most of the houses described above. Even here, however, some of the basic features of the Romano-British house can be recognised. A rear reception room is evident (Room R), whilst a main range of rooms incorporated a larger suite (Room Q) which could have functioned as an audience chamber.

Villas

Recent studies of the Romano-British villa have correctly concentrated on the place of these establishments within the broader landscape. Excavation at sites such as Stanwick in Northamptonshire have shown how houses and farm buildings could be spread wide across the countryside. The larger villa estates supported sizeable communities engaged in a range of specialist activities. In this study, however, we are chiefly concerned with the principal houses of the estate, where leading members of the community are likely to have lived.

Most previous attempts to describe the types of building found in Roman Britain have been based exclusively on the evidence of villas. Defining characteristics have been taken to be the addition of corridors, wings and courtyards to a nuclear main block: hence cottage villas, corridor houses, winged-corridor houses and courtyard houses (Collingwood and Richmond

1969). John Smith has offered an extensive critique of these attempts to classify villa plans, and proposed a refined typology and terminology (1997: 6–9). His description of the architecture is structured to lend weight to his argument about social structure, and emphasises a contrast between buildings dominated by central 'halls' and those that were instead divided into rows of more evenly sized units. In this the architectural significance of the portico is considered a secondary feature. Other architectural features, such as baths and reception rooms, are not given weight in either system of classification.

Where several variables compete to give defining identity to the house it will always be something of an arbitrary decision which to treat as the more important. I have followed the structure set out by Richmond, amended to absorb some of the terminological improvements suggested by Smith. This is in part because the Richmond classification dominates the published litera-ture and in part because there is no compelling evidence to believe that the provision of a central hall is more socially revealing than the use of a portico.

The simplest Roman-style houses built in the British countryside were rectangular halls, similar to the simpler strip buildings. There were also a few row-houses based on a standard suite of living rooms. Although it was exceptional for such suites not to be set behind a portico or corridor this had been the case at a few early villas, as at Park Street in the late first century (fig. 24a, O'Neill 1945). A feature of these early villas built without a portico was the lack of emphasis on either a central or end reception room. These buildings contained the core domestic suite (for which see Chapter 11), but lacked the reception features that were subsequently to form such an important part of the Romano-British house. Porticoes were frequently added to these early buildings in later phases of alteration and improvement, as for instance at Farningham in Kent where a narrow front portico was built *c.* AD 100, at which time a bath-house was also added (Meates 1973).

There may also have been one or two later buildings where porticoes were not provided (as at Rudston). There is no obvious reason why this was the case, although in some instances lightweight timber structures may have eluded identification. Most Romano-British villas were instead built con-taining the standard ranges of rooms set behind a portico or corridor. In the simplest such design (fig. 24b) the architectural emphasis was on a central reception room, and although these houses could contain a heated end room, such end rooms were generally smaller. The importance of the central room could be further indicated by a substantial porch looking out over the forecourt or garden (fig. 24c). An alternative approach involved placing the emphasis on a large reception room at the end of the main block (fig. 24e). On the whole a preference for a central reception room was evident in the southeast in earlier periods, whilst the use of end reception rooms was particularly popular in the west of Britain in the fourth century.

Normally a small room flanked the portico at one or both of its ends (fig. 24d–e). These rooms formed the corner pavilions characteristic of the winged-

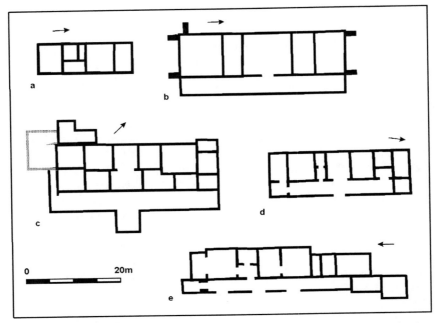

Figure 24 'Cottage' and 'corridor' villas. a: simple row villa, Park Street (O'Neill 1945). b: portico villa with central reception room, Feltwell (Gurney 1986). c: portico villa with central room and porch, Ashtead (Lowther 1929). d: portico villa with pseudo-pavilions and central reception rooms, Sparsholt (Johnston 1969). e: portico villa with pseudo-pavilion and end reception room, Pitney (Haverfield 1906).

corridor facade. In several buildings these corner rooms did not project beyond the line of the corridor, and it is not known if they were given architectural emphasis. The evidence of the stone shrines from the Rhine suggests that such rooms could have been separately roofed to present gable-end pediments (fig. 48, J.T. Smith 1997, Massy 1989). The most popular villa design in Roman Britain involved making an exaggerated architectural feature of the corner pavilions, and setting these forward from the line of the portico to establish a full winged-corridor facade. This style of villa made its first appearance in Britain in the late first century AD. At many sites the arrangement was a second-century addition to a building of simpler form, but from the middle of the second century it was normal for new-built villas to include the winged-corridor facade (Neal 1974: 90–1). A similar development is documented in Belgium (Van Ossel 1992), and the building type was a characteristic feature of the northwest provinces. It is likely that these developments in the arrangement of villa facades were related to the introduction of reception rooms to the rear of some town houses. Projecting rooms were much in fashion in the second century.

The standard arrangement of space within winged-corridor houses involved a central reception room flanked by living rooms with further reception rooms at the ends of the house forming the wings (fig. 25a). The villa at Newport on the Isle of Wight is a classic example of this type (fig. 67). Although there were differences in the degree of emphasis placed on the respective reception facilities, it was usual for houses to have both a central reception room and an end reception room. At some villas the winged-corridor facade was irregularly arranged, with a projecting room found at only one end of the portico (fig. 25b). This demonstrates that the important

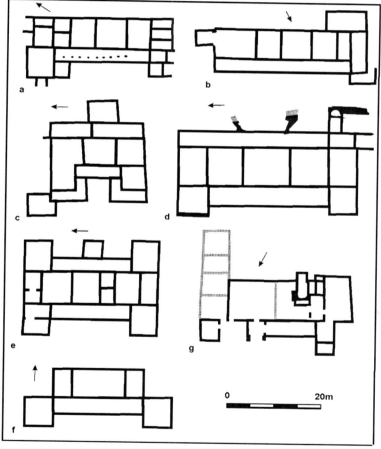

Figure 25 Winged-corridor villas. a: Lockleys (Ward-Perkins 1938). b: Cobham Park (Tester 1961). c: Ely (Wheeler 1921). d: Walton-on-the-Hill (Lowther 1950). e: Hambledon (Cocks 1921). f: Great Staughton (Greenfield 1959). g: Barnsley Park (Webster and Smith 1983).

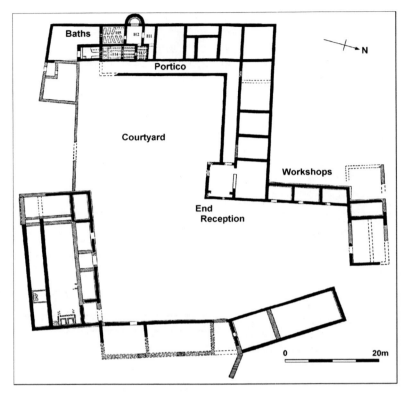

Figure 26 An L-shaped villa at Llantwit Major (after Nash-Williams 1951).

feature of this arrangement was to provide a projecting room, often a large heated room with a mosaic pavement suitable for a dining room, rather than to establish a symmetrical facade. This particular plan closely followed the L-shaped arrangement typical of the town houses of this period. Projecting rooms at the back of the house sometimes allowed for the enlargement of the principal reception rooms. In a couple of examples these included impressive apsidal projections to the central reception room (fig. 25d). The second portico built to the rear of some villas could also be flanked by corner-pavilions, to produce an H-block villa plan (fig. 25e).

A few winged-corridor villas did not have an imposing central reception room, and either a suite of smaller rooms or a large hall was found at this location. The hall villas were of two main types. Some presented a symmetrical facade and emphasised a principal end reception room (fig. 25f), others were of more irregular form where the reception rooms were arranged in a row added to the rear of the house (fig. 25g).

There were several L-shaped villa houses, a building class missed by

Collingwood in his classification (Branigan 1976: 51). Like their urban counterparts these buildings were usually the result of setting the main reception rooms in a separate wing. The villas at Llantwit Major and West Park (Rockbourne) were both grand houses of this type and contained impressive end reception rooms in a separate wing from the main residential suite (fig. 26). Most L-shaped houses were composed of two separate buildings linked by a portico. In many of these the principal part of the villa, recognisable from its privileged location within the compound and by the presence of better mosaic pavements, was unusually small. Much of the accommodation had been displaced to the adjacent structure, often a part-converted aisled building or hall. At Whittington Court the domestic and service quarters were relegated to the back of the house and the adjacent hall exploited as a large reception room (O'Neill 1952).

Most villas with three principal ranges were extended versions of the winged-corridor villa, in which further rooms had been added to the corner pavilions to form extended wings. It was frequently the case that one side range contained a hall and associated service rooms, whilst the other was occupied by a group of end reception rooms. A central reception room flanked by two suites of private rooms usually dominated the main range (as at Spoonley Wood, fig. 62). In most of these buildings the portico extended around all three sides of an enclosed central courtyard with an unusually

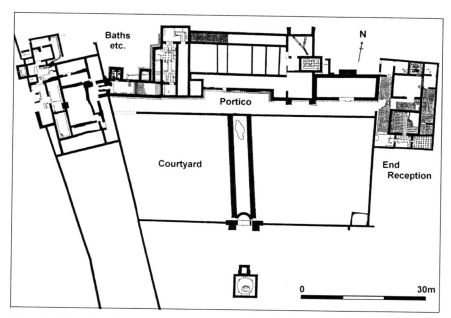

Figure 27 The villa at Darenth, Kent (from Payne 1897).

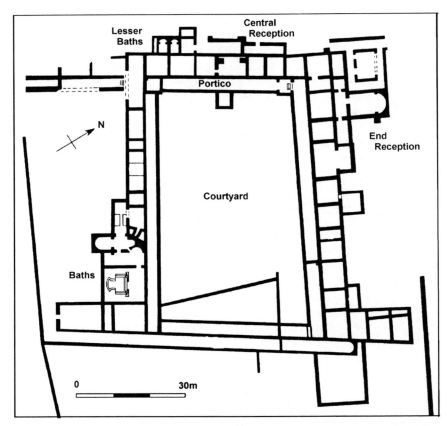

Figure 28 The principal building ranges of the courtyard villa at Bignor, Sussex (after Frere 1982).

close regard to symmetry. Bow-fronted wings were a particular feature of winged-corridor villas and buildings of this type in Kent.

A more complicated layout was represented by the villa at Darenth in Kent, in which the wings were formed by separate ranges linked to the central range by a portico (fig. 27). Notwithstanding the scale of this building, which contained 63 rooms, the arrangement of space followed a common pattern. The west wing contained baths and kitchens, the main range contained audience rooms and a principal suite of living rooms, and the east wing included numerous hypocaust floors and a possible dining suite.

Although courtyard villas were built at Angmering and Fishbourne soon after the conquest, these early constructions may not have had an important influence on the subsequent development of Romano-British villa types. These first-century villas were formally laid out around a central peristyle and included a bewildering complexity of room suites (fig. 6) (Cunliffe 1971a,

Scott 1938). The great villas of the later Roman period were also laid out around a central courtyard but this was the end result of several phases of rebuilding, in which the central peristyle was not part of the original design (fig. 28). These houses had started life as L-shaped or winged-corridor buildings to which porticoes and walls had been added to enclose the central yard (Clarke 1982: 219, Todd 1978: 205). The approach finds parallel elsewhere in the later Roman world. The magnificent fourth-century villa at Piazza Armerina (fig. 54, Wilson 1983) was built not as a single block but as a series of separate units loosely arranged around a central open space designed as an irregular peristyle. Here too the main reception wing stood opposite the entrance and included a centrally located audience hall. These larger buildings could contain several suites of living rooms. At some sites rows of such rooms were laid out at some distance from the core of the house.

In this chapter we have described a wide range of different types of building plan. Several common features and approaches have been identified, and these will be given more attention when we consider how the individual rooms in the house might have been used. Before doing so, however, we turn our attention to the ways in which the houses of Roman Britain were built. This structural evidence gives insight into the progress of technological change in Roman Britain and offers useful clues about the influences that were brought to bear in the creation of new architectural traditions in the province.

5

BUILDING TECHNIQUES

This chapter is dedicated to an exploration of the different ways in which Romano-British houses were constructed. The choice of whether to build in timber or in clay, in brick or in stone, was critical. All of these materials were used in Roman Britain, and the different techniques employed involved sophisticated craftsmanship. The methods adopted were the consequence of cultural, social and economic choices; and the result was a varied architectural landscape, incorporating diverse colours, forms and textures. Previous studies have understated this variety and it is consequently worth exploring the evidence in some detail. The nature of archaeological survival is such that this chapter is mostly about walls and foundations. A hierarchy of choice can be described, from the versatility of timber to the monumentality of masonry.

The study of how buildings were made, held and exchanged has a significant contribution to make to our understanding of provincial economies. Private houses better reflect changing fortune than most other types of building. Public architecture is comparatively unresponsive to the passage of time. By contrast, domestic buildings are likely to be altered, replaced or rebuilt whenever they change hands. Each new generation has new requirements of a home, and is likely to refurbish and redecorate before taking possession. Houses are therefore restructured at frequent intervals. They provide a more sensitive measure of settlement dynamics than most other forms of archaeological evidence.

The building trade was a major industry and property speculation was an important economic activity. Investment in land was a vital means of creating, storing and transmitting surplus. The scale of investment has been illustrated by a recent survey of quantities involved in the building of the fortress at Inchtuthil. Shirley (2000) suggests that a team of about forty men would have taken four weeks to build a barrack block. Although there are more variables involved, and the estimates are consequently more speculative, this approach can also be used to establish the level of resources involved in building Britain's first towns (e.g. Faulkner 1997). The use of more durable construction techniques usually involved a greater initial investment, but promoted the accumulation of wealth since such real estate could be passed through the generations and established the preconditions for a property market.

The choice of what and how to build did not always rest with the owner. Roman litigation and legal codes show that planning controls were exercised over the height, boundaries, ownership and maintenance of buildings, and over rights of access and light. Town magistrates were also concerned to record property holdings for the purposes of taxation and to define the various rights, liabilities and responsibilities that stemmed from property ownership. This necessitated the keeping of detailed public records. The private use of records is also implied by the replication of elements of building layout from one phase to the next at both London and Verulamium (Frere 1983: 29, Perring and Roskams 1991: 69–70). Boundary ditches marking out plots, and from which measurements could be made, are common features. At Dorchester ditches were used to define plot boundaries when the town was first laid out and were respected by all subsequent phases of alteration (Woodward *et al.* 1993). Some Roman architects' plans have survived, although none from Britain (Evans 1994: 163–4, Haselberger 1997, Alston 1997). Baths and funerary monuments were popular subjects, but houses were not. Although plans may have been employed in the design of some Romano-British houses, it is unlikely that measured drawings were used.

Buildings were often laid out to set proportions (Evans 1994), and a general survey of the plans of Roman houses suggests a preference for rooms with a width to length ratio of 2:3. It is less certain that standard measures were regularly employed. The study of the use of measurement in Romano-British architecture has been complicated by the fact that more than one unit of measure was available. Hyginus describes both a standard Roman foot, the *pes Monetalis* (*pm*) equivalent to 291–7 mm; and a longer northern foot, the *pes Drusianus* of 332/333 mm. Considerable effort has been expended on finding buildings laid out to one or other of these measures, but without convincing results (Millett 1982). Replicated measures were, however, used in town planning and in the prefabrication of building materials. An *actus* (120 feet) based on the standard Roman foot (*pm*) can be identified in the layout of Roman Colchester, and had broader currency in town planning (Crummy 1988). The design of several public buildings can also be described in terms of ratios and proportions derived from the use of this standard foot. Multiples of integral measures, notably 8, 12 and 20 feet, may have had greater currency (Dilke 1985: 9). The same standard was used to make fired bricks and tiles: most brick dimensions are based on a multiple of 148 mm (0.5 *pm*). This was also used in the on-site manufacture of air-dried bricks in early Roman Britain. The study of a timber-framed building found in the southern suburb of Roman London, has shown that timbers were cut to standard dimensions including 1 *pm*, 1.5 *pm* and 3 *pm* (Brigham *et al.* 1995: 25). The elevation of the aisled building at Meonstoke was also planned using this foot, with the facade divided into decorative registers 7.5

pm high (King and Potter 1990). It would be an unnecessary inconvenience to plan a building using a different type of measure to that used for the prefabricated materials or in town planning. It is therefore likely that most buildings were laid out according to a scheme of relative proportions specific to the site, but that when measurements were taken these were normally in the *pes Monetalis* (*pm*).

We know little about the people involved in the building of Romano-British houses. Architects named in inscriptions include Amandus at Birrens (*RIB* 2091) and Quintus at Carrawburgh (*RIB* 1542). Other inscriptions mention surveyors and craftsmen. But it is unlikely that these figures were much involved in private constructions. Roman patrons were usually involved in the design process and could command the services of freedmen and slaves, but in Roman Italy hired building contractors were normally employed (Cicero, *Ad Quintum fratrem*: 3.1.1–2, *Ad Atticum*, 14.3.1, Cato, *de re Rustica*, 14, see Ling 1985). Many specialist artisans were involved, and there were Roman *collegia* (guilds) of *fabri tignuarii* (woodworkers and subsequently general construction workers), *pavimentarii* (paviers), *structores* (builders), *subrutores* (demolition men) and others. In Roman Britain a lower level of demand might have reduced the scope for the development of trades, but many areas of work required specialist competence. Skills introduced to Britain after the Roman conquest included those of mosaic laying, fresco painting, heating engineering and stonemasonry. The use of materials in the villa at Fishbourne illustrated an early appreciation of the potential of different kinds of local stone, even in the absence of a local masonry building tradition (Greene 1986: 152–3). The construction of earth-built structures needed skills unavailable locally prior to the conquest, and post-conquest changes in joinery witness the arrival of specialist carpenters. The sophistication of the building trade is illustrated by some of the builders' tools introduced to Britain after the Roman conquest. One of the most valuable of these is the joiner's try-square (*norma*) found in construction levels of a second-century building at Canterbury (Chapman 1979: 403–7). Saws, chisels, planes, adzes and plasterers' floats also arrived in the Roman period (Liversidge 1968: 188–90).

Another architectural sophistication unlikely to have been in much demand prior to the Roman conquest was the use of timber scaffolding. Putlog holes are sometimes found in Roman structures (e.g. Frere 1983: 249). These housed horizontal beams socketed into the rising walls that served as joists beneath temporary working floors. The absence of putlog holes from many masonry walls suggests, however, that scaffolds were often built without taking support from the masonry wall under construction. A painting in the tomb of Trebius Justus at Rome illustrates a Roman building site with men working from a free-standing scaffold (MacDonald 1965: 147). Postholes likely to have supported the uprights of such scaffoldings were evident in the construction of the fourth-century villa at Feltwell (Gurney 1986: 1–48). Scaffolds used in the construction of the Roman forum at London were built over timber base-plates, set parallel to and some 600 mm distant from the wall under construction (Milne 1992: 22). These temporary constructions were chiefly employed during the building of substantial masonry structures.

Timber buildings

Most Romano-British houses were built of wood. Until recently we knew comparatively little about timber buildings, but campaigns of excavation in London and Carlisle have uncovered some remarkably well-preserved structures. As a result of this recent work we are now able to describe such buildings in surprisingly close detail.

Most timber used in London had been obtained by coppicing within managed woodlands, although wildwood sources were also exploited (Goodburn 1992). A writing tablet found in London describes an early second-century dispute over ownership of a wood in Kent, reflecting the importance of this resource (*RIB* 2446). Unseasoned oak from young, fast-growing trees was preferred for structural work (Hanson 1978). Such timber could be felled on demand, or speculatively against sale. Hazel and birch rods from short rotation coppicing were extensively used in wattle panels. Ash, alder and elm were also used in structural work (Dark and Dark 1997: 38–40). A trend towards the use of younger and smaller trees in later London waterfronts might indicate that the earlier profligate use of massive timbers had taken its toll but could equally reflect changes in carpentry practice (Brigham 1990: 150–1). Even late in the third century large timbers were abundantly available for use as oak piles in the construction of London's public buildings and waterfronts (Milne 1985: 65–7).

The conquest brought about a radical advance in woodworking skills. Simple mortice and tenon joints had been widely used beforehand (Coles *et al.* 1978, Bulleid and Gray 1911), but the equivalent Roman joint was much more precisely cut. A wide range of new joinery techniques now made its first appearance (fig. 36, Goodburn 1995: 45, Goodburn 1992: 197–8, Brigham *et al.* 1995: 50, Weeks 1982). These advances in carpentry technique were facilitated by the introduction to Britain of the carpenter's plane and frame-saw (Liversidge 1968: 188–91). New techniques of sawing along and across the grain appeared. The frame-saw, with its teeth set in a straight blade, offered significant advantage over concave-bladed pre-Roman equivalents. Planks were sawn over a trestle by cutting from both ends of a square-hewn saw baulk. Further to the widespread use of wooden pegs, nails were used to reinforce Romano-British timber joints although this was not standard practice (Goodburn 1995: 45, Frere 1972: 8). Nails were also commonly used to attach wall planking to studs and were used in fixing roofing materials. Their use on this scale was a Roman introduction.

Clusters of short cleft oak piles were widely used in circumstances of ground instability. Most timber-framed houses were also built over consolidated construction platforms that offered some protection from movement. An occasional indifference to the risks of subsidence (e.g. Perring and Roskams 1991: 69) is more likely to reflect a lack of interest in durability than technical incompetence.

Earth-fast post constructions

The simplest and most widely diffused form of timber construction involved setting uprights into the ground and using these earth-fast timbers to support the roof. Some such constructions were built without principal posts, and relied for support on wattle and daub walls built around stakes set at irregular intervals. These were typically small buildings with walls no more than 100 mm wide, in which round-sectioned timbers, infrequently more than 80 mm in diameter, were driven into the ground at 150–500 mm intervals. These uprights served as rods for horizontally woven wattle sails, which were usually coated by clay daub (figs 29a, 30 and 41.3). Basketwork walls of this type, in which the support of the roof did not rely on the rigidity of individual vertical members, had been used in Britain since the Bronze Age (Bell 1990: 51–3). A four-roomed building of this type was built outside the fort in Carlisle *c.* AD 73. Substantial parts of the collapsed wattle and daub wall from a similar building, of Claudio-Neronian date, were found at Colchester (Crummy 1984: 23). Contemporary circular structures in the suburbs of London were built with wattle and daub superstructures, again without any use of principal posts (Perring and Roskams 1991: 74–6).

Another of the buildings erected in London's early suburb was rectangular with irregularly spaced timber posts, including squared and circular elements, set up to 3.3 m apart. Burnt daub from destruction layers indicated that diagonal bracing elements were also used. The posts served as a framework for wattle and daub walls. It is possible that these irregular walls were capped by longitudinal wall-plates supporting rafters (Smith 1982, Charles 1982). Apart from the occasional use of nails there is little to separate these buildings from pre-conquest wattle and daub structures such as those found at Skeleton Green (Partridge 1981).

Irregular buildings were common in the earliest phases of settlement, but were often replaced by structures with larger posts set out with greater regularity. In these the uprights were typically 100–350 mm across, set at intervals of 500 mm, although there is considerable variation and larger buildings used bigger posts set further apart. These buildings were still frequently built with circular-sectioned uprights supporting horizontally woven wattle walls (e.g. Wilson 1970: 281). A common design variation involved using a narrow palisade trench, subsequently backfilled with soil or

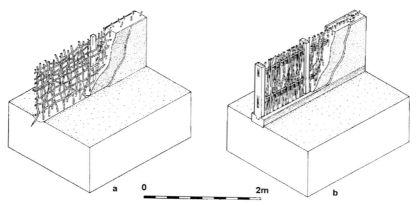

Figure 29 Different types of wattle and daub walls represented by evidence from early Roman London (Perring and Roskams 1991). Copyright Museum of London.

Figure 30 Circular structure with basketwork wattle walls from Castle Street, Carlisle. Photograph courtesy of Mike McCarthy. Copyright Carlisle Archaeology Ltd.

gravel, along the wall-line to assist in the setting out and planting of the individual posts. A late first-century building from Carlisle was built with round-sectioned posts set in a continuous trench at 360 to 400 mm intervals with horizontally woven hazel rods (figs 31 and 32, McCarthy 1991). Few of these structures have been studied in sufficient detail to permit an analysis of post spacing, from which evidence it would be possible to reconstruct elements of superstructure and roof. Some houses were, however, built with the posts on one side of the building paired by posts on the other, such that the weight of the roof could have been carried by pairs of rafters resting on the opposed posts and joined together in an A-frame (fig. 33). This was not standard practice.

Buildings with earth-fast posts and wattle and daub walls remained popular on low status sites throughout the Roman period, although such buildings were rare in larger cities after the second century. This may reflect the rarity of low status buildings in these settlements rather than any change in building fashion. These buildings were generally short-lived, and the widespread use of sapwood suggests that durability was not a primary concern. On several sites in London there were three or four phases of timber building in the decade before AD 60 and the average life-span of late first and

Figure 31 A timber building with wattle walls: Building 1090 at Castle Street, Carlisle. Photograph courtesy of Mike McCarthy. Copyright Carlisle Archaeology Ltd.

Figure 32 Close up of the wattle wall illustrated in fig. 31. Photograph courtesy of Mike McCarthy. Copyright Carlisle Archaeology Ltd.

early second-century post-built houses at Ironmonger Lane was less than ten years (Perring and Roskams 1991: 57–61).

Timber-framed houses

The Romans introduced timber framing to Britain, and many town houses built prior to *c*. AD 150 contained close studded oak frame partitions with wattle and daub or mud brick infill (mud and stud). These partitions were made of timbers cut to lengths which allowed the construction of panels about eight foot high (in *pm*), and close studded at one or two foot intervals. The wider spacing was preferred where a wattle and daub panel was to be inserted.

Timber-framed constructions of this nature were commonplace in Claudio-Neronian Colchester and Verulamium (Crummy 1984: 8, Frere 1972: 8), but the best evidence derives from a study of timbers re-used as piles in a masonry building at Cannon Street in London (fig. 34). These timbers had been removed from a late first- or early second-century structure. Most had been cut from whole logs taken from young trees. The walls that they had formed were built over base-plates jointed together. Studs about 2.2 m long, with projecting tenons, were set into mortices cut into the base-plate at intervals of 520–620 mm (edge to edge). A top-plate was inserted over these upright studs, and diagonal bracing inserted. The top- and base-plates were 110 mm deep, such that in total the wall stood about 2.4 m high. Tie beams were used to brace the building at ceiling level. The jointing

87

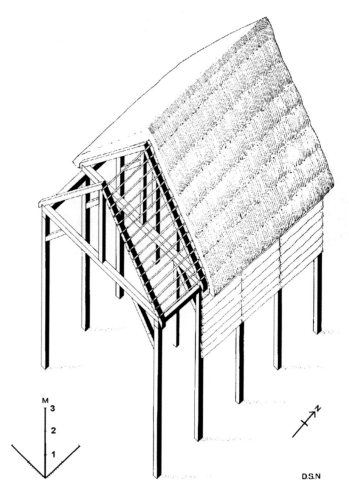

Figure 33 Reconstruction of the superstructure of Building 53 at Gorhambury, illustrating the possible use of an A-framed roof construction. Drawing by David Neal (1990). Reproduced by kind permission of English Heritage.

shows this to have been of normal assembly, in which the top-plate was laid before the tie beams. It was the combined mass of the wall, as much as the load-bearing capacity of individual studs, that supported the roof. The nature of the joints and the lack of pegs suggest that the walls were not pre-assembled, but built piecemeal on site. Wattle and daub panels were inserted between the uprights and the wall further reinforced by nailing planks to its outside face. Almost identical timber-framed structures had been built in AD 40–1 at the Roman auxiliary fort at Valkenburg on the Rhine (Glasbergen

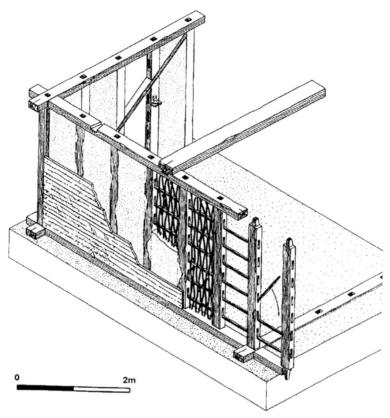

Figure 34 A timber-framed building reconstructed from the evidence of the timbers found at Cannon Street, London (Goodburn 1992). Copyright Museum of London.

1972). The casual approach to rectilinearity evidenced by the buildings at Valkenburg seems inconsistent with the requirements of pre-assembly and it is probable that the final carpentry took place on site.

Part of another well-preserved timber-framed structure built c. AD 153 was found at the Courage Brewery site in Southwark (fig.35, Brigham et al. 1995). Wall posts with tenons were set into a ground beam at 0.9 m centres: lesser uprights (scantlings) measuring 110–20×40–60 mm alternated with larger timbers measuring 135–40×60–80 mm. The corner posts of the building were more substantial, measuring up to 100×180 mm. There was no evidence of cross-bracing, but the building was clad with boards which reinforced the structure. This building may have been prefabricated in an assembly yard before being brought to site. Three strands of evidence can be presented: the cut timbers had dried and warped before use, no wood-

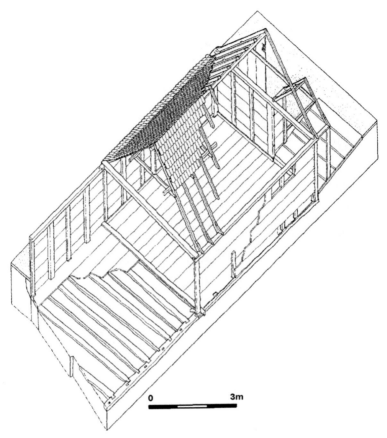

0   3m

Figure 35 The timber-framed building with a semi-basement found at Courage Brewery
warehouse (Brigham *et al.* 1995). Copyright Museum of London.

working debris was found on site and the building had been laid out in a
regular fashion to standard measures. This building employed slighter
timber uprights than was normal. These were set wider apart than was
typical, at 3 ft. intervals. These differences show that a higher level of technical
skill was employed than in the earlier framed buildings, allowing for a more
economic use of materials. Carpentry techniques had perhaps evolved over
the previous half-century to allow these improvements.

Timber chocks and stone pads were also sometimes used for base-plate
levelling (e.g. Anderson and Wacher 1980: 119–21). Not all framed
buildings relied on the use of continuous timber base-plates. An alternative
foundation treatment consisted of lining narrow foundation trenches with
planks, reinforced with paired wooden piles, and using these to hold the

studs fast. Walls of this type were used in London before the Boudiccan revolt of AD 60/61 (Philp 1977: 7–9), and were still being built down to the middle of the second century. In another variation studs were jointed into discontinuous timber pads. At Watling Court, London the principal uprights of a wattle and daub building, destroyed c. AD 60, had been built over timber pads about 600 mm across and 1.2 m long, set at intervals of 1.2–1.5 m (Perring and Roskams 1991: 72). These features were similar to those employed in the construction of a building in the villa compound at Gorhambury (Neal et al. 1990: 29). At Vindolanda short pad-like lengths of sleeper beams were used beneath squared uprights (Birley 1977: 113), and this was also the case in a mid second-century construction at Verulamium, where less deeply buried timber ground beams supported the wall infill (Frere 1983: 204–5).

Villas were more often built with timber-framed walls than is generally recognised. A good example is the early timber-framed wattle and daub building at Boxmoor (Neal 1974–6: 57–8). Many such timber-framed structures were set over stone footings. In most cases the ground beams rested on the smooth upper surface of the masonry (although see Williams 1971a: 175). It is often difficult to establish whether the concrete foundations encountered on archaeological sites had supported superstructures in earth, timber or masonry. Smith (1982) has drawn attention to the fact that the broad concrete footings interpreted as foundations for timber-framed structures would often have supported earth-walled superstructures. Since timber-framed walls were unlikely to be any wider than 300 mm there is no good reason why footings for such walls should be wider. There are, however, instances where offset courses were used to reduce broad masonry footings, often about 600 mm wide, to narrow sleeper-walls that supported timber-framed buildings (Zant 1993: 80–1, Bushe-Fox 1916: 4–5). At Colchester foundations 450–500 mm wide preserved the imprint of a timber base-plate (Crummy 1984: 131). In these cases timber-framed superstructures were built over unnecessarily wide footings. Perhaps the builders of these houses believed that these wider footings helped spread the building load or compensated for local ground instability.

The use of a timber frame represented an enormous improvement over earth-fast construction. It is normal to find that the first phase of Romano-British urban settlement relied extensively on earth-fast structures, in which squared timbers and carpentered joints were exceptional, but that these were soon replaced by timber-framed buildings employing sophisticated carpentry (fig. 36). The changes in building techniques were often accompanied by a greater level of expenditure on interior decoration. The framed buildings were not, however, very durable. Small, unseasoned timbers might last no more than five years in load-bearing walls (Goodburn 1992: 192). These were cheap buildings, popular in contexts where short-term values prevailed. Many of London's first inhabitants evidently chose to rebuild their properties

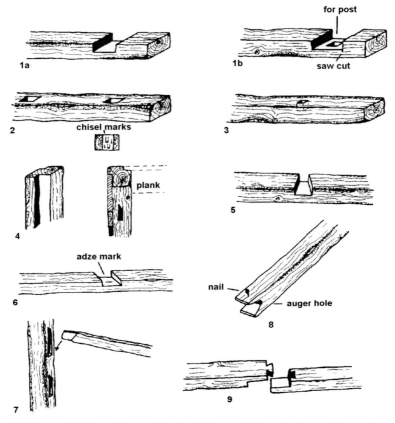

Figure 36 Range of timber joints used in London, mostly from the Cannon Street site (Goodburn 1992). 1–3: square mortice and bareface tenon (including through and not through mortices) for joining studs to plates. 4: rebate, for receiving cladding planks into corner posts. 5: lap dovetail, for top-plates, tie beams and ends of major joists. 6: cross halving to join base-plates. 7: sloping rectangular recess for insertion of lathe/stave into studs. 8: bird's mouth (examples from waterfront quays in Southwark). 9: edge halved scarf with one dovetail butt for joining base-plates. Copyright Museum of London.

once every 5–10 years, and in Insula 14 at Verulamium the timber-framed buildings were rebuilt four times in the period AD 75–150 (Frere 1972: 5).

Wattle and daub

Some timber-framed buildings incorporated wattle panels similar to those used in earth-fast constructions. These consisted of a lattice of round-sectioned rods and sails (e.g. Frere 1972: 6–8). Frequently, however, a different type of

92

wattle construction was associated with the use of timber framing (Perring and Roskams 1991: 74–7, Goodburn 1992). Circular-sectioned sails (10–18 mm in diameter) were woven vertically around square-sectioned horizontal rods slotted into vertical notches cut in the sides of the studs (figs 29b, 34, 37 and 41.2). The horizontal rods measured 12 mm deep by 25–42 mm wide and were set at intervals of about 550–600 mm, such that there were four of these cross members between base-plate and top-plate. It is possible that the wattle panels were pre-assembled and dropped into place. Similar vertically woven panels involving squared rods have been recorded at London, Verulamium and Corbridge (Frere 1972: 6–8, Richmond and Gillam 1953: 218). Panels of this type were used in Colchester before AD 60, and were still being built in early second-century Verulamium. A variation on this type is represented by daub fragments from Watling Court in

Figure 37 Stud and wattle wall from Lion Walk, Colchester. Photograph courtesy of the Colchester Archaeological Trust.

London, which preserved the impressions of a series of overlapping horizontal squared rods or lathes (Perring and Roskams 1991: fig. 65).

All of these wattle and daub walls were about 100 mm thick, exclusive of any plaster, timber or clay facing. The daub, which was well mixed and grass tempered, encased the wattle and was taken across the outside face of the timber frame, which in some cases was subsequently faced and secured with horizontal 'weatherboard' planking. The Cannon Street timbers illustrate that the inside face of the timber frame remained exposed within the rooms of the house (Goodburn 1992: 201), but elsewhere this face too was daubed over in preparation for the decorative finish (Crummy 1984: 22).

Vitruvius was clearly aware of the several limitations of wattle and daub buildings (*On Architecture* 2, 8.20). Such walls were prone to subsidence, posed a fire risk and would rot if in contact with the ground. But they were also quick and cheap to assemble and saved on space. The context in which wattle and daub was used in Roman Britain reflects this attitude, and in most high status buildings the technique was relegated to internal partitions, or the walls were protected by means of masonry plinths. At Watling Court in London timber-framed walls were only used as internal partitions within the Flavian adobe-walled houses, following a design adopted in Augustan houses at Lyon (Desbat 1981: 55–8).

Mud and stud

In mud and stud walls the infill between the timber uprights was formed of mud or clay rather than wattle and daub. The mud was usually introduced in the form of air-dried bricks, the use of which was apparently a Roman introduction to Britain. The earliest such walls are found in pre-Boudiccan levels (Crummy 1984: 20–4). In one building of this period in London timber studs were set into a plank-lined palisade trench packed with cobbles set in brickearth, with mud brick infill above (Hammer 1985: 7–9). Partitions within the first-century barracks at Gloucester were also of mud and stud construction (Hassall and Rhodes 1975: 20).

Most bricks used in mud and stud partitions measured 420–80 by 150–80 by 70–80 mm: equivalent to 1 ft. 6 in. long by 6 in. wide and 3 in. deep (Perring and Roskams 1991: 77–8). There was considerable width variation, however, and some walls used bricks as narrow as 100 mm across, and others bricks up to 250 mm wide (bricks used in adobe walls showed even greater variation). Bricks were made by mixing clay with water and grass, and pressing the resultant slurry into a wooden mould before leaving it to dry (McGann 1987: 1). The moulds were open at top and bottom, and the underside of the bricks sometimes retain the impressions of the straw or sand on which they were placed while drying.

Contextual evidence suggests that mud and stud was superior to wattle and daub, since its use was initially confined to a small number of high quality buildings. The technique became more widely diffused during the Flavian period, gaining particular currency in the early second century. Partitions used in the rear extension of an early second-century commercial property in Newgate Street showed the use of mud bricks within close-studded partitions set over timber ground beams. The studs were set one brick length apart (fig. 38). The volume of destruction debris from the building suggested that the walls here had originally stood some 3.3 m high (Perring and Roskams 1991: 77–8). Collapsed mud and stud partitions at Verulamium had stood over 3.66 m high (Frere 1983: 238–9). In some instances the technique was still used on high status sites into the later Roman period. The late second- or early third-century clay-walled building at Bignor may have been of this type (Frere 1982: 146).

Mud and stud walls were not always built over timber base-plates. In a minority of constructions the studs were instead set into trenches lined with planks which held them in place. In other cases the uprights were earth-fast. In many such buildings there was no evident order to the spacing of the uprights, and it is possible that the roof had been supported by the mass of the wall rather than by specific structural timbers. In most cases the timbers and bricks were encased by a skim of daub applied with a float.

Figure 38 Collapsed brick and stud partition to the rear of Building K at Newgate Street (destroyed by fire *c*. AD 125). Copyright Museum of London.

Masonry nogging

The use of stone as an infill between timber uprights, known otherwise as masonry nogging or in classical contexts as *opus gallicum*, is well represented in pre-Roman contexts in Gaul. But the technique was rarely employed in Roman Britain. At Cirencester a collapsed half-timbered wall was built with dry laid stonework between closely spaced studs (fig. 39, Goodburn 1976: 354). Other examples include partitions at Caerleon and Verulamium (Zienkiewicz 1993: 40–43, Wheeler and Wheeler 1936: 140), although in these the masonry construction probably supported a wattle and daub superstructure. At Colchester a watching brief at the Cups Hotel site uncovered part of an early timber-framed building with close set studs (0.3–0.35 m apart) where the infill consisted of broken tile set in mortar (Crummy 1992: 330).

Stave building and timber cladding

The main walls of a second-century building in York consisted of squared timber uprights, some earth-fast others set over timber base-plates, with horizontal planks nailed onto their outside face (Frere 1985: 279). This is a structural approach reminiscent of the balloon-frame structures popular in

Figure 39 Masonry nogging. A collapsed partition from a third-century shop at Cirencester. Photograph by J. Wilson.

the United States in the nineteenth century. A similar second-century building found at the Old Grapes Lane site in Carlisle, had a wall of oak uprights supporting horizontal planking (fig. 40, McCarthy *et al.* 1982: 82). Several late first- and early second-century stave-built walls have also been found in London (Frere 1991: 266, Milne and Wardle 1995: 38). The external face of the timber-framed walls of the mid second-century sunken building found at the Courage Brewery site in Southwark were reinforced with horizontal square-edged boards, 35–8 mm thick and 250–450 mm wide set on edge (fig. 35, Brigham *et al.* 1995). These were chamfered at the ends to improve the join and housed by a rebate in the corner posts. Boards were also used to form a skirting on the inner face of one wall. It is not known if this pattern of wall planking continued above ground level, although this seems likely. Boarded walls have also been noted at Vindolanda and Heronbridge and account for several other discoveries of collapsed planking nailed to structural timbers (e.g. Mason 1989: 129, Drury 1975: 165, Frere 1972: 75 and fig. 3, Hammer 1985: 7–8, Burnham and Burnham 1991). In some cases planks formed both sides of the wall. Flavian wall lines at Ironmonger Lane in London were represented by parallel lines of decayed timber planking 100 mm apart and this approach was adopted in the construction of timber-walled cellars in Colchester (Crummy 1984: 23).

Figure 40 A collapsed wall of oak uprights supporting horizontal planking from a second-century building found at the Old Grapes Lane site in Carlisle. Photograph courtesy of Mike McCarthy. Copyright Carlisle Archaeology Ltd.

Internal partitions formed of planks nailed to both sides of a row of small studs have been recorded in earth-walled buildings in London.

Planks were commonly employed to clad timber-framed buildings with wattle and daub infill. This added to the structural stability of a building, and offered security against pests and other potential intruders. A timber-framed wattle and daub wall in Southwark was reinforced by horizontal planking applied to its outer face, and held in place by further squared uprights (Graham 1988: fig. 13a). Iron nails were used instead to fasten external plank sheathing, 200–350 mm wide, to the timber-framed building from Cannon Street, London (fig. 34, Goodburn 1992: 193, 201). The nailing pattern suggests that the planks were set edge to edge, and not overlapping. Similar planking was also frequently attached to mud and stud walls. It is not clear if the planking was confined to the lower parts of these earth walls, where it protected the clay from eavesdrip splash, or extended to the eaves. The examples illustrate that the standard approach involved the use of horizontal planks nailed into place without overlap. Overlapping weatherboarding was, however, reportedly used in military constructions at Wroxeter and vertical planking has also been recorded on some military sites (Frere 1986: 391, Hanson 1982: 180).

Cruck construction

Cruck construction may have been employed in Roman houses although the evidence is inconclusive. This alternative to timber-framed construction involved curved or angled timbers such that the rafters supporting the roof effectively sprang from, rather than rested on, the load-bearing uprights. Possible instances of cruck building are largely confined to a group of small agricultural buildings in and beyond the German borders (Trier 1969, van Es 1967). It has also been suggested for some small towns and rural sites in East Anglia (Green 1982). Cruck building was not, however, a mainstream building type amongst the Romanised communities of Britain.

Building in earth and clay

Earth walls were superior to timber ones for their greater durability and better resistance to fire. There was no pre-Roman tradition of earth-walled construction in southeast Britain, and the use of such walls was a Roman innovation of Hellenistic inspiration. Both Cato (*On Agriculture* 14) and Vitruvius (*On Architecture* 2, 3.2) gave practical advice on how to build with the material, emphasising the problems of settlement and the value of masonry foundations. The use of these techniques on high status Italian sites is illustrated by the evidence of early imperial buildings at via Tomasso Grossi in Milan (Perring 1991a), and the villa at San Giovenale (Poulsen 1960: 313ff.). Although better represented in republican contexts, earth-walled buildings continued to be found into the later Roman period (as at Ventimiglia, see Pallarés 1986), by which time building in timber had returned to popularity. Britain was most influenced by Gallic practice, and the Augustan buildings of Lyon provide numerous parallels in matters of construction detail to the Flavian houses of London and Verulamium (Desbat 1985).

The sandy clays best suited for mud-wall constructions are found throughout much of southeast England. Clay pits were dug as near to the construction sites as was practical. The quarry at Newgate Street, London is a good illustration. About one hundred cubic metres of clay were extracted from a pit 7 m in diameter and 2.2 m deep, at the back of the building site (Perring and Roskams 1991: 67). The manufacture of dried bricks took place nearby. Access to suitable quarry sites diminished through time, and more complex mechanisms of supply were developed. Before the end of the first century AD some earth walls in the more intensely developed parts of London were built with material recovered from earlier constructions, as indicated by fragments of wall plaster re-mixed through the brickearth.

Mud brick

Adobe or clay lump construction involved building load-bearing walls from air-dried bricks, without timber supports. It is sometimes difficult to distinguish between adobe walls that contained non-structural timber elements, and mud and stud walls where the timber frame and not the bricks carried the roof load. The earliest Romano-British mud-walled buildings were found in pre-Boudiccan contexts in both London and Colchester and were probably built by the army (Boddington and Marsden 1987, Crummy 1984: 22, 37, Perring 1991b: 12). The main walls of these buildings were formed of brickearth bonded air-dried bricks, set over timber base-plates that rested on trench-built concrete foundations (580–650 mm wide, and 0.3–1.10 m deep) (figs 41 (2) and 42c). The colonists at Colchester inherited the building type from the fortress and some early civilian use of the technique is known.

In London the bricks in these walls were similar to those used in mud-and-stud walls, but at Colchester the clay may not always have been grass tempered and a wider but thinner brick was used. Here the standard was approximately 430 by 290 by 50 mm, equivalent to 1 ft. 6 in.× 1 ft.×2 ft.: the 'Lydian' brick. These walls find close parallel in Augustan constructions at Lyon where adobe walls (with bricks measuring 1 ft. 6 in. × 1 ft.) were set over concrete footings (Desbat 1981: 55–8, 1985: 75). Coincidentally, air-dried bricks of similar dimensions (460 by 230–300 by 150 mm) were used in nineteenth-century Cambridge (McGann 1987), at which time it took approximately two days to make the 1,000-odd bricks needed to make a house. Smaller bricks have also been found in early contexts at Colchester.

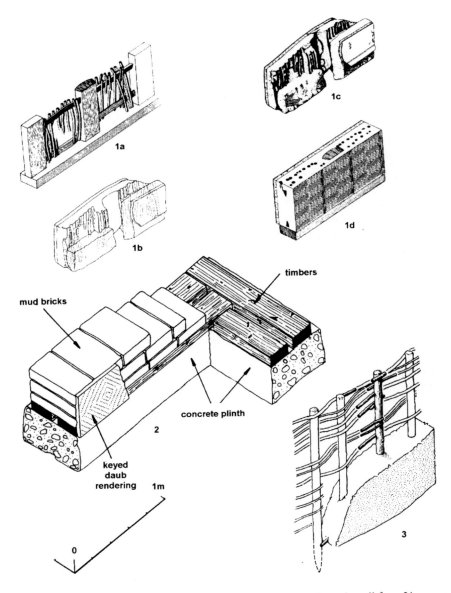

Figure 41 Types of wall from excavations in Colchester. 1: stud and wattle wall from Lion Walk. 2: daub block wall from Culver Street. 3: stake and wattle wall from BKC (Building 44) (from Crummy 1984).

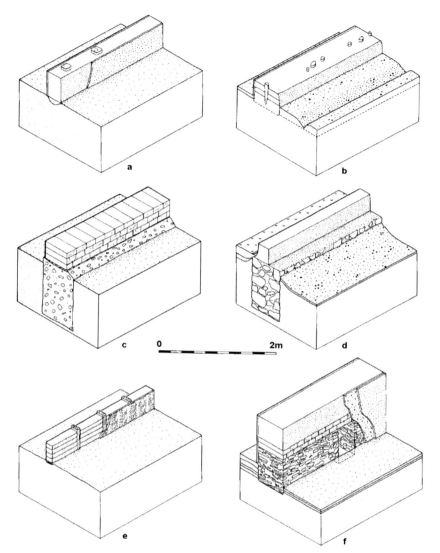

Figure 42 Earth walls from early Roman buildings in London. a: mud and stud wall from Building F at Watling Court. b: cob wall from Building K at Newgate Street. c: adobe (mud brick) wall from 160–2 Fenchurch Street. d: clay wall over stone footings from Building D at Watling Court. e: stud and mud brick wall from rear extension to Building K, Newgate Street. f: tile footings and mud brick wall from Building H at Watling Court (from Perring and Roskams 1991).

101

Examples include bricks measuring 222 by 185 by 95 mm at Lion Walk, and 330 by 279 by 38 mm at North Hill (Crummy 1984: 22; Dunnett 1966: 31). The practice of making the bricks on the construction site permitted significant variation of brick size from one site to the next.

The best earth-walled town houses were built in the late first and second centuries. In contrast with the short-lived timber-walled buildings some of these earth-walled town houses stood for over forty years. Clay-walled buildings of this date have also been noted in London, Leicester, Dover, Canterbury, Verulamium and Cirencester (Philp 1989, Wacher 1995: 196, Frere 1983: 161–6, Wacher 1963: 16–19). These better town houses found contemporary imitation in the villas at Farningham and Lullingstone, where thick clay walls were set over stone foundations in the period from *c.* AD 80 and in the second-century villa at Norfolk Street, Leicester (Meates 1973, 1979, Mellor and Lucas 1980). These buildings were similar to the early buildings referred to above, although it was no longer usual to find a timber base-plate intervening between the masonry dwarf wall and the mud brick superstructure. It was also usual to find that the masonry elements incorporated a greater proportion of better quality stone, and less cement. These footings were typically 0.40–0.60 m wide and 0.5–1.2 m high, of which 0.35–0.55 m projected above the ground level. Wider bricks were also widely favoured in later adobe constructions, as in the town house at Blue Boar Lane in Leicester (250–300 mm wide), and the villa at Norfolk Street, Leicester (400–500 mm wide). Many of the construction details find parallel in Gallic architectural practice (e.g. Coulon and Joly 1985: 98–9).

A late first-century earth-walled house from Watling Court in London illustrates the level of sophistication that could be achieved in such houses (Perring and Roskams 1991). It had been built over two stories and was decorated with mosaics and painted walls. The main walls were set over foundations of re-used roofing tiles (*tegulae* laid with the flanges facing outwards to form the side of the wall, and bonded by brickearth) built-up some 300 mm above ground level (figs 42f and 43). Air-dried bricks were laid lengthways across this foundation in a header bond to form a wall about 480–500 mm wide. Tile within the collapsed building debris is likely to have come from another tile course, perhaps at eaves level where it may have formed an architrave. A villa at St Osyth appears to have been built using the same style of tile plinth. Evidence of a masonry architrave set over a clay wall has also been recovered from a Roman building excavated at Great Chesterford in Essex (Brinson 1963).

Lesser partitions within these buildings were formed of timber-framed walls with wattle and daub infill, and by walls of dried bricks laid end-on-end, stretcher fashion, both with and without timber uprights. The buildings described above were unusual for the width and solidity of their walls. Most of the mud brick walls of early Roman London were narrower and made of

Figure 43 Early second-century clay block wall from Watling Court, London. Copyright Museum of London.

bricks laid end-to-end with occasional timber uprights. Early in the second century most walls were of this type. A similar picture emerges from the evidence of both Verulamium and Colchester, although there are contexts in which timber-framed buildings with wattle and daub infill remained more popular.

Pisé

There is some debate as to the extent to which walls of true pisé construction were found in the Roman west (Desbat 1981, 1985). The technique makes use of dry earth rammed into compaction between strong shuttering, usually without the addition of straw. The characteristics of such walls are that they are at least 400 mm wide. This width was required to allow the builders to gain access to the wall to tread and pound between the boards. Battens used to hold the shuttering in place also leave narrow slots through the wall (Odouze 1985: 85). Although Pliny and Varro describe the construction technique, suggesting it to have a Spanish origin (Varro, *De Re Rustica* 1,14, Pliny, *Natural History* 25, 48), efforts to find evidence for its use in Romano-Gallic constructions have failed.

The main advantages of pisé over adobe are that it can use a greater variety of types of earth, and it requires less water. Neither of these advantages would have carried much weight at most of the sites considered here, where clays suitable for adobe could be found and water was plentiful. One building alone suggests that this technique can be identified in Romano-British domestic architecture. The 480–560 mm wide masonry sleeper-walls of House 21,2 at Verulamium, built about AD 180, supported an earth superstructure. In the upper part of the wall-thin horizontal transverse slots had contained timber battens up to 100 mm by 76 mm which crossed the wall at 1.2 m (c. 4 ft.) intervals (fig. 44). It is difficult to know what other purposes these might have served other than to hold a timber shuttering in place.

Figure 44 Verulamium House 21,2. The masonry footings of a wall containing narrow slots that may have housed the wooden battens used to fix shuttering in place during the construction of a terra pisé wall. The fallen plaster in the foreground (in Room 4, see also fig. 59) also illustrates the chevron keying of the clay wall (Frere 1983). Reproduced by kind permission of the Society of Antiquaries of London.

Cob

In cob walls the mixed clay and straw, once adequately puddled, was used directly in the construction of the walls rather than formed into bricks. The wall was built up in layers, or lifts, each of which had to be properly beaten down and dried out before the next layer could be laid. Although cob walls did not have the same breadth of appeal to Romano-British builders there are some clear examples of their use.

It seems likely that the technique was more widely diffused on the less Romanised and more British sites. Cob walling was common in the Fens (Phillips 1970). At Godmanchester cob walls 0.6–1.2 m wide were commonly built around wattle hurdles in continuation of pre-Roman practice (Green 1982: 96). The technique was also used in an early second-century strip building at Newgate Street in London (Perring and Roskams 1991: 78–9). Although of modest design and status, this was evidently a Roman-style building. The east wall of the building survived best and consisted of a 6.5 m length of brickearth built with converging rather than parallel sides (fig. 42b). Thin layers of trample within the body of the wall marked the differences between lifts no more than 100–200 mm thick. A series of small stake-holes within the body of the wall may have been the remains of a skimpy wattle framework.

The earth-walled building that replaced the early timber-framed villa at Boxmoor in the early to mid second century has also been described as cob-walled, set over chalk foundations 450 mm (18 in.) wide and 600 mm (2 ft.) deep. This house was furnished with painted walls and hypocausts before being rebuilt sometime in the third century (Neal 1970: 159). Cob walling on stone footings has also been described as the most common construction type in Dorchester on Thames (Rowley and Brown 1981: 3). At Vindolanda a variation on this type involved the use of timber and wattle hurdles either side of a 600 mm (2 ft.) wide trench, with the gap between filled by puddled clay (Birley 1977: 113).

Earth and gravel foundations

Earth-filled foundation trenches were employed in the construction of some first-century buildings. The technique is well documented in late republican and early imperial contexts in north Italy, where it was identified during excavations in Milan (Perring 1991a: 135–6), and was also employed in early Roman buildings in Cyrenaica (Lloyd 1985: 57). These foundation trenches removed poorly consolidated and/or poorly drained soils and replaced them with compacted gravel and silt. This reduced the risk of settlement and was used in preference to timber piling where timber was in short supply. The technique was most commonly found in earth-walled buildings.

Three possible instances of earth-filled foundation trenches have been found in first-century contexts in London. At Philpot Lane vertical-sided earth-filled trenches 1 m wide and 0.65 m deep may have served this function (Williams in preparation). At 15–23 Southwark Street trenches 2.5 m wide and 0.5 m deep marked out the plan of a complicated structure of the period prior to AD 70 and have tentatively been identified as earth foundations (Cowan 1995). More recently work at 68–71 Fenchurch Street has identified rammed gravel foundations beneath timber ground beams (Esmonde-Cleary 1998: 410). At Lion Walk, Colchester, the walls of Building 20, were set over packed gravel in continuous foundation trenches: the upper 300 mm of one foundation contained fragments of tile bedded horizontally, with other tiles laid over this with upright flanges coinciding with the limits of the wall (Crummy 1984: 62–3). In a variation on this technique several late first-century buildings at Colchester were built over closely spaced gravel-filled pits up to 0.6 m deep, set out along the lines of the timber ground plates (Crummy 1992: 30–1). Gravel bedding layers continued to be used beneath later masonry foundations in Colchester. A gravel-filled foundation trench was employed in the foundations of a second-century building at Canterbury (Esmonde-Cleary 1997: 452), and rammed-earth foundation pits may have been used beneath wall foundations at the Brooks site in Winchester (Zant 1993: 59).

Masonry and concrete constructions

Whatever the advantages of building in timber or earth, masonry was preferred for aristocratic houses after circa AD 120 and in many regions even the most humble buildings came to be built with stone walls. Only particular need or rare extravagance obliged the Roman builder to go more than twenty miles in pursuit of stone (Blagg 1990b: 48, Williams 1971a and 1971b, Buckland 1988, Vitruvius, *On Architecture* 1, 2.8). The luxurious early villa at Fishbourne was something of an exception and made use of a comparatively wide range of imported stone for particular architectural details, as in the Corinthian capitals used in the colonnades. Even London with its easy access to a major port relied on the poor range of building stone on offer in the Kentish hinterland (Perring and Roskams 1991: 67). Throughout Britain the favoured stones were those that were not only the most readily available but the most easily worked.

The best materials were needed by the greatest patrons, and the most important quarries were in imperial ownership. The exploitation of materials for public projects established mechanisms that subsidised their use in private construction projects. This was no doubt the way in which more expensive marbles found their way to Britain (Branigan 1976, Pritchard 1986, Buckland 1988), and on a more modest scale may have contributed to the distribution of Purbeck marble. Marble imports, always a rarity, were most common in the late first and early second centuries. Domestic architectural fashion was influenced by the availability of materials, and this in turn reflected the changing patterns of supply developed for public construction projects.

Many quarries were located within the property of the house under construction. Where local stone was not suitable for finer detail, as was often the case, greater effort was made to import suitable building material from the nearest convenient source. As a consequence different types of stone were sometimes used for quoins and architectural details. The procedures adopted for quarrying depended on the character of the material being addressed. The tools (chisels, axes, adzes and files) and techniques (wedging, splitting, etc.), that stonemasons deployed in extracting and shaping the stone blocks have been described in detail by Blagg (1976) and Adam (1994). Much of the stone working was carried out at the quarry rather than on the building site, in order to reduce transportation problems. In later construction projects the disused walls of earlier buildings frequently provided the most convenient source of stone, and this contributed to the more heterogeneous nature of later stone walls.

The supply of brick and tile is an even more complex subject (Greene 1986: 150, McWhirr 1979). Brick was required in military and public building projects, and this had a major impact on the early development of the industry. Military kilns were in operation in Britain by the end of the 50s and brick was used in the Neronian bath house at Exeter. Private demand was both stimulated and supported by such public initiatives. The concrete constructions and plasters also depended on the lime produced in kilns. Wood burning periodic or 'flare' kilns, perhaps large enough to have produced lime on a commercial scale, have been excavated at Weekley, Northants and Helpson (Jackson 1973, Wild 1974: 157).

Three kinds of masonry foundation are commonly encountered: concreted rubble, pitched stone or coursed stone. These differences in approach were essentially dictated by the availability of building materials. Where stone was in short supply a rubble concrete was more likely to be preferred, whilst where there was plentiful, good quality stone there was no problem in laying the foundations in regular courses. The use of pitched foundations prevailed where the available stone was of poor quality (Williams 1971b: 115). The foundations usually filled the width of a purpose-built trench.

Concrete foundations could be formed by pouring cement slurry between timber shuttering (Bateman 1986, Frere 1972: 6), but usually consisted of roughly coursed masonry rubble. Sprung arch foundations were rare, but not completely unknown (Wheeler and Wheeler 1936: pl. 99B). In later Roman London pile rafts capped by alternating courses of crushed chalk and ragstone were used in the foundations of masonry structures, as in the construction of a large apse-ended fourth-century building at 25–30 Lime Street. Foundations of a second-century chalk walled extension to a building excavated at One Poultry in London were set over a lattice of crossed timbers at the base of the construction trench (fig. 45). Close piling at the base of masonry foundation trenches was a particular characteristic of late third and fourth century construction (Crummy 1992: 112).

Most Romano-British masonry walls consisted of mortared rubble concrete (*septaria*), faced by small squared blocks laid in regular (or near regular) courses (*petit appareil*). In better constructions the quality of the dressing is such that the walls can be termed ashlar, but most walls are more properly described as rough-faced coursed rubble (Hill 1981: 2–3). A common practice, developed for use in concrete rather than masonry constructions, was to insert tile or stone bonding courses across the full width of the wall at regular intervals up its height. This technique had appeared in Roman Gaul prior to the Claudian conquest of Britain (Desbat 1992), and was initially a feature of public architecture before being widely adopted in domestic architecture in the second and third centuries AD. The tile courses,

Figure 45 Chalk and timber lattice footings used in the foundations of a masonry building at One Poultry, London. Copyright Museum of London.

usually two or three tiles thick, were used to provide even lifts and spread weakness, and helped dry off the lifts of concrete whilst work was in progress. Apart from offering a certain convenience during construction they were perhaps more decorative than functional, and indeed in some cases would have introduced fault lines to the structure. At Feltwell in Norfolk a collapsed flint wall at least 2.6 m high, set over a tapered plinth, had contained two tile bonding courses within its height (Gurney 1986). A wall that had collapsed into a cellar at Colchester consisted of concreted stonework with double tile courses at 400–500 mm intervals (Crummy 1984: 66). A cellar wall at 25–6 Lime Street (c. AD 125–50) was typical of the masonry constructions of London, with its roughly coursed squared ragstone blocks separated by tile string courses at 650 mm (2 ft.) intervals. In this particular example tegulae were vertically mortared to the exposed inside wall of this cellar, perhaps as part of a damp-proofing exercise. Box-flue tiles which were primarily used to form conduits for the hot air generated through the firing of hypocaust systems, were also on occasion used within the thickness of masonry walls as a form of cavity walling.

Romano-British concrete walls were given visual and structural character through the use of stone quoins at corners and around doors and windows. Examples include Colliton Park, Dorchester and a house at Winchester where limestone ashlar quoins were employed on walls of coursed flint set over chalk and flint footings (Zant 1993: 61). Elsewhere, and prevalently in urban contexts, brick was used for this purpose. For instance the 600 mm wide flint wall footings at Silchester were typically reinforced with brick quoins. Concrete walls in Roman Italy were frequently faced with tiles and bricks, laid in one of a distinctive range of styles, as *opus incertum*, *opus reticulatum* and *opus testaceum* (Sear 1982: 74). Although such wall types were found elsewhere in the empire in the first and second centuries AD, they did not appear in Roman Britain.

Herringbone and pitched stone walls were inferior to coursed rubble. One such wall was found in the villa at Barnsley Park, where rough courses of counter-pitched stones were employed alongside coursed rubble con-structions (Webster 1981). Similar herringbone constructions were found in houses at Caerwent, and in villas at Lufton and Chilgrove, as well as being popular in the Nene Valley area (Wild 1974: 159). In House 22,2 at Cirencester both standing elements of walls, and parts of wall collapse, illustrate the use of courses of pitched stonework, herringbone fashion, alternating with coursed rubble string courses (McWhirr 1986: figs 38 and 46). At Redlands Farm, Stanwick a gable wall of herringbone construction had been heightened with a rather crudely executed coursed rubble addition, with a course of tegulae and imbrices marking an offset at the base of the pediment (Keevill 1995). It has already been noted that repairs and rebuilds were often of poorer quality than the original constructions, as at Chedworth and Whittington Court, where the later stonework was larger and not so well dressed (Williams 1971b: 102). This was often a consequence of the reuse of earlier building material, and cannot be assumed to be evidence of decadence.

In this chapter we have reviewed a mass of detailed evidence for a wide range of different building techniques. It is a testament to the progress of archaeological research over the last half-century that we now know so much about the ways in which these Romano-British buildings were put together. We can now describe in close detail how the Roman conquest introduced many new skills in the development of an increasingly monumental approach to domestic architecture. Simple timber constructions, supported by earth-fast posts and basketwork wattle walls, had long been used in Britain. But the first towns and villas owed much to techniques of timber framing that arrived with the army and immigrant craftsmen. Greater sophistication and permanence was achieved by building first in clay and then in stone. The ideas and techniques employed in such buildings were rooted in earlier Romano-Gallic practice, adapted to local circumstance.

6

APPEARANCE AND SUPERSTRUCTURE

Our attention now turns to the more difficult question of what might have stood over the foundations and walls revealed in archaeological excavation. What did these Romano-British houses actually look like? The extent to which upper stories were found in Romano-British houses is hotly disputed (Neal 1982, J.T. Smith 1997: 10), and the first question that needs to be resolved here is whether or not the houses described here were generally built over one or more floors. There is no doubt that several Romano-British aisled buildings were tall enough to have accommodated an upper storey. A collapsed fourth-century gable wall found in excavations at Carsington in Derbyshire had stood 11.5 m high to the gable (Ling 1992). Similar evidence shows that the gable wall of an aisled building at Meonstoke in Hampshire had been some 10 m high (fig. 46). The Meonstoke wall, which is now on display in the British Museum, has provided a mass of new information about the appearance of such structures (King and Potter 1990). It was built as part of a fourth-century addition to the southeast facade of the building, and had been set over foundations 1 m thick and 2 m deep. The remains show that the aisled building was designed as a basilica with a tall nave lit by clerestory windows set above the line of the aisles, and not with a single roof span over both nave and aisles. The collapsed wall included a register of three clerestory windows separated by mortared columns, some 2.5 m above ground level. A projecting tile cornice, about 200 mm deep, protected these windows from the rain. Above this, in the gable of the building, there was a register of blind arcading with tile arches separated by pilasters with greenstone bases and capitals. Most of the architectural details were executed in red tile separated by thick bands of white mortar. This monumental building drew inspiration from the public basilica, and the use of rows of linked arches in Romanesque style witnessed considerable architectural sophistication.

In many aisled buildings in the Nene valley the foundations of the gable walls were wider than those of the side walls. Typically the gable footings were reinforced with pitched stone footings 900 mm wide, whilst the sides were built over foundations 600 mm wide (Wild 1974: 159, Jones 1981:

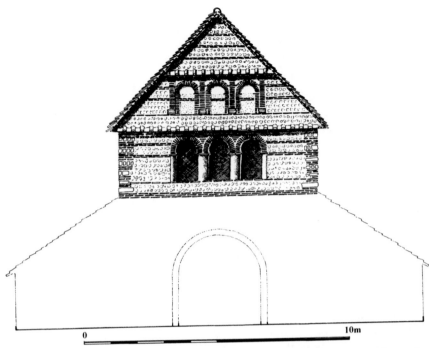

Figure 46 Reconstruction of the collapsed gable wall from the aisled building at Meonstoke. Drawing by S. Crummy. Copyright The British Museum.

94). In a house at Silchester the end walls were twice the width of the side walls (Fox and St John Hope 1894: 205). Elsewhere buttresses were sometimes used to support gable walls (e.g. Gurney 1986: 1–48). The reinforcement of end walls was thought by Smith to illustrate a weakness in roof construction (Smith 1982: 9), and it is perhaps no coincidence that several collapsed gable walls have been found. The implication is that the end walls took a substantial part of the roof load, and were consequently more prone to collapse and in need of structural reinforcement. This has implications for the nature of roof construction.

These large aisled buildings were designed as impressive structures, and we have already explored some of the reasons why this may have been the case. Roof-venting hearths found in many such buildings suggest, however, that upper floors were unlikely to have been inserted within many of these lofty interiors. Reception rooms placed in such buildings may also have extended to the full height of the building to exploit the clerestory lighting. Mezzanine or upper floors were therefore probably restricted to certain bays. This is the arrangement of the modern Italian *portico rustico*, which offers a close structural parallel. In these modern buildings the upper areas are designed for storage and reached by ladders rather than fixed stairways. Archaeological proof of such use would be difficult to obtain.

Aisled structures were not the only imposing houses found in the Romano-British countryside. The unusually deep foundations supporting the central block of the villa at Frocester (up to 2.6 m deep) suggest that this was a particularly massive structure (Gracie 1970). Wall collapse from a reception room in the eastern wing of the villa at Redlands Farm, Stanwick shows that here the room had stood 6.6 m high from ground level to the gable (Keevill 1995). In this case the ridge of the roof ran along the central axis of the wing, at right angles to the main block. Here, as was perhaps normally the case, the wing room had been designed to present a gable-end to the facade. Wall collapse from Building 1 in Colliton Park, Dorchester shows that here too the end reception room stood over 5 m high (fig. 20). In both these cases it is likely that the greater height was exploited to create a lofty reception area and that upper floors were not present.

At several sites, buttresses were added to heighten or emphasise the reception rooms (Walters 1996). This is likely to have achieved dramatic effect in towering octagonal rooms at Lufton and Maidstone, and in the large apse-ended reception room added to the corner of the villa at Box in Wiltshire (Brakspear 1904: 18). Buttresses also supported heated 'pavilion' wings in the winged-corridor facades of the houses at Darenth and Stroud near Petersfield (fig. 10: Room 12, D.J. Smith 1978: 126). Some evidence can be adduced for the reinforcement of walls in several other wing pavilion rooms: and it is possible that these were built to stand taller than other parts of the houses (Neal 1982: 153–70). This is suggested by the illustrations of villas found in some North African mosaic pavements, where the corner pavilions sometimes appear as small towers (Sarnowski 1978). It is unlikely, however, that this was always the case. Reinforced foundations were the exception and not the rule, and other illustrations of villas show the corner pavilions as smaller structures (fig. 48).

Terraces at the villas at Great Witcombe, Lockleys and Gadebridge Park were exploited to allow the insertion of lower floors beneath at least one wing (Neal 1982: 154–6). At Lockleys the presence of an upper floor above the terraced room was illustrated by the collapse of two concrete floors, as if the roof had fallen first and carried the ceiling of the lower room as it fell (Ward-Perkins 1938). The buttresses recorded at some other sites appear to have been built to counteract downward pressures due to the terraced location of these villas (Williams 1971b: 117), but may also have been exploited for decorative effect. There is therefore abundant evidence for the construction of lofty halls and reception rooms in the Romano-British countryside, especially in the earlier part of the fourth century. But there is good reason to believe that in many of these cases upper floors had not been provided as a matter of course. Most villas were probably single storied.

Figure 47 Pottery stand found in Sherborne Lane/King William Street, London. Apparently in the form of a building (Chapman 1981). Copyright Museum of London.

The urban evidence is of a different character but points towards a similar conclusion. The early second-century destruction debris of Building H at Watling Court in London included a tessellated pavement that had probably collapsed from an upper floor. This unusual discovery was consistent with the evidence of the structure itself, which was built with unusually sturdy mud brick walls. Although some of the mud and stud structures in Lyon are likely to have supported two-storey structures, as at the Verbe Incarné site (Desbat 1981), this was not usually the case in Britain. The surviving timbers from London's timber-framed houses were all from single-storey structures about 2.4–2.5 m high. The volume of brickearth used in the construction of buildings at Newgate Street and Watling Court, as estimated from both the extraction quarries and the destruction horizons, is also consistent with buildings of this height (Perring and Roskams 1991: 78). The volume and character of the destruction debris from many of the buildings at Verulamium supports the argument that most of the timber buildings were bungalows. The design of the wall paintings from House 21,2 at Verulamium indicates that the corridor wall they had decorated was only 1.82 m high (Davey and Ling 1982: 31), although the rooms reached by the corridor would have had higher ceilings.

Strip buildings, like the aisled buildings to which they were closely related, are more likely to have had upper stories or mezzanine floors. Not only would this be consistent with evidence from the shops of Pompeii and Herculaneum, but would also account for the porticoes at Caerwent and Wroxeter which are likely to have supported upper floors. This was not a universal feature and some of the timber strip buildings from London and Verulamium were single-storey constructions.

At Pompeii upper floors were often later additions and lower status rooms. In Roman houses upper floors were usually lesser floors. The best rooms, the dining rooms and halls, were on the ground floor (although see Pliny, *Letters* 2.17 on a dining room and bedroom on an upper floor in his villa at Laurentum). Only in densely populated towns, such as Ostia, was space at such a premium that reception rooms were placed in upper floors (e.g. the Caseggiate del Serapide 3,10,3, where a mosaic was laid in a third-floor apartment). It reflects on the crowded nature of early Roman London that houses such as Building H at Watling Court were provided with decorated upper rooms. This was exceptional.

We have few illustrations of Romano-British buildings with which to supplement the archaeological evidence. A graffito found on wall plaster from Hucclecote had, until recently, been thought to illustrate the gable-end of a half-timbered house. It is alternatively possible that the features shown, two arches beneath a pair of parallel horizontal lines divided by a series of vertical elements, were brick and tile elements within a masonry wall similar to that found at Meonstoke (Davey 1961: 41). A mosaic pavement found in the villa at Brading, in the Isle of Wight, shows a small single-storey structure with a low pitch roof, entered by a large door in the gable-end. This is perhaps most likely to represent a small shrine or temple (Witts 1994: 114–15). A couple of pottery stands manufactured in the London area are of greater interest, and appear to show small single-storey buildings with round-headed doors and windows pierced through walls divided into a series of cross-braced panels (fig. 47, Chapman 1981). The best overall impression of what some Romano-British houses looked like is, however, given by a group of stone shrines (*aediculae*) from the Rhine area (fig. 48, Massy 1989: 107, Boon 1983: pl. 6). These portray rectangular houses with winged-corridor facades. In most cases the buildings were shown as single-storey structures, with clerestory lighting represented by small square windows set above the line of the portico facade. The main entrance is shown at the centre of the facade, and distinguished by a pediment. The wings are shown as comparatively small structures with ridge lines at right angle to the main

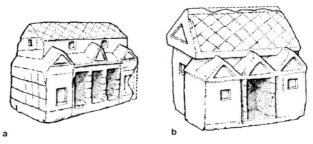

Figure 48 Two monolithic stone shrines in the form of wing-corridor houses. a: Fontoy-Moderwiese. b: Titelberg (from Smith 1997).

block, terminating in gable-ends of similar scale and height to the pediment set over the central porch. These representations may not be accurate, but the evidence is consistent with what we know from other sources. Since pressures on building space in Britain did not necessitate the use of upper floors, and the building traditions imported by Rome preferred to place facilities on the ground floor, it is likely that upper storeys were an exception and not the norm.

Doors and windows

Important doorways were emphasised by flanking columns or pillars supporting an entablature and pediment. Only the foundations of these features survive. Doorways in timber buildings are usually represented by timber thresholds 1.0–1.75 m wide. This is somewhat wider than is typical today. Stone thresholds were used in masonry constructions and these provide additional information. For instance the entrance to House 3N at Caerwent was through a double door 1.2 m (4 ft.) wide, hung on pivots and with a central bolt-hole (Ashby *et al.* 1904: 101–3). Iron pivot-shoes and sockets have been found at several sites (Boon 1974: 204), although the absence of such finds from extensive destruction horizons in London and Verulamium suggests that doors were more commonly hung on unreinforced timber pivots (Perring and Roskams 1991: 95–6). A folding door found at Dewlish represents a rare discovery. Three planed and rebated oak boards were held together by horizontal oak ledges secured with hooked iron nails, but nothing survived of the hinges or pivots. Other traces of doors have tentatively been identified at Batten Hanger, reused as the floor of a mortar mixing pit at Leadenhall Court in London and in burnt debris at Wroxeter (Milne 1992: 21, Webster 1988: 139–40). Part of a door was also found at One Poultry in London and a plank-built cross-braced Roman door was found reused as a floor in the Roman fort at Chesterholm (Burch *et al.* 1997, Hanson 1982: 180). Excavations in Bucklersbury in London in 1987 produced evidence for the use of removable shutter partitions (Rowsome, personal communication), and at Catterick a threshold supporting timber uprights with a slot for wooden shutters was found in a street-side shop (Burnham and Wacher 1990: 45–6). Such removable shutters were a common element in shops and workshops elsewhere in the Roman world. The timber shutter of a shop in via dell' Abbondanza at Pompeii has been preserved in a plaster cast and shows how the vertical interlocking planks were socketed into a groove in the base-plate and secured by horizontal iron bars.

The arch was a popular motif in Romano-British domestic architecture. Fragments of several windows and arches have been found in the collapse and destruction debris of stone built houses. Arches were commonly used to divide multi-chambered reception rooms. A fragment of one such arch built of tile and tufa, and originally 1.75 m wide by 2.5 m high, had collapsed into a hypocaust at Boxmoor (Neal 1974–6: 57–8). Another, from the villa at Woodchester, had a span of *c.* 1.5 m (Lysons 1797). An arcade divided the hall and corridor of the villa at Kingsweston (Boon 1950). Fallen masonry in front of the veranda at Dewlish included the shattered remains of a semi-circular brick arch together with fragments of a plaster cornice, and at Combley on the Isle of Wight a round-headed tufa arch had fallen in mass from a doorway (Putnam and Rainey 1975, Goodburn 1976: 364–5). An arch with part of a fallen wall and vault was also found in the baths at Sparsholt (Johnston 1969).

Small windows, both round- and square-headed were commonly installed in the upper parts of walls to provide clerestory lighting. Such windows were shown in the architectural fantasies used to decorate rooms in Italian and North African houses, as most famously in the fresco used to decorate a bedroom in the Campanian villa at Boscoreale, now on display in the New York Metropolitan Museum. There is abundant archaeological evidence for their use in Roman Britain. We have already mentioned the evidence of the collapsed wall at Meonstoke, which contained an arcade of three round-headed tile clerestory windows measuring 2.8×1 m (fig. 46). Clerestory windows above the line of a corridor roof are also implied by chalk voussoirs (the wedge-shaped stones used to form arches) 700 mm in diameter from Verulamium House 21,2 (Frere 1983, 161–4). This offered raised lighting for a reception room, likely to have been more than 4.9 m high. Voussoirs have also been found associated with several villa houses, and a small round-headed window was identified in the collapsed gable wall of the Stanwick villa (Keevill 1996). Arched window heads carved from stone slabs, and sometimes decorated to illustrate spandrels, are known from forts in the north of Britain (Blagg 1996: 11, Bidwell 1996: 26). Round-headed windows may even have been used in comparatively modest establishments, such as the late Roman building at Bradley Hill (Leech 1981: 182).

The archaeological record is biased towards these round-headed openings since these were usually executed in robust masonry. Squared openings are more likely to have been formed by timber frames. These do not survive, but the pictorial evidence shows that they were common throughout the Roman world. Even if the evidence is unrepresentative it is still clear that the arch had particular significance in house design. The apse and arch were familiar icons from Roman public architecture, and were transmitted into the design of the western church. These motifs had currency in places where Roman authority was most evident, especially in civic and religious architecture (Baldwin Smith 1956: 10–11). The apse was particularly suited to sacred use, where it could represent the vault of heaven. The domestic architecture of Roman Britain sits firmly within this tradition, where the apse and arch located and framed the activities of the Romano-British magnate (Bek 1983: 91).

Few town windows overlooked the street, but where they did we assume that the windows would have been small, high and protected. Wooden window frames were sometimes employed (for which see the mouldings on the stone sill of the window at Colliton Park, Dorchester). Iron window grills of a type used throughout the western provinces have been found at various sites (Webster 1959: 10–14). These consisted of three or four horizontal bars fixed to a similar number of vertical ones, with the ends turned over to fit into the wooden frame. The windows that they had protected were rectangular, almost square, and measured 500–700 mm across. Window glass was used across a range of sites but sparingly (Boon 1974: 207). Panes of glass up to 400 mm across have been found on Romano-British sites (Harden 1961). Early window glass at Colchester was cast, but by the fourth century was blown. Where larger quantities of window glass are found on domestic sites the provenance is likely to have been the baths. The windows at Meonstoke were unglazed, but were in part protected from the elements by a projecting tile hood 200 mm deep.

Further ventilation was perhaps provided by small ground-level openings. Small rectangular openings, 300–460 mm across, were set at floor level through the walls of houses at London and Verulamium (Perring and Roskams 1991: 103). A hole formed by an imbrex at floor level through the wall of a house at Silchester and similar features in reception rooms at Chedworth and Brading may have been vents and drains (Fox and St John Hope 1890: 738, Price and Hilton Price 1881: 18, Richmond 1959: 10).

Roofs

Most Roman roofs were supported on a timber framework, although concrete vaults were used in the heated rooms of baths and a few other rare instances. Since no antique roofs have survived in Britain it is necessary to draw heavily on the evidence from other parts of the ancient world in order to describe roofing arrangements.

Most simple houses in Roman Britain had no need of complex roof carpentry. In some earth-fast post constructions there is clear evidence for post-pairing, and such paired supports are most likely to have taken coupled principal rafters (fig. 33). Similar paired rafters could also have rested on the close-studded wall plates used in timber-framed constructions. The absence of substantial supports within the framed walls of the building found at Courage's Brewery in Southwark indicates that this roof had not been supported on heavy principal rafters or trusses (fig. 35, Brigham *et al.* 1995: 31). The use of paired rafters braced by collar beams to form A-frames, has instead been suggested. Tie beams were not used, although tie-beam assembly is likely elsewhere. It seems likely that simple close-coupled roofs of this sort were the most common in Roman Britain.

A more complex form of timber roof, sometimes known as the double-roof, involves the use of horizontal timbers or purlins to support the rafters. Simple roofs at Pompeii consisted of rafters resting on purlins that ran from one gable wall to the other (Adam 1994: 205–13). The use of such techniques has been suggested in the construction of Greek temple roofs (Hodge 1960). These were primarily purlin roofs, with short-length rafters slotted onto large axial purlins resting on walls and struts from below. The evidence of the reinforced gable-end walls found on various sites in Roman Britain suggests that these had been designed to carry the weight of the roof, and the pressures brought to bear by a sagging purlin roof would also account for their occasional collapse.

The king-post roof was possibly a Hellenistic innovation, but is first positively attested by a bronze copy in the second-century AD porch of the Pantheon at Rome. In this form of roof large principal rafters supported lesser purlins and rafters. These rafters were prevented from lateral move-ment by tie beams across the width of the covered area. These were in turn prevented from bowing by a king-post suspended from the apex of the roof. This roof type allowed the construction of large buildings, such as the basilica at Trier with a span of 27.5 m. Constructions of this type are found in early Christian church architecture, and the Constantinian roof of Old St Peter's, Rome would appear to have rested on double trusses with a scarfed tie beam and pendant king posts (Choisy 1873). In St Paul's (fuori Lateran) at Rome, trusses were formed of paired rafters braced by both a tie beam and above this a straining beam which supported a central king-post (Adam 1994, Rondelet 1814: pl. 76). These trusses spanned a width of 24.25 m and were set at 3.33 m intervals along the length of the church. Vitruvius provided a description of roof carpentry broadly consistent with this evidence (*On Architecture* 4, 2.1). Although there is no conclusive evidence that trussed roofs were ever built in Roman Britain, the probability is that they were.

The discovery of reused Roman hip rafters at Scole in Norfolk indicates that hipped roofs were sometimes used (Flitcroft and Tester 1994: 324), but this was not the case in those buildings where collapsed gable walls have been found. The shrines built in the form of small houses that were used in the area of Luxembourg also illustrate a general preference to take roofs to a gable-end (fig. 48).

Roof pitch was largely determined by the nature of the roofing material employed. Thatch and shingles benefit from a steep pitch. Slate roofs are also usually given a steep pitch. At Meonstoke the slate roof had a pitch of 47.5 degrees, the roof at Welney one of 45 degrees, and at Carsington one of 40 degrees (King and Potter 1990, Phillips 1970: 233, Ling 1992). Tile roofs are more stable if a shallow pitch is chosen and this reduces the need to nail tiles into place. The gable-end wall found collapsed at Redlands Farm, was pitched at 22.5 degrees and supported a tile roof (Keevill 1995: 28). Roof pitches below 20 degrees are unlikely to have been water-resistant.

The eaves did not normally project significantly beyond the wall line. This was even the case with earth-walled houses: the eavesdrip gullies from Newgate Street and Watling Court were set 100–300 mm from the wall (Perring and Roskams 1991: 95).

It is assumed that thatch was commonly used on lower status Romano-British sites, and a collapsed thatch roof has tentatively been identified in London (Grimes 1968: 97). The absence of tile or stone collapse over houses destroyed by fire in London and Colchester c. AD 60 and AD 125, similarly implies the use of organic roofing materials. The regional use of thatch is supported by Caesar's description of his winter quarters having been built with 'roofs of straw in Gallic fashion' (Caesar, DBG 5,43). Shingles are likely to have been favoured in the early Roman forts because more easily obtained (Shirley 2000: 26). At the Courage Brewery site in Southwark four square fragments of oak board pierced by nail holes may have been wooden shingles. These were 2 mm thick and measuring 250–350 mm by 115–40 mm, but might have been broken clapboards (Brigham et al. 1995).

Ceramic tile was used as a roofing material soon after the conquest and appeared on timber-framed wattle and daub buildings in pre-Boudiccan Colchester (Crummy 1984: 22). In most cases such roofs consisted of squared flanged tegulae capped by curved imbrices. It is possible that imbrex only roofs were used, although this has not been established. Nails were used to secure tiles in more vulnerable locations, with perhaps as many as 20 per cent of the tiles fixed in this fashion (Shirley 2000: 27). In southwest Britain stone became a more popular roofing material than ceramic tile from the middle of the second century (Williams 1971b). This fashion extended east to Hampshire (Boon 1974: 203, Zant 1993: 80), and has been documented in the suburbs of Lincoln where slate replaced tile on the roofs of strip buildings in the fourth century (Jones 1981: 97). It was less marked in the southeast where ceramic tile remained common in the later Roman period. Stone slates were commonly nailed into place, as illustrated by slates found in Cirencester and at the villa at Tarrant Hinton where traces of lichen indicate the manner in which the slates had overlapped (McWhirr 1986, Giles 1981: 91). Roof tiles were sometimes hexagonal or pentagonal rather than rectangular. The use of tiles of different colours in the same roof has been noted at Fishbourne and London (where red and yellow was used) and Piddington (which featured blue and yellow), and these colours may have been exploited to form different decorative patterns (de la Bedoyere 1991: 25–6). At Sparsholt, the roof was composed of grey limestone slates and red tiles (Johnston 1969: 17).

Decorative finials or ventilators, made of terracotta or carved stone, have been found on some sites (Lowther 1976: 40–1, Blagg 1979 and 1977: 52–4). In a couple of instances these had clearly been attached to the roof. Ceramic finials were conical or square, with vents that allowed them to function as small louvers or chimney pots, although it cannot be shown they were used as such. Blagg has identified two regional groupings of stone finials. In some high status sites in the southwest of the province tower shaped finials were used. These sometimes took the form of a four-way arch, surmounted by a roof or pediment. In contrast military sites, especially along Hadrian's wall, favoured pinecone finials. More rarely a phallus was used. All three motifs – gateway, pinecone and phallus – were potent boundary markers. These finials would have been placed prominently and their limited range of circulation suggests that their use marked particular local fashion.

The hot rooms of baths were usually vaulted, as in the second-century complex at Winchester Palace, Southwark (Mackenna and Ling 1991: 159). In most cases these would have been concrete barrel vaults constructed over a timber frame, as shown by the collapsed vaulting of the bath-house at Beauport Park (Brodribb and Cleere 1988: 226). Ceramic box tiles and hollow voussoirs were sometimes used to line the insides of the heated rooms, allowing the hot air to circulate upwards towards chimneys and vents and establishing a form of cavity insulation, but also allowing for the construction of lighter vaults (Black 1987: 13, Williams 1971a: 195).

Some cellars were also vaulted, as illustrated by the roof at Burham (Jessupp 1958). The sockets and putlog holes found in masonry cellars might have supported frames used in vault construction. Vaults were otherwise rare in Romano-British houses, in contrast with their wide-spread use at Ostia and Rome. The vaulted room found in House 34,1 at Silchester was an exception (St John Hope 1907: 442–3). The room had unusually thick walls (up to 900 mm across). Its roof, which had collapsed over the floor, had been formed of hollow tile voussoirs cemented with thick mortar joints and plastered over to form the ceiling. A similar roof may have been built over an underground corridor at Verulamium (Frere 1983: pl. 47).

7

DECORATION AND THE MEANING OF MOSAICS

Aristocratic houses in the Roman world were extravagantly decorated with marbles, mosaics and wall paintings. These schemes of decoration have received wide attention from both archaeologists and art historians, and their study offers insight into the social use of the Roman house. British patrons never achieved the high standards of the wealthier parts of the Roman world, but there is none the less a substantial body of decorative art from the province (Henig 1995). This chapter offers two rather different approaches to the study of interior design and decoration in the Romano-British house. In the first place it offers a brief review of the range and character of the decorative techniques employed. This completes our description of the fabric and craft of Romano-British houses. This evidence is best presented according to the technique employed, and for this reason we treat separately with the evidence of walls and then floors, rather than attempting to describe complete schemes of decoration within individual rooms.

The second and perhaps more interesting part of this survey explores some aspects of the meaning of the subjects used by way of decoration. Although there are some wall paintings of relevance to this argument, most of the better information is found in the mosaic floors. This evidence is particularly valuable for the insight it offers into the cultural affiliations and belief systems that supported elite society. This chapter therefore concludes with a fairly lengthy, if rather selective, discussion of this evidence.

Walls

Lime wash rendering was widely used in Roman Italy, as at Pompeii, and has been documented in several instances in Roman Britain. Exteriors of timber- and clay-walled houses were often plastered and painted in white. Some masonry structures were similarly treated. The columns of the villa at Piddington were instead painted in three colours: red with purple-brown bands and white details (Bidwell 1996: 27). Colour was also employed to create a red base to the exterior wall of the Painted House at Dover (Philp

1989). These were unusual treatments, but illustrate that the exteriors of some Romano-British houses may have been highly colourful.

The use of timber cladding has already been described (see p. 96) and would have had an important visual impact in the earlier Romano-British towns. Many masonry walls, especially those of better ashlar construction, would have been left exposed. Rendering of a wall at Gadebridge Park involved the use of scored lines to imitate ashlar blocks for decorative effect (Neal 1974: pl. 5b). Similar effects were achieved in the cellar at Burham. Visual effects were also achieved through the different approaches adopted to pointing: ribbon pointing and heavy scoring are both attested in Roman Britain, although the evidence has been obtained from public buildings (Bidwell 1996: 20, Blagg 1996: 14).

Decorative keying – pargeting

Two or three clay scrims were commonly applied to the faces of earth walls, and sometimes also to wattle and daub and mud and stud constructions. These were often finished off with an impressed herringbone, diamond-lozenge or, more rarely, circular pattern (figs 41, 42e and 44). The design was commonly applied by a roller die, which at Lullingstone measured 300–70 mm wide and was operated upwards (Meates 1979). Most of the diamond patterns were formed in this manner. The chevron designs were more frequently incised directly onto the clay scrim. Decoration of this character was widespread in first- and second-century Romano-British contexts. This was a construction detail imported from Gaul, closely paralleled in Augustan Lyon (Desbat 1985). The patterns sometimes provided a keying for plaster decoration, but frequently served as decoration similar to the pargeted wall plaster designs popular in Tudor England. At Colchester pre-Boudiccan keyed daub in Building 8 at Lion Walk involved a dado, probably formed by a roller stamp, of the diamond-lozenge pattern 280 mm wide. This was separated from an upper wall decoration of incised diagonal bands by horizontal lines formed by impressing string into the still wet clay.

Painted wall and ceiling plaster

In his review of the social arrangements of the Pompeiian house, Wallace-Hadrill emphasised the importance of wall paintings in the study of social flow within the house (1988: 77). Unfortunately the poor state of preservation of Romano-British remains means that schemes of decoration can only rarely be reconstructed for individual rooms and never for whole buildings.

The best frescos were executed on a wall plaster about 10 mm deep, laid in two or three coats of thoroughly slaked lime mortar with a fine aggregate, to which hydraulic materials such as crushed brick were sometimes added. Powdered marble or calcium was used to produce the final surface, which could be polished to a high sheen, possibly helped by the addition of calcite to the pigments. Red, black and green schemes of decoration were preferred, and were usually set in panels above a dado no more than 800 mm high that was decorated in imitation of stone or marble cladding. A cornice border would generally have been found above the coloured panels (Davey and Ling 1982: 52–62). The inspiration for this decorative approach was architectural: drawing in particular on the lavishly decorated interiors of public buildings and palaces. The use of colour reflected a hierarchy of status, in which white was the least valued colour, yellow and red were of medium status, and blue and black schemes were restricted to the very best rooms. Ceilings were also painted, and where evidence survives the decorative schemes involved repeat patterns of geometric shapes, including roundels, octagons and squares, mostly on a white ground.

Painted wall decorations are found in a small proportion of the earliest town houses to have been built in Britain. In London fragments of red- and green-painted wall plaster were recovered from beneath Boudiccan destruction debris in the town centre (Philp 1977). Less than one house in ten had painted walls at this time. At Verulamium the decoration of a corridor or portico of a stone-founded building, perhaps a bath house, included a polychrome still-life featuring a lyre, quiver and bow, the symbols of Apollo (Davey and Ling 1982). At Lion Walk, Colchester, a contemporary civilian building had a wall of red, green and black panels above a marbled dado (Crummy 1984: 42). Neronian painted wall plaster has also been recovered from select villas, most notably Fishbourne (Cunliffe 1971b: 52). Flavian decoration of this character was more widespread. Good urban examples have been recovered from London and Cirencester (Perring and Roskams 1991: 85–7, Davey and Ling 1982: no. 8), and villas so decorated at this time include the timber-framed villa at Boxmoor, where the scheme comprised a dado with red panels with green borders separated by black fascia.

A painted lunette in what was probably a bath suite in the second-century building complex at Winchester Palace, Southwark, had originally shown a winged Cupid at the centre of an elaborate framework of flimsy pavilions (Ling 1989). The quality of the painting is shown by the use of luxury materials such as red cinnabar and gold leaf, and it bears comparison with contemporary work in Italy (Yule 1989: 35). Other architectural illusionistic schemes were found in early second-century London (Rhodes 1987: 169–72), and elsewhere in the province they appear from the mid-second century (as at Leicester Blue Boar Lane: Davey and Ling 1982). Such schemes were widely popular in Roman interior decoration, and boasted power, status and order (Kuttner 1993: 341–7). It is no coincidence that these scenes became popular in Britain at a time when much greater emphasis was being placed on reception facilities within private buildings.

These early painted decorations were generally more technically accomplished than later works, which were coarser in their execution with an increasing dominance of low-status white ground decoration from the end of the second century (Davey and Ling 1982). This was partly a consequence of the less exclusive nature of later wall decorations, although the third-century remains something of a 'dark age' for painted wall plaster. In some higher status houses few rooms were left unpainted, as in the villa at Winterton where at least eleven of the sixteen rooms in the main house were painted (Stead 1976).

Large figure compositions were popular in high status contexts in the third and fourth centuries. The earliest known large-scale figure subject is that showing water nymphs or goddesses set in the niche of the cellar at Lullingstone, a painting probably executed c. AD 180 (Liversidge 1987). The best paintings were usually found in those rooms that also had the best floors, and these complex decorative schemes are found in the major reception rooms. The painted scenes would have complemented the images found in the mosaic floors. Centrally placed reception rooms with important decorative schemes of this period include rooms in the villas at Sparsholt (architectural illusion), Bignor Room 28B (rich use of imitation marbles), Rudston room with charioteer mosaic (perspective decoration) (Davey and Ling 1982). Figurative and mythological scenes were more popular in the heated end reception rooms (e.g. Swain and Ling 1981, Henig 1995: 162). One of the most interesting decorative schemes was that found in the room above the Lullingstone cellar. These fourth-century paintings showed a row of six robed figures with their arms raised in prayer, and on another wall a large painted chi-rho, the symbol of Christ.

The other main place in the house where wall paintings were likely to be placed was the portico or corridor (fig. 49). Examples include the peopled scroll from in House 21,2 at Verulamium and a fresco with people in an architectural landscape in the corridor of a house at Leicester (Frere 1982: 161–3, Wacher 1995: 353–5). The baths were also decorated, with marine scenes often preferred (Davey and Ling 1982: nos. 37, 34 and 49).

Stuccos and veneers

Stucco was rarely used in Britain under the Romans, and its domestic use was restricted to a select group of lavishly decorated villas where architectural details and figurative decorations were sometimes sculpted in plaster (Ling 1976). The use of imported marble cladding was similarly an unusual extravagance. In London wall veneers of continental marbles were first used in buildings of the late first century – Purbeck marble had been used in the decoration of a pre-Flavian building – but are found with greater frequency in early to mid second-century deposits (Pritchard 1986: 185–6). The early palatial villas of the south coast were also provided with walls veneered with imported marble (Cunliffe 1971b: 33). Wall mosaics are even more rarely attested. Some second-century plunge baths were lined with white tesserae,

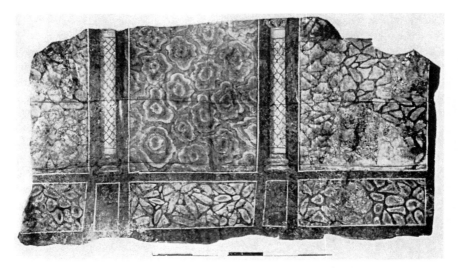

Figure 49 Restored panel of painted wall plaster of Antonine date from the corridor of House 28,3 at Verulamium. Reproduced by kind permission of the Society of Antiquaries of London.

sometimes above a coloured border, but no examples of decorative wall mosaics have survived (Liversidge 1968: 284).

Floors

Different degrees of care were exercised in laying earth floors, and these could sometimes be comparatively sophisticated constructions. At Watling Court the floors were built over brickearth construction slabs up to 800 mm thick laid in two or three bands of compacted earth, separated by thin gravel spreads. This laborious approach is paralleled in contemporary constructions at Chartres and Milan (Coulon and Joly 1985: 98–9, Perring 1991a: 126). It is likely that rushes and grasses covered many earth floors, but evidence is difficult to obtain. Straw floors have been recorded in a military building of Flavian-Trajanic date at Ribchester (Wilson 1970: 281). Timber floors can be also be difficult to identify on dry sites, but there is mounting evidence to suggest that they were widely used in Roman Britain. At the Courage Brewery site in Southwark a plank floor was laid over joists at 500 mm intervals. The planks were 300 and 450 mm wide and the joists were dove-tailed or lap-jointed into the sill beams. The planks were rebated into a central beam across the middle of the building (Brigham *et al.* 1995). Oak floorboards, some 180–280 mm wide, in a building in the fort at Pumsaint were nailed onto underlying joists by large iron spikes (Burnham and Burnham 1991).

Earth floors were standard, but higher status rooms were provided with something more impressive. In earlier periods mortar and *opus signinum* floors were generally more frequent than tessellated ones, whilst the reverse was the case after the middle of the second century. Stone-flagged floors are found in areas where suitable paving stone was readily available. Such floors were preferred in working and service areas. This is illustrated in the houses of Caerwent, where flagged floors were commonly found in corridors and work-rooms. Another type of floor used in porticoes and other busy areas consisted of tiles laid in a herringbone pattern, otherwise known as *opus spicatum*. Such floors are rare in Roman Britain where most examples date to the second and third centuries (Williams 1971a: 179). Although normally composed of red tiles only, a floor laid in a house at Colchester was executed in both red and black (Dunnett 1966: 39). Tessellated pavements, usually executed in red, were widely used in similar contexts to the mortar and tile floors. Durable tessellated pavements were particularly popular in the corridors of later Romano-British villas, where simple mosaic designs were also sometimes used.

Lime-based cement floors, employing a wide range of different types of aggregate according to circumstance, were common in better Romano-British houses. In modest houses a mortar floor was more likely to mark out a high status room than be an indication that the room in question was subject to greater use. The use of a high proportion of crushed and broken tile in the aggregate is the characterising feature of *opus signinum* (or terrazzo), a particularly durable type of mortar floor in which polished tile fragments gave the floor a red (or occasionally buff) finish. The earliest dated urban appearance of this floor type is from pre-Flavian contexts in London (Richardson 1988: 387). In slightly later contexts in the same part of London a mosaic inlay pattern had been set into the *opus signinum* (Smith in Perring and Roskams 1991). This floor type, particularly popular in Italy in the late republic, was used on a few other early Roman sites in southern Britain but did not see widespread adoption. At Verulamium *opus signinum* floors were rare before the second century, where a variation on the type involved mixing the pounded tile with chalk rather than mortar (Frere 1972: 78, 80). Quarter-round red-painted cement and *opus signinum* fillets were used as a form of skirting around the borders of decorated rooms.

Stone inlay pavements composed of imported marble (*opus sectile*), were an early but short-lived fashion restricted to luxurious houses and little known after the end of the first century. The best evidence for this type of floor comes from Fishbourne and other villas along the south coast. A few houses in London, Silchester and Canterbury were also decorated in this fashion.

Hypocausts

Underfloor heating was first introduced into Britain *c.* AD 60–5 in the baths attached to forts (e.g. Bidwell 1979), and subsequently in the public baths of the emergent towns. Heated baths houses were also found attached to some better pre-Flavian villas, but only towards the end of the first century were heated rooms found in other domestic contexts.

Hypocausts were heated from furnaces set in an adjacent room or against an outside wall of the building, from which hot air was circulated beneath the floor and up through flues set within the walls. There were three principal types of underfloor arrangement: pillar hypocausts where the floor was raised by a series of columns (*pilae*); channel hypocausts where the hot air was directed along channels radiating from the main flue; and composite hypocausts where a central pillared chamber fed a series of radiating channels.

There were several variations on these types. Pillars were most frequently formed of stacks of tiles nine inches square, but circular and octagonal tile *pilae* are also known. The use of circular pillars waned in popularity through the Roman period, and the few Romano-British examples date to the earlier period. Box tiles set on end and filled with clay or mortar were also used. Stone plinths often supported hypocaust floors, and were preferred to ceramic where stone was available. The use of stone in hypocausts mirrors the use of stone tiles on roofs.

Rooms with pillared hypocausts were hotter than those with channels, and were most usually found in hot baths. Pillared hypocausts feature in some early houses, although heated rooms were rarely found outside baths throughout the first century. The absence of hypocaust floors from the late first-century town houses in London, as those at Watling Court, is notable. Even at Fishbourne the earliest heated rooms were restricted to the baths, and we know of only one small pillared hypocaust in the domestic quarters of the late first-century villa.

Heated domestic rooms were found in early second-century London (fig. 50). London was characteristically precocious. Domestic heated rooms did not appear in Winchester until towards the end of that century (e.g. House 23,1), and in Verulamium were not widely found until the third century (e.g. Houses 18,1 and 28,1). Channelled hypocausts first appear in mid second-century villas. Their introduction seems to have been linked to the increased emphasis placed on rear reception rooms. This type of hypocaust was less difficult to fire and offered less intense heat. Lined in stone or tile according to the availability of these materials, these heating systems were widely used in later villas and town houses, especially in the fourth century. In this later period pillared hypocausts were generally restricted to the baths, although there were also some small heated rooms where pillared floors were preferred. There has been speculation as to the function of these rooms which gave a heat that perhaps exceeded the needs of domestic comfort (Black 1985), although it is possible that this preference reflects problems that obtained in making efficient use of small channel hypocausts.

One of the earliest Romano-British channelled hypocausts was laid in the early second century in a reception room in the villa at Gorhambury (fig. 7).

Figure 50 Pillar hypocaust in a clay-walled building at 15–23 Southwark Street (Cowan 1995). Copyright Museum of London.

Channels were formed between a series of parallel sleeper walls that supported the floor. This was one of a small and generally early group of hypocausts of close set channels, usually laid out in parallel rows although sometimes of labyrinthine design. These provided almost as much under-floor circulation as the pillared hypocausts. Hypocaust floors with less closely set channels were being built from the end of the second century (Williams 1971b: 112). After this date most channelled hypocausts were of a dendritic form, with a large central flue leading from the furnace to a chamber at the centre of the room feeding smaller channels directed towards its corners. In these floors it was normal to establish a rectangular chamber in the middle of the room, and these chambers were often large enough to require the insertion of pillared supports for the floor (fig. 51). This composite form of heated floor involving the use of both channels and pillars, sometimes referred to as the 'union-jack' hypocaust, was widely used in the larger heated rooms of later Roman houses. When the villa at Gorhambury was rebuilt *c*. AD 160–80 the main reception room was laid out with one of these 'union jack' hypocausts (fig. 7), whilst a similar floor was laid in the early third-century rebuilding of the north wing of the villa at Fishbourne. An alternative approach involved dispensing with the central chamber but adding a range of further secondary channels to a broad central flue.

Mosaics and their meanings

As with the opus sectile pavements, the early use of mosaic reflects a precocious and expensive taste. The Claudio-Neronian, or early Flavian, 'proto-palace' at Fishbourne included a series of the black and white geometric designs characteristic of this period. Other fragmentary pavements of first-century date, also in monochrome, have been found in some town houses in London (Perring 1991b: 41). Colour, chiefly red and yellow, and a range of somewhat more fluid motifs had been introduced to the decoration of high status rooms at both of these sites before *c*. AD 120. A trend confirmed by a recently discovered pavement at Gresham Street, London.

During the second century, mosaics were increasingly common in houses in the more prosperous towns but remained rare in the countryside (about twenty villas with mosaics of this period are known). Pavements of this period were generally coloured, and involved the use of geometric backgrounds, panels of vases and sometimes animals. Symbols of conviviality and of plenty (vine leaves, *cantharii*, etc.) were especially popular and would have been particularly suitable in dining rooms. There were stylistic links between the pavements laid in Colchester and Verulamium, and these were distinct from the contemporary designs favoured in the western parts of the province (Ling 1997).

Most Romano-British mosaics were laid in the fourth century, in particular in the first half of the century. The better mosaic designs incorporated figures and scenes drawn from Graeco-Roman mythology and showed a detailed understanding of the complex iconography of the period (D.J. Smith 1977). Villa mosaics of this date considerably outnumber those known from urban contexts. This partly reflects the exaggerated archaeological attention that villas have received and the greater ease with which their pavements can be uncovered, but it also represents a real disparity in numbers.

Regional fashions in mosaic design can be identified on the basis of the range of motifs employed. Six such groupings have been described, each subsuming a more complex series of inter-related local styles (D.J. Smith 1969, Scott 2000). These different stylistic groups are often described as schools, on the questionable assumption that they were produced by separate workshops (*officinae*) from which customers ordered pavements for their homes. It seems more likely that the craftsmen involved would have worked

Figure 51 A 'union-jack' hypocaust from the villa at Fishbourne. Photograph by David Baker (Cunliffe 1971). Reproduced by kind permission of the Society of Antiquaries of London.

directly for a single patron over a period of several years, and that one commission would have led to the next through aristocrat networks of families, friends and clients.

However the craft was organised, it seems reasonably certain that the designs would have been selected by the patrons commissioning the work (Dunbabin 1978). It is therefore probable that the different regional traditions represented different circles of patronage that had inspired different local fashions. The mosaics described shared tastes and identities that differed slightly but significantly from one villa-owning community to the next. It is therefore no surprise to discover that the distributions of different types of mosaic define territories that are similar to those of the different pre-Roman tribal communities (fig. 71, Millet 1990b: 176). The design choices may therefore reflect on the ways in which the communities of Britain maintained distinct regional identities based on traditional affiliations, within the common language of Roman art. Two communities in the southwest of Britain most vigorously adopted the fashion for expensively designed mosaic pavements: the Durotriges and Dobunni.

It can also be inferred that these identities would have been sustained by more than just a shared preference for particular abstract symbols or decorative scenes. The commission of a series of mosaic pavements represented a major choice not lightly undertaken. The images were important. It must be borne in mind that very considerable sums were invested in making these floors. It has been estimated that just one pavement at Colchester was the product of at least 700 man-hours work (Crummy 1980: 8). A pavement in London was considered so valuable by its owner that it was protected during the demolition of the building in which it was housed, and restored to use as the floor of a new home built on the same site (Rowsome 2000).

It has long been noted that several fourth-century pavements reflect an allegorical preoccupation with the afterlife (Toynbee 1964). The subjects taken from Roman mythology were held to represent the quest for truth and salvation, the triumph over death and the liberation of the soul. Even the lesser decorative motifs and geometric designs could carry significance (Henig 1995: 152). Ling (1997) has urged caution in reading too much into images of ambivalent meaning that may simply have been chosen to vaunt erudite taste, and has even gone so far as to suggest that the choice of topics may have been random and without significance (1991). This is difficult to accept (as Scott 2000: 113). This was a world where images were known to carry layers of meaning, and where social standing was reinforced by educated good taste. Some patterns may have been selected in ignorant ostentation, but only at the risk of inviting ridicule on a patron unable to explain his or her choice to more learned guests. The complex and peculiar choices of subject matter are much more likely to have been the product of a deliberate and informed choice. The images therefore reflect on the philosophy of those for whom they were prepared. Where life after death is the implied subject, then the way in which this subject was illustrated must surely identify the belief systems and cosmological understandings of the patron. Unfortunately we do not have direct access to the learning deployed in designing these expensive and communicative works of art, and it is not always possible to decipher the hidden texts that they contain. This is a complex issue and one that cannot be addressed in full here. Several important surveys of this subject have already been prepared (summarised in Scott 2000). But the subject is of such importance to our study of the use and meaning of the houses that it merits our further if somewhat selective attention.

The rich combination of both pagan and Christian elements that were found in some of these houses has, in particular, occasioned much comment (as Henig 1995). One possibility that has not yet been fully explored is that these illustrate the adoption of aspects of Gnostic belief (Stupperich 1980: 300). This raises some important questions about the nature of architecture and society in late Roman Britain, some of which have already been addressed in Chapter 3. The rest of this chapter is therefore given over to a speculative review of the evidence for Gnostic imagery in some late Romano-British pavements.

Gnosticism and the design of the Romano-British pavements

In the second century the Gnostics had formed an important strand of thought within a heterodox Christian community. But by AD 180, Irenaeus, Bishop of Lyon, was publishing attacks on the belief as heresy (*Against Heresies*). There were many different traditions within Gnosticism, but at core was the idea that the spirit (*pneuma*) was trapped in a hostile world and that release from the chains of matter was the accomplishment of a higher mystical knowledge (*Gnosis*). Followers of the cult had to master secrets and sacraments that revealed to them the soul's way out of the world, opening a path through the different spheres of existence (Jonas 1958: 45, Rudolph 1983). This, therefore, was the religion of an educated elite. The possessors of *Gnosis* were set apart from the common mortal. Following the syncretic tendencies of the time, Gnostics avowed that truth was to be found in many places not just in the gospels (Clement of Alexandria, *The Stromata or Miscellanie*). Accordingly they turned to the natural philosophers and mystery religions in search of enlightenment, and drew heavily on diverse sources in their allegorical cosmography. They were particularly taken by revelations obtained in the worship of the ecstatic god Dionysus (Bacchus) and the mystical Orpheus (Rudolph 1983: 286). Greek and Roman myths were also widely drawn upon, especially where antithetical contrasts could be drawn: as between life and death, good and evil, spirit and matter, male and female. The religion was highly dualistic in its theology, and many aspects of worship were designed to achieve synthesis through posing antithetical contrasts.

One charge laid against the third-century Gnostics was that: 'professing themselves to be wise, they became fools, and changed the glory of the uncorruptible God into images of the likeness of corruptible man, and of birds, and four-footed beasts, and creeping things' (Hyppolitus, *Refutation of all Heresies*, 5.2). Hyppolitus also observed that 'among the Gnostics the Ophites were particularly fond of representing their cosmogonic speculations by diagrams, circles within circles, squares, and parallel lines, and other mathematical figures combined'. This fondness for allegory, images and geometric patterns is suggestive, since these elements feature strongly in late Romano-British pavements. Of course Gnostics had no monopoly in the use of such designs, but some pavements also hint at a sophisticated understanding of Gnostic theology.

The mosaics at Frampton, which probably date to the period AD 335–55, present the strongest case for such interpretation (fig. 52, Lysons 1813). The main room in this house was divided into three separate parts: an antechamber, a main room and an apse. The mosaic floor in the outer room contained a central panel showing Bacchus accompanied by his leopard. Scenes of the hunt were placed to either side of the room, channelling attention towards the chamber beyond. Hunting was a popular aristocratic pursuit, and there is no particular need to search for hidden meaning in these images. The chase was, however, widely used as a metaphor for the quest for truth (Clement of Alexandria, *The Stromata or Miscellanie* 1.2, Scott 2000: 156 and Henig 1995: 155–6). The arrangement of this antechamber and the subject matter of the panels that lay beyond, suggest that in this case the allusion was intended.

The mosaic in the main chamber contained several elements that appear to refer to the Gnostic resurrection beliefs of the Ophites or serpent-worshippers (and perhaps specifically to the sect of Sethites). These beliefs are most comprehensively described in the anti-heretical writings of Irenaeus and Hyppolitus (see also Schaff 1889), although a wealth of further detail can also be found in the cache of Gnostic texts discovered at Nag Hammadi in Egypt in 1945 (Meyer and Robinson 1981). The message of this mosaic

Figure 52 The mosaic pavement from Frampton (from Lysons 1813).

appears to have been the struggle of ethereal spirit against matter and mortality, as represented by watery depths. The central part of the floor showed Bellerophon seated on the winged Pegasus and slaying the Chimaera. On a straightforward reading this myth represents the heroic quest, deliverance from temptation and the victory of good. The taming of the immortal Pegasus, the flight over the seas and the defeat of the Chimaera represent man's attempt to escape from the mortal cycle. Four smaller figurative panels surrounding this central scene have only survived in part, but contained paired figures drawn from Graeco-Roman mythology. One of the panels perhaps illustrates Adonis with Venus, a mythological coupling used in Gnostic texts as a commentary on the nature of pure soul. Another shows Attis and Sangaritis, or perhaps Paris and Oenone.

A border of dolphins enclosed the pavement, and brings to mind a Gnostic prayer quoted by Hyppolitus where the soul is described as 'encircled ... within aqueous form'. A four-line verse exalting Cupid over Neptune was placed next to this outer border. To Gnostics this particular antithesis, the victory of Cupid over Neptune, represented the desired victory of soaring hermaphroditic spirit over mortality. In this pavement this message was reinforced and made specific to Christian teaching by the placement of a chi-rho, the symbol of Christ, facing the head of Neptune. Here Christ provided the spark of life in opposition to the Stygian Ocean. The paired oppositions in this pavement described the struggle of spirit (Pegasus-Cupid-Christ) against matter (Ocean in its diverse forms). A pavement elsewhere in this villa included two separate mythological references to the heroic slaughter of serpents and sea-monsters (Cadmus and Perseus), and this was a critical theme in Sethian theology.

Other elements of the design of these mosaics can be related to the celebration of the resurrection and life eternal based on the synthesis of contrasting forces. One of the most important clues to the reading of this group of pavements, and to our understanding of the room in which they were placed, is given by the large *cantharus* that occupied the place of honour at the centre of the apse. This was the ultimate symbol of conviviality: the cup from which all could drink. But in this particular context, set above and beyond the sign of Christ, the *cantharus* must surely also represent the mixing of water and wine that played a central part in the celebration of the Eucharist at this time (Schaff 1889, Rudolph 1983: 230–43). An under-standing of the purpose of the Gnostic Eucharist gives coherence to the entire series of mosaics. The antechamber was dedicated to Bacchus and this was wine, whilst the inner chamber was held by Neptune and this was water. The apse, defined by its architecture as the most potent and sacred space, offered a synthesis of these conflicting elements. This was where wine and water became one. This was the purpose of the Eucharist, a miracle of transubstantiation that could only be achieved by passing through Christ.

The Eucharist itself was but a means of representing an even more profound truth. It was a mythic ritualisation of the cycle of life, death, resurrection and ascension, where earthly substances were transmuted into divine ones and people were similarly transformed (Jung 1955: 314). The tripartite division of space and ritual presented in this group of mosaics can be interpreted as representing the three Gnostic classes of existence and of man: sensual, material and spiritual (Schaff 1889). The antechamber was the place of sensual man ruled over by the Demiurge: the god of matter who had created the imperfect world and was here personified in the figure of Bacchus. This was where catechumens might have waited as the Eucharist was celebrated, reminded of the purpose of their quest by the hunt scenes and of their miserable state by the intimidating presence of the powerful god who ruled them (Esmonde-Cleary 1989: 125). The main room was for mortal man bound by the chains of earthly matter, although the mosaic here also offered the promise of escape and explained some of the means by which it could be achieved. The third space, the apse, was reserved for spiritual man, for the elect who through their knowledge of Christ and the celebration of his secret rites had achieved the necessary synthesis of sensual and material. The mosaics described the path to eternal life, and these rooms represented the ultimate ascent of privilege. It is reasonable to conclude that the goal of the quest described on the floor of the villa at Frampton was symbolised by the Eucharistic chalice containing the blood of Christ. This, therefore, was the Holy Grail. On the basis of this identification there is some scope for speculation about the extent to which the dragon/serpent-slaying, grail-seeking myths of fourth-century Gnostic-Christians in this part of Britain might have influenced the subsequent elaboration of Arthurian myth. It would be entertaining to discover that these elements of Celtic folklore were actually rooted in ideas developed in the Hellenistic east. These are subjects for future research, but give partial encouragement to the suggestion made here that Gnostic belief may have been far more important in late antique Britain than has hitherto been supposed.

Returning to the various images and themes illustrated on the floor of the villa at Frampton, it strains credulity to believe that any Christian other than a Gnostic could have commissioned such vivid and explicit images. Orthodox and Gnostic communities had been engaged in an increasingly bitter dispute for nearly two centuries before this pavement was laid and these arguments were increasingly central to intellectual life in the Roman world (Pagels 1979: 103–4). This pavement shows every sign of having been designed by someone that understood these arguments and had taken a decided position.

Several other villas were decorated with mosaics that also seem to hold Gnostic meaning. This is the most obvious conclusion to draw where Christian elements were introduced alongside pagan images promising liberation and salvation. The Hinton St Mary mosaics show a range of close parallels with those at Frampton, and must surely represent a similar expression of faith (Toynbee 1964). The highly unusual use of the image of Christ as the central motif in the main pavement here fits more comfortably within a Gnostic approach to Christ than an orthodox one.

The villa at Lullingstone, with its Christian wall paintings, is another prime candidate for Gnostic interpretation. Although the mosaics were laid before the wall paintings were executed it is likely that they were in use at the same time. The central panel of the mosaic in the main room of this villa presented another interpretation of Bellerophon slaying the Chimaera. Here too dolphins encircled the scene. Stylised bivalves placed next to the dolphins drew exaggerated attention to the fact that Pegasus first appeared at the sources of Oceanus: this was another pointed reference to the contrast between soaring spirit and mortal sea (D.J. Smith 1977: 111). The womb-like central panel was framed by the four seasons representing the cycle of life, death and regeneration (Scott 2000: 145–54). A second scene was set in a panel in the apse of the same room. As at Frampton the allegorical theme emphasised at this point of the room was that of the ascendancy of the spirit freed from mortality. At Frampton this idea had been represented by the victory of cupid over Neptune. Here, instead, Europa was carried heavenwards by the god Jupiter in the form of a bull with only her foot left trailing in the dark blue sea (the contrast between light and dark is significant). Cupids were on hand to help in the process. The scene was accompanied by a couplet alluding to the story of the Aenead, which described how jealous Juno would have had even greater justification in resorting to the help of Aeolus had she seen the bull (Barrett 1978: 311). Here then we have the quest of Aeneas introduced in support of the arguments presented by the mosaics in this room. The *Aenead* was popular with Romano-British patrons, and scenes from this story appear on several pavements. This story was also well suited to Gnostic interpretation. In this particular couplet we are first reminded of the recourse made by a jealous god to the powers of wind and sea in a futile attempt to stop the pilgrim from reaching his or her goal. Recent research suggests that the text might also contain cryptic Christian references (Henig 1997).

Elsewhere the evidence for Gnosticism is generally somewhat more ambiguous. The lyre-playing Orpheus, surrounded by concentric circles of animals and birds, featured in a series of some of Britain's most impressive fourth-century mosaics. Stupperich (1980: 300) has already identified Gnostic elements in one such mosaic at Cirencester. This took the form of a serpent-like figure, possibly Abraxas or Naos, accompanying Orpheus at the centre of the mosaic. Another important Orpheus pavement was found in a triconch reception room in the aisled building of the villa at Littlecote. Walters has suggested (1984) that the scenes in this mosaic described a syncretic cult involving Orpheus, Apollo and Bacchus. A case can be pressed for considering the general tenor of the decorations here to be Gnostic in character, although the other alternatives are not to be dismissed. The panel containing a *cantharus* flanked by sea beasts is certainly suggestive, as are the references to Bacchus and Orpheus. Hypollitus dedicates a whole chapter to his description of how the Gnostic Sethians were particularly dedicated to the worship of these two figures: conflation of Bacchus with the Demiurge and of Orpheus with Christ would go some way towards offering an explanation of this particular Sethite preference. Scott (2000: 159–60) considers the second of these possibilities in some detail, finding some evidence in support but without reaching a firm position on the matter.

There are several other pavements that would have suited Gnostics better than most other possible patrons (examples include the floors in the villas at Brading and Bignor). Elsewhere the general popularity of scenes involving tritons, sea creatures and serpents in the villas of Dorset and Somerset is consistent with the concerns of the Sethian 'serpent-worshippers'. One of the earliest Roman-British pavements that might possibly lend itself to Gnostic interpretation is the splendid Cupid and dolphin mosaic at Fishbourne laid shortly after AD 160. The use of sea dragons and *cantharii* to frame the central panel is strongly suggestive. Although the motif and its message were popular, and it is therefore impossible to establish a Gnostic connection, the date is about what might be expected for the first appearance of such scenes. This was a period when Gnosticism was being vigorously propounded by some of its leading exponents, hence the first denunciation of the sect as heretic by Iraneus in Lyon some twenty years later. It is equally significant that the latest pavements that were arguably of Gnostic inspiration date *c.* AD 360/70. The last period when such ideas were easily tolerated was under the pagan emperor Julian who died AD 363. His eventual successor, Valentinian, had little tolerance of Gnostic heresy, and the religion was firmly suppressed after Theodosius made orthodox Christianity the sole faith of empire in AD 380.

This raises an important question about the fate of such meaningful images once the ideas that they had supported were on the verge of anathema. Mosaics could be damaged and buried not through decadent neglect, but because they bore false testimony. The selective destruction of some panels at Frampton may have been a consequence of the re-evaluation of the meaning of the images that they presented. The elements removed from the floor include most of the *cantharus* that dominated the apse and four panels in the main room. Might these have contained sea serpents? Some lead tanks bearing Christian symbols were also discarded at about this time, and it is perhaps more likely that these were destroyed to prevent heretical baptism rather than out of some generalised pagan disrespect for Christianity (*contra* Frend 1992: 130). Politically incorrect church plate, such as that represented by the Mildenhall treasure with its scenes of Bacchus and sea creatures, might also have been buried for much the same reason that the precious Nag Hammadi texts were concealed, as treasured but damning evidence of deviancy.

In this chapter we have given a disproportionate amount of attention to one particular reading of a rather unusual mosaic pavement. Most pavements of this period were deliberately, almost irritatingly, ambiguous. The reading proposed here does, however, provide a coherent explanation for a series of otherwise confusing images and suggests new readings for a series of other finds. The argument made here is that Gnosticism gained adherents amongst Britain's villa-owning aristocracy, and that the emphasis that the cult placed on allegorical scenes drawn from pagan mythology contributed to fourth-century fashion in the use of mosaics and wall-paintings. There is a danger, however, in placing too much emphasis on one particular set of beliefs. Gnosticism was one cult amongst many. Some of the images held to be significant by Gnostics would also have suited other mystery cults; especially those inspired by neo-Platonist thought.

Although the images selected might carry different and specific meanings, the general taste for rich interior decoration pervaded all areas of elite society where status was declared through Roman culture. Beyond the obscure ambiguities of the inner beliefs of the educated few, many more accessible messages were conveyed. The patron announced good taste and education, represented an authority rooted in the traditions of the Roman world, and suggested a mastery over the forces of nature on which prosperity relied. The mosaics that survive, and the paintings and statues that do not, gave symbol to space. They created a theatrical space of hints and declarations, a place of exploration and enlightenment (Lefebvre 1991: 186–9). Roman interior design enriched the temporal dimension of space, stressing the processional nature of the architecture, describing boundaries and defining rites of passage. The Frampton mosaic may present a rather extreme example of the way in which space was structured to serve such rituals, but it is unlikely to have been an aberrant invention. The idea of ascending through meaningful space towards potent inner realms had been a feature of Roman architecture before the conquest of Britain, and was a guiding influence on the design of domestic space in the Romano-British house.

8

ADMITTANCE TO THE HOUSE

The purpose of this chapter is to descrbe the architecture of approach, entrance and movement within the Romano-British house. By modern standards a disproportionate amount of space in the Roman house was set aside for public and social functions. In the villa at Boxmoor in Hertfordshire, for instance, almost two-thirds of the floor space was taken up by the portico and principal reception rooms (Neal 1974). This was not unusual. In a fourth-century house at Cirencester a third of the house was occupied by the baths whilst another third was given over to a large end reception room (McWhirr 1986). Ancillary structures and upstairs rooms may have provided additional space, but the relative importance of reception space cannot be denied.

Emphasis was placed on three main facilities: dining halls, porticoes and baths (fig. 53). The development and improvement of these parts of the house was a prime concern, and in this the British patron was following established Roman practice. Juvenal, in passing ironic comment on the way in which Rome's aristocrats lavished fortunes on their houses, singled out the exaggerated attention given to baths, porticoes and dining halls (*Satires* 7, 178). These were the areas of the house where wealth and status were most likely to be displayed. In a famous passage the historian Tacitus explains how 'the Britons were seduced into alluring vices: to the lounge, the bath, the well-appointed dinner table' (*Agricola* 21). This form of cultural imperialism made architectural demands, and archaeology shows how the leading families of Britain invested their wealth in similar facilities to their Roman counterparts.

Orientation and aspect

Villas were usually enclosed by a bank and ditch, which like the walls of a town offered a symbolic protection that could be converted to practical use. Such boundaries announced the status of the site and emphasised its surrogate urban character: a feature taken to extreme in the imitation town

ENTRANCE ARRANGEMENTS
E: Porches
  E1: Simple porch
    a - flanking pedestals/piers
    b - projecting flanking pedestals
    c - projecting side walls
  E2: Deep porch
    a - projecting from corridor
    b - within line of corridor
  E3: Gatehouse porches
  E4: Wing Entrance
  E5: Garden porches
  E6: Garden pavilions
  E7: Pseudo porches
  E8: Entrance lobbies
C: Porticoes
  C1: Street-side porticoes
  C2: Domestic porticoes
    a - standard
    b - taken around wings
    c - winged
    d - courtyard
    e - internal
  C3: Covered walks
    a - between street and open area
    b - bisecting garden space
  C4: Apsidal ended corridors
T: Lodges
  T1: Gatehouse Lodges
  T2: Wing Lodges
    a - independent entrance
    b - entrance from corridor
  T3: Corridor Lodges

PRINCIPAL RECEPTION ROOMS
Q - Central rooms
  Q1: standard
  Q2: extended to rear
  Q3: bipartite/chambered
R: End rooms
  R1: Large 'end' room
  R2: projecting 'pavilion' room
  R3: wing
  R4: bipartite.
  R5: suite
    a: central room
    b: facade projection
    c: rear/side projections
M: Reception in strip buildings
N: Reception in aisled buildings
  N1: main room
  N2: smaller rooms
D: Front rooms

OTHER RECEPTION AREAS
H: Baths
  H1: changing room/entrance
  H2: cold room
  H3: warm room
  H4: hot room
    a: outer chamber
    b: inner chamber
  H5: dry-heat rooms
H/R: reception room next to baths
J: Octagonal and circular rooms
  J1: circular
  J2: octagonal
K: Cellars
  K1: full cellars
  K2: half cellars
  K3: terraced
G: Gardens
  G1. Peristyle courtyard
  G2. Courtyard without peristyle
  G3. Irregular courtyards
  G4. Yards
  G5. Forecourts
  G6. Enclosures/precincts
S: Garden Buildings

LIVING QUARTERS
P: Lesser reception rooms:
  P/D: Front of wing
  P/Q: Middle of wing
  P/R: End of wing
A: Antechambers
B: Rear chambers (bedrooms)
Y: Other small chambers
  Y1: In place of A/B rooms
  Y2: At end of wing
L: Narrow rooms
  L1: Transverse lobbies.
    a - leading to baths
    b - linking street to portico
    c - flanking principal room
    d - services
  L2: Central lobbies
F: Bedsitting rooms

HALLS KITCHENS AND SERVICES
X: Central Halls
W: Workrooms
  W1: main room in wing/outhouse
  W2: associated smaller room
  W3: front rooms
  W4: in strip buildings
  W5: in aisled buildings
U: Kitchens
V: Rear corridors and service areas
  V1 Corridors
  V2 Small rooms/stores
  V3 Furnaces
Z: Latrines

Figure 53 Description of room types (see Perring 1999b).

wall built around the Roman villa at Settefinestre (Carandini and Ricci 1985). The attribution of potency to significant boundaries was not a peculiarly Roman practice, and a long prehistoric tradition of ritual deposition at liminal contexts in Britain is well documented.

By contrast urban plots were constrained by the street system, and arrangements could be influenced by the commercial value of street frontages (Laurence 1994a). This was a significant factor in the evolution of the strip buildings, which exploited narrow plots of land beside busy streets. None of these constraints applied to villas, which were located with respect to a variety of social and topographic concerns but avoided main roads (Hodder and Millett 1980, Sheldon *et al.* 1993, Columella 1, 5.7).

Villas were consistently located to take advantage of southerly or easterly views. A Romano-British house that caught first light was more salubrious than one that could not, and architects strived to obtain this advantage. Some nine out of ten villas in Roman Britain faced south, southeast or east; with most of the rest orientated to exploit southwesterly views. A similar pattern has been identified in the villas of Roman Picardy (Haselgrove 1995). These houses were turned to the sun. Several Roman texts explicitly acknowledge the importance of a sunny aspect (Vitruvius, *On Architecture* 6, 4.1, Pliny, *Letters* 5,6). This had also been pre-Roman practice: the doorways of most British round houses were orientated towards sunrise and especially in the direction of midwinter sunrise and the equinox (Oswald 1991). Significantly the pattern of orientation favoured in Roman Britain was less concerned with the point of sunrise and of the winter solstice than had been the case in the British round house. Pre-Roman foundation rituals and belief systems, that gave emphasis to the precise point of sunrise, had not survived to influence Romano-British practice.

Given the evident value of a southerly or easterly aspect in villa architecture the orientation of town houses is also a subject of interest. The study of the plan of Silchester is particularly rewarding. It has long been recognised that a number of properties in Silchester were not aligned with the street grid (Berry 1951). Having dismissed the possibility that this was a consequence of different phases of urban planning, Walthew (1975) suggests that issues of cardinal orientation might influence property alignments. There was a consistently applied interest in arranging the houses in Silchester around open space in such a way that the principal wings faced either south or east. Reception quarters were generally at the southern ends of wings with an easterly aspect, whilst the main residential quarters were within a south-facing range. In order to achieve this arrangement the plans of houses with a west entrance mirrored those of houses with entrances to the east. A similar, if less marked, emphasis emerges from the study of the layout of houses at both Wroxeter and Colchester (Wilson 1984, Hull 1958: fig. 81). In town, therefore, cardinal aspect was clearly more important than left–right distinction.

In the countryside there was a slight preference for using the western or left–hand side of villas for functions found at the front of town houses, such as the baths or audience room. By the same token the eastern or right-hand side of the villa was more likely to contain the private reception rooms usually found at the back of urban properties. This separation of the house into three components, with the main range of rooms flanked by the baths at the front/left/west and an end reception room at the back/right/east, was not a feature peculiar to Romano-British architecture. Its abiding influence in the layout of high status buildings can be seen in both the first-century Villa of the Mysteries at Pompeii (fig. 4) and in the fourth-century villa at Piazza Armerina in Sicily (fig. 54). There are aspects to this arrangement of space that merit further consideration. The western side of the house, at the setting of the sun, can be considered mortal. It often made practical sense to place the baths, which had little need of windows, at this less favoured spot. In ecclesiastical architecture the baptistery took the equivalent site: a place of ritual death before a rebirth in Christ. By the same token the palaeo-Christian basilica was placed with an east-facing apse, where mass could be celebrated beneath the rays of the rising sun. The design and orientation of such ecclesiastical buildings was influenced by earlier domestic practice, in which apse-ended basilical rooms were preferred at the eastern end of the house. The cardinal orientation of the Roman house betrays a growing interest in the cosmographic significance of the different parts of the house, which interest was later fossilised in church architecture. It can be argued that in its ideal form the house, by following the cycle of the sun was also following the cycle of life and death. Clerestory windows in the reception rooms on the eastern side of the house were placed to catch the first rays of the rising sun. Rooms of this sort were ideally suited for the celebration of the Eucharist, and perhaps for the equivalent ceremonies of the other mystery cults of the period. In such houses the portico might have been conceived of as a place that represented man's passage through life, leading eventually to mortal death. The villa at Whittington Court in Gloucestershire seems to have been designed with these concerns in mind. A handsomely decorated portico linked a large basilical reception hall to the southeast with an octagonal cold plunge bath to the northwest (although the baths were later restructured). These particular features were given unusual emphasis in a contrived layout that appears to have divorced the three principal components – baths, portico and end room – from the rest of the house. This was, however, a rather unusual building. Even in the later period many Romano-British houses were built without any particular concern for the distinction between east and west. Other issues, of location and aspect, were of greater importance.

One of the main arguments developed in this book is that the winged-corridor facade can be explained through reference to the architecture of the peristyle house, and that a principal concern was to obtain a proper range of

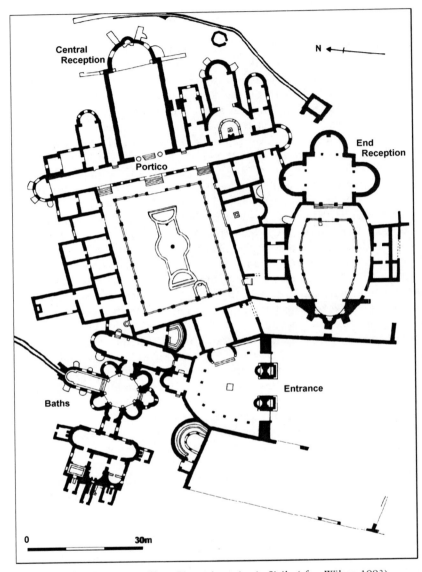

Figure 54 The fourth-century villa at Piazza Armerina in Sicily (after Wilson 1983).

aspects and views from the building. Several studies have properly stressed the importance in the Roman house of the views of landscapes that patrons and guests could enjoy from the main reception rooms (Clarke 1991: 16, Ellis 1995: 168, Dickmann 1997). The premium that the Romans placed on a sea view has already been noted, and was probably an influence in the

144

location of coastal villas like that at Folkestone (Winbolt 1925). Other Romano-British villas were located to take advantage of river views and headwater locations. Sources and views of water were of evident importance in Roman Britain and influenced garden design. Views of the house obtained from a distance were probably of secondary importance.

The portico or corridor has often been viewed as a superficial decorative addition to the house facade, designed either to display the house or to conceal its private rooms, but of indifferent importance to the function of the building. This view derives from the work of Swoboda (1918), reinforced by the evidence of the villa at Mayen where there was little evident relationship between the portico facade and the hall-house to which it was attached (Oelmann 1928). It has been widely adopted in descriptions of Romano-British domestic architecture (as Blagg 1991: 10, Smith 1997: 13). The importance of the portico as a setting for reception activities such as the *ambulatio*, and to frame views obtained from the house has instead been understated.

A pair of adjacent town houses in Roman Herculaneum, the House of the Stags and House of the Mosaic Atrium (Tram Tanh Tin 1988), provides useful points of reference (fig. 55). These houses commanded an impressive view of the Bay of Naples, and to exploit this the main rooms were arranged along a garden terrace overlooking the sea. As was normal the main entrances to the house were found against the street and so the terrace could only be reached by passing through the house. The reception rooms were therefore only easily visible from the garden itself. The design of the building facade built on this terrace was almost identical to the winged-corridor arrangement favoured by Romano-British architects. Projecting rooms (T) were placed at opposite ends of the facade, at the centre of which stood an imposing free-standing porch. Here the central porch was not a principal entrance but a garden feature, and the facade was not designed to impress those approaching the house. The projecting rooms were instead placed where the best views and prospects could be obtained, and the central porch provided a focal point at which house and view met. The owners of these houses may have enjoyed knowing that an impression of architectural refinement might be obtained from the sea, but the pleasing facade was a happy consequence of arrangements designed for the benefit of those entertained in the house rather than the chief object of architectural contrivance.

Symmetry matters in classical architecture and was emphasised in the writings of Vitruvius, but its importance to domestic architecture can be exaggerated. The symmetrical arrangement of the villa and its subsidiary buildings along a central axis was a feature of some palatial houses, particularly in early empire villas in Gaul, but was not widely adopted in either Italy or Britain (Agache 1975, Blagg 1990c, Rodwell and Rodwell 1985). J.T. Smith, in a series of influential but contentious papers

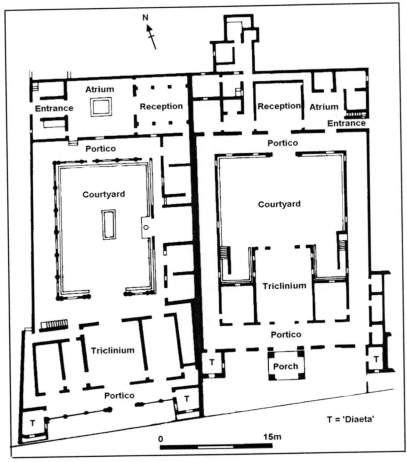

Figure 55 The House of the Mosaic Atrium (left) and House of the Stags at Herculaneum (after Ward Perkins 1981).

(culminating in 1997), suggests that classical symmetry demands an axial central entrance and that its absence can be taken as evidence of un-Roman practice. The argument is not helped by the fact that in several of the villas that he describes as having two entrances access circumscribes rather than bisects a forecourt. This approach to the house follows the spatial arrangement inherent in the design of peristyle houses and is therefore a normal feature in many Roman houses.

Few surviving Roman houses present a fully symmetrical facade and none a wholly symmetrical plan. What mattered more was the social flow around the house, and this depended on patterns of entry, movement, pause and welcome. Symmetry was not a primary objective in the layout of Roman houses, and when found addresses the harmony of individual spaces and vistas but not the whole. The example of Hadrian's villa at Tivoli springs to mind.

Romano-British houses, like their counterparts elsewhere in the Roman world, defined a hierarchy of reception and movement. Three types of signal were employed: lighting encouraged movement towards and through public spaces, decorative order marked areas of higher and lower status, and thresholds channelled movement. These signals defined entrances, pathways and destinations. In the ideal Roman house peristyles, gardens, archways, views, paintings and mosaics marked a progression towards a dining room (Wallace-Hadrill 1994). The visitor to some Romano-British houses had to travel some eighty metres from the street, passing through half-a-dozen or more doorways, in order to reach the main room (fig. 56). The object of this lengthy passage was not to deter or impede, since the route was clearly marked: it declared the importance and standing of the host and reflected on the ritual nature of social encounter. The house mirrored the city and offered an armature of focal spaces articulated by porticoes that guided the visitor from a formal gateway to its ceremonial heart (MacDonald 1986).

Entrances and porches

For the house to work in this fashion the main entrance was critically important: no grand effect could be achieved if the innocent visitor arrived at the tradesman's entrance. Houses could have more than one entrance, but the articulation of reception space demanded that one took precedence over the others. The main entrance to the house was therefore a place for architectural emphasis. Long before the Roman conquest Iron Age round houses had been entered through an imposing porch, but there is no evidence that Roman fashion was influenced by this native practice. Although porches were found in some early Romano-British houses, as at the late first-century villa at Fishbourne, they were actually quite rare before the start of the second century. Indeed only in the fourth century did the porch become a standard feature of the new-built villa. This was an architectural fashion that grew in importance through the Roman period.

Entrances were found at two main locations in the house: next to its gable-end or through a porch located near its middle. Town houses were usually set perpendicular to the street, and the principal entrance was therefore most conveniently placed at the gable-end frontage. In many such houses the front door opened directly into a portico or corridor along the side of the house. At Verulamium, in particular, little effort seems to have been made to mark this entrance with a separate porch (fig. 17a and c). Villas, instead, were usually entered halfway along the length of a front portico. A porch at this central location had vital importance in defining views onto the gardens, and elaborate structures were placed here even when they could not have been used as main entrances. But even in the countryside the end

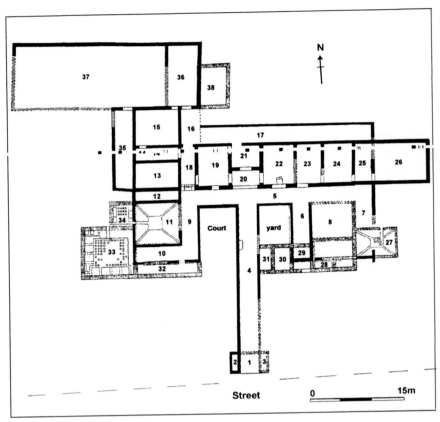

Figure 56 House 24,2 at Silchester (from Fox and St John Hope 1901). This shows the complex entrance arrangements typical of Silchester. A porch next to the street (Room 1) was linked to the house by a long portico (Room 4 – and note also the space given over to other corridors and porticoes, including Rooms 5, 6, 7, 9, 10, 16, 17 and 18). The house itself was composed of two main ranges. Within one of these can be seen the suites of smaller rooms characteristic of the principal living quarters of the Romano-British house (Rooms 18, 20, 21 and 22 might have formed the most important domestic suite). The other wing included a series of heated rooms at its far end (Rooms 11, 33 and 36). A large barn-like structure (containing Rooms 36 and 37) stood as an independent building.

entrance was more common than is recognised in the literature. For instance a reconstruction of the original layout of the Northchurch villa indicates that the entrance may have been from the end of the corridor-portico rather than from a centrally placed porch (Neal 1974–6). Main entrances, marked by pillars flanking the main doors, were found in the wing 'pavilions' of several villas. Several other end entrances can be reconstructed from the evidence of paths leading to the house. Doors at these locations are likely to have provided a more useful entrance where the formal porch was relatively inaccessible.

Most porches were comparatively small affairs with rectangular pedestals or foundations flanking the doorway. These most probably supported columns or pillars surmounted by a gable-end pediment (fig. 57a–c). These simple structures were characteristically no more than one metre deep. Some were given added emphasis by being slightly elevated and approached by a flight of low steps. In several buildings, however, a much larger chamber was placed at the entrance. Some of these rooms were formed within the depth of the portico, whilst others projected forward from the building facade (fig. 57d). They were probably given visual emphasis by projecting a gable at right angles to the line of the portico, and they might even have been raised above the flanking portico to form a low tower. A good impression of the likely appearance of these rooms is obtained from the Romano-Gallic sculptures of winged-corridor villas (fig. 48).

At Silchester rectangular entrance chambers, emphasised by flanking pier bases, were instead set beside the street some distance from the house, to

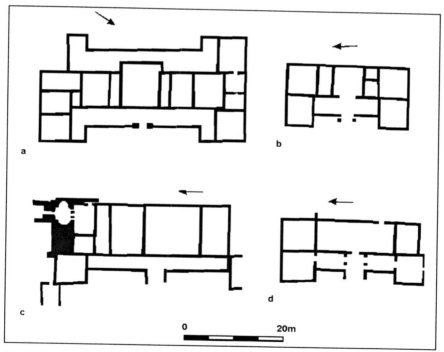

Figure 57 Winged-corridor villas, illustrating also some of the principal types of porch. a: Gayton Thorpe (Atkinson 1929); b: Winchester 23,3 (Zant 1993); c: Bancroft (Frere 1984); d: Boughspring (Neal and Walker 1988).

which they were joined by an extended portico (fig. 9). These chambers were roughly square, 3.8–4.2 m across, with substantial pier or column bases flanking an entrance almost as wide as the room. In some cases the arrangement of corridors meant that these gatehouses, when viewed from within the building, resembled the corner pavilions employed in winged-corridor facades. This distinctive style of entrance was popular in the aristocratic houses of Silchester but rare elsewhere.

Entrances to courtyard buildings differed from those of other houses, since the courtyard could only be reached by penetrating the front range of the building. Small cross passages were usually preferred in this situation (fig. 58, room 4), but larger entrance halls have also been found. The entrance in the east wing of the villa at Fishbourne was by far the grandest of such entrance halls (fig. 6, Cunliffe 1971a: 110). This measured 30 m by 13.4 m and may have included a peristyle. At the far end of the room stood a pool. The late third- or fourth-century courtyard house in the fort at South Shields offers a parallel (Hodgson 1996: 135). Here the entrance to the house was effected through an entrance court 7 m by 6.50 m in which six columns defined a central area containing a water tank. This building, like that at Fishbourne, stands outside the mainstream of Romano-British architectural fashion and betrays a range of more explicitly Mediterranean influences.

Street-side porticoes

Porticoes open to the street, of the kind that provided a covered shopping arcade, were rare in Roman Britain. Some of the early shops in Verulamium and Colchester were separated from the street by a covered passageway (Crummy 1984: 62–6, Wacher 1962), and equivalent structures at Caerwent incorporated a flagstone floor (Ashby et al. 1902: 121–36). At Gloucester a more imposing structure was built in the second century. This consisted of a colonnaded portico over 5 m deep with columns measuring 0.51 m in diameter set at 3.6 m intervals (Hunter 1981). An even more imposing public portico was built along a Wroxeter street (fig. 58). This was 5–6 m deep, with a colonnade set over irregular pier bases formed of re-used cramped stones at intervals of 4–6 m (centre to centre), with corresponding piers in the front wall of the building. Fragments of a tile arch had collapsed from the arcaded superstructure.

At Caerwent porticoes 3–4 m deep with rectangular piers at 3–4 m intervals were added to the facades of two adjacent strip buildings (fig. 11g). A similar arrangement was noted in the strip buildings excavated at Sites 1–5 in Wroxeter. In both examples the objective was to provide a covered pavement in front of individual stalls, not a continuous ambulatory from shop to shop. These constructions might have supported first floor balconies, similar to those from Delos and Pompeii (Bruneau 1978: 120, Spinazzola 1953: 115, 123). In all cases porticoes were an adjunct of the property to which they were attached, as was the case in most western provinces. This contrasts with practice in the east where the portico was a significant class of public building (Ward Perkins 1981: 143).

Rooms attached to entrances

In several houses square rooms were found attached to the entrance. Rooms of this type have been identified as offices, waiting rooms, gatehouses or porters' lodges. They could equally have been used to receive guests or clients at some remove from the main reception and residential quarters. A parallel might be drawn with arrangements noted in Islamic houses where a separate room near the entrance was reserved for the reception of guests and protected the privacy of the inner courtyards (Revault 1967). Small rooms were commonly attached to the porches at Silchester. One of these rooms was heated by a hypocaust floor (in House 31,1), which suggests that it served a significant role in the reception activities of this house. In a few cases a second room was also provided at this location.

There are several instances where one of the pavilion wings of a portico facade was entered independently of the rest of the house, or was poorly integrated with the main reception or living quarters. In a significant number of cases these rooms had hypocaust pavements. Masonry foundations were built to one side of several wing pavilion rooms, either as rectangular platforms or as walls set parallel and close to one of the sides of the room. It is possible that in some instances such features had supported timber stairs. Stairways at Ostia were generally built of timber and set over masonry platforms (Packer 1971: 29), and at Pompeii it was not unusual to find a stairway inserted into one of the small square rooms flanking the entrance (as in the House of the Menander). This explanation fails to convince. The rooms were of higher quality than might be expected for stairwells and the masonry constructions were excessive for timber stairs. These foundations might alternatively have buttressed tall walls (Neal 1982). One further possibility, and perhaps the most attractive, is that these features supported fixed benches. If this were the case these rooms might possibly have been places where supplicants paid court on the villa proprietor, in local interpretation of the morning *salutatatio* that cemented ties of patronage in imperial Rome.

Garden porches

In many houses an imposing porch was built not to mark the main entrance, but to overlook enclosed gardens or courtyards (fig. 9: Room O and fig. 58: Room 31). These garden porches were generally open to the main corridor or portico and were often placed opposite a central reception hall. Such rooms were often fairly large: at Verulamium they ranged in size from 1.75×3.6 m

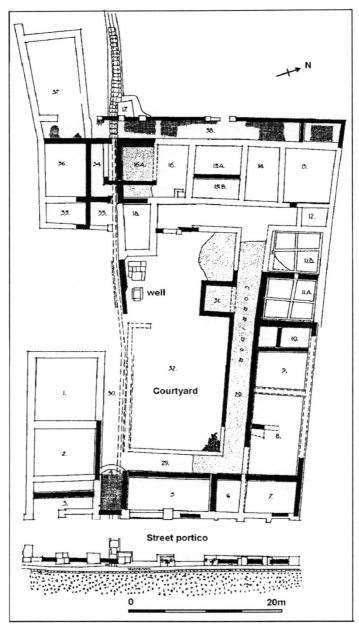

Figure 58 The elongated courtyard house at Wroxeter Site 6, illustrating also a street-side portico (Bushe-Fox 1916).

to 4.6×4.6 m, with the shorter length representing the depth of the projection and the greater one the width of the entrance. In town these rooms were often decorated with mosaics and were usually better decorated than the corridor onto which they opened. The earliest recorded examples date to the period *c.* AD 120–50. The preferred arrangement placed these rooms symmetrical to both internal and external space. In town internal symmetry was the chief concern whilst in villas it was more important that the rooms were placed central to the external facade. House 21,2 at Verulamium illustrates the relationship between the portico, main reception room and projecting garden porch (fig. 59). Superficially the layout recalls the positioning of a chancel beyond transepts formed by the corridor. There were some villas where similarly placed porches were unlikely to have been principal entrances (e.g. Bignor and Chedworth). These rooms were somewhat smaller than their urban counterparts, and were less likely to be decorated with mosaic pavements. Pliny describes a similar arrangement in his villa at Laurentum where a room opened onto a portico on the opposite side of

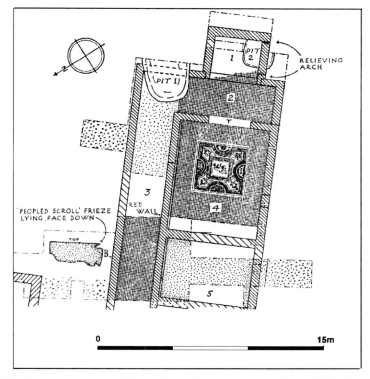

Figure 59 The reception wing of House 21,2 at Verulamium (after Frere 1983). The main portico or corridor (Rooms 2 and 3) of this late second-century house reached a rear reception room (Room 4) which faced a garden porch (Room 1).

153

which was a smaller chamber overlooking the sea. Folding doors and curtains were used to unite or divide these three related spaces. In this description the porch was a place for a couch and some chairs (*Letters* 2,17). This description suggests that such rooms were places to sit and admire the view.

It has been suggested that some of these projecting rooms may also have been used as cult rooms (Rodwell 1980: 219). It is true that they were set at an important boundary between house and garden, and that this might have been accorded ritual significance. It is also the case that these rooms provided a focus for circulation space within the Romano-British house, much in the fashion of Pompeiian *atrium*, and this was a favoured place for the location of household shrines. So the suggestion has some merit, but there is no evidence with which to test the hypothesis.

Two garden porches from Silchester were of a slightly different form to those described above. They had been built as free-standing structures linked to the main corridor or portico by a short passage. In the villa at Great Witcombe the porch was set above a terrace line and could not have been used as an entrance. The associated drainage system suggests that this projecting room had contained a fountain or water basin (Neal 1977). A close parallel for this style of pseudo-porch, an architectural feature that provided a visual but not physical link between house and garden, was attached to a terrace veranda overlooking the garden of the house of Loreius Tiburtinus at Pompeii. The design of this Pompeiian garden terrace could easily be copied to the facade of a Romano-British house without seeming out of place.

Porticoes and corridors

The corridor or portico was one of the most important parts of the Romano-British house, as demonstrated by the amount of space it occupied and the close attention given to its redesign in phases of alteration. The significance of this feature has been much discussed in considerations of the evolution of provincial building types. Such discussions have concentrated on evidence for the introduction of corridors and on the evolution of winged-corridor facades, but surprisingly little attention has been given to the social meaning of this distinctive architectural feature.

Because of the incomplete nature of the archaeological evidence it is not always possible to establish whether the feature that we are talking about was actually a corridor or an open portico. In most aristocratic houses they were probably porticoes, but it was not always sensible to build open-fronted structures in crowded urban surroundings. Wall-plaster collapse from Verulamium shows that a decorated corridor could substitute for the portico, although the decorations employed offered some architectural reminders that these rooms drew inspiration from the classical peristyle (fig. 49, Frere 1983: 164). It is likely that the social character of this space differed from house to house, and as its use became more widely diffused.

Porticoes were present on civilian sites in Britain as early as AD 65–75 (Blagg 1990c). Initially they were not standard features, but by *c.* AD 100 it was exceptional for villas to lack a portico. They were usually built to face south or east onto a courtyard or garden and either extended the full length of the house or were taken to projecting pavilions or wings at one or both ends. In town some care was taken to avoid overlooking the street or the wall of an adjacent property. Buildings laid out over several wings were linked and articulated by these passageways. Some houses had porticoes at both front and back, and in a few rare cases a veranda-portico completely encircled the house. Some porticoes crossed open space to link porches and out-buildings (fig. 56, O'Neill 1952). In contrast to the arrangement represented by the above examples several properties at Caerwent could only be reached from the street by crossing an open courtyard. Some corridors were terminated by an apse perhaps in order to focus attention on an object framed at this point (fig. 28). The transverse corridor at the entrance to the Caerwent temple offers a parallel (Ashby *et al.* 1910). Rooms of this type were placed at the entrances of aristocratic villas elsewhere in the late Roman world, a famous example being the room with the mosaic of the Great Hunt at Piazza Armerina (Wilson 1983: 24). Too few examples have been found from Roman Britain to add usefully to the chronology of the form.

The porticoes and corridors established a linear progression from the front entrance to the main rooms to the rear. They defined focal points where important rooms could be accessed or views of the garden obtained. The importance of the Romano-British domestic portico reflects a wider Roman obsession with processional architecture. The peristyle mediated between natural and human domains and the portico penetrated a series of potent thresholds (Knights 1994: 140–3). This was liminal space with ritual connotations. The absence of axial views through the building is consistent with classical practice. From the fifth century BC the typical Greek house had been secluded from public view by an indirect entrance (Lawrence 1973: 238ff.). In many Roman houses the more magnificent reception rooms could only be approached by similarly navigating an L-shaped entrance route (e.g. fig. 3).

Notwithstanding the elaborate nature of the entrance arrangements, the courtyard and corridor house created permeable space. It was relatively easy to get from one part of the building to another. Most rooms within the house could be reached from the corridor, and the main patterns of access did not differ significantly between town and country (fig. 60). Normally the portico gave direct access to the most important reception facilities: the baths, dining rooms and reception halls. The need to provide a controlled street entrance and to exploit the garden views, added to the complexity of the town house and reduced the accessibility of domestic and reception quarters in the houses at Silchester and Verulamium. This illustrates a real difference between town and country living, where the villa precinct was more effective

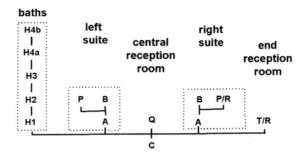

a. Newport

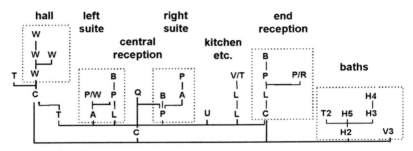

b. Spoonley Wood

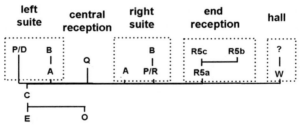

c. Silchester, House 8,1.

Figure 60 Interpretative access maps for some better preserved Romano-British houses (for letter codes see fig. 53). a: Newport (for plan see fig. 67). b: Spoonley Wood (for plan see fig. 62). c: Silchester 8,1 (for plan see fig. 9).

in establishing social controls than the town wall, and permitted a more open building plan as a consequence.

The suggestion has been made that less secure householders, in communities under greater social tension, are inclined to protect domestic space and introduce more blocks on entry and movement (Glassie 1975). Sarah Scott (1994) has ventured to suggest that the use of the corridor facade was a demonstration of just such stress. The matter is not straightforward. On one hand the corridor served to unite and integrate the domestic space, and can be viewed as an important area for social interaction, but on the other it controlled and influenced movement within the house. The hierarchy of space described in later houses in Roman Britain certainly introduced distance between a patron and his clients. Changes in the domestic architecture of the second-century, when many of the more structured approaches to reception activities were first adopted, illustrate the ritualised nature of social encounter. This might be seen as a distancing mechanism adopted in response to the stresses that accompanied the economic changes of the period. The emphasis placed on the portico-corridor also witnesses the ongoing Romanisation of British social practice. It is possible that the introduction of the portico may simply represent the introduction of new social practices, such as those that might have been attached to new belief systems, and that allowed for the architectural realisation of precedent social distinctions.

There can be little doubt that the porticoes and corridors described here were inspired by the Romano-Hellenistic peristyle, but full-scale colonnades were only found in select aristocratic houses. At Fishbourne the peristyle was built with columns 0.42 m in diameter and 3.96 m high, set at 3.58 m intervals over a ground-level stylobate (Cunliffe 1971a: 121). Another house with a substantial colonnade was House 3S at Caerwent, where the columns were 0.43 m in diameter and set at 3.35 m intervals, whilst at Ditchley in Oxfordshire columns at least 3.5 m tall are thought to have belonged to the villa facade. Porticoes at Chedworth and Kingsweston were more modest in scale, with columns 0.3–0.35 m in diameter set 2.10–2.5 m apart (Blagg 1982: 137). At Kingsweston an arcade set over columns divided the corridor from the hall behind. Pillars forming the portico of the villa at Ridgwell were set over rectangular tile bases about 2.15 m apart, whilst that at Brixworth was built of posts at close intervals (Walford 1803, Wilson 1972: 322). Some structures were formed of small columns set over a low wall in the fashion of a monastic cloister, as illustrated by arrangements at Piddington and Llantwit Major. Fragments of curved parapets with open-work S designs have been found at Chedworth and Great Witcombe.

Lathe-turned stone columns, used in both porticoes and porches, have been found on only one in four of villa sites with mosaic pavements (Blagg 1996: 11). Nearly two-thirds of Romano-British column shafts have diameters no more than 350 mm, and these 'dwarf' columns were most probably used in the portico (fig. 61). Miniature Tuscan columns, 0.8–1.21 m high, perhaps designed to stand over a low wall have been found at Dorchester, and in various villas, including Bignor, Spoonley Wood, Westcotes and Great Witcombe (Blagg 1982). Corinthian capitals were the most frequent alternative to the Tuscan and their design shows Gallic influence (Blagg 1984). Indeed in the period down to c. AD 75 it seems likely that immigrant Gallic craftsmen were responsible for sculpting the few items of decorative architectural ornament known from Roman Britain

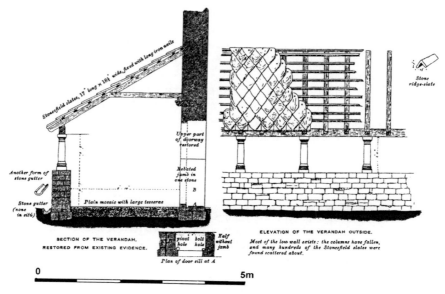

Figure 61 A reconstruction of the Roman villa at Spoonley Wood, Gloucester, illustrating the suggested arrangement of the portico (from Middleton 1890).

(Blagg 1980: 28). Such capitals were not often found in domestic contexts, and the villa at Fishbourne remains a rare example.

Where lathe-turned columns were absent, other materials were employed in their place. At Piddington the columns of the portico were made of stone discs which had been plastered over, with crude mouldings to form bases and capitals (Selkirk and Selkirk 1996). These columns were set over a low stone wall. Plastered brickwork columns were widely used as an alternative to stone shafts, especially in urban contexts as at Colchester and Verulamium (Williams 1971a: 192, Blagg 1979). Other architectural features were also executed in brick and plaster, as the engaged pilaster from House 27,2 at Verulamium (Frere 1983: 216), and the comparative fragility of such structures is likely to have ensured their under-representation in the archaeological record. In other cases carved wood may have been employed, although no proof for this has yet been obtained.

The occasional presence of ovens, including corn-drying ovens, in porticoes has already been touched on in Chapter 3. These features were added towards one end of some corridors, usually in the course of the fourth century. Hearths and ovens are also evident in some of the later town house corridors. These may reflect changes in practice towards the end of the Roman period, with the *ambulatio* ceasing to be an important part of social ritual in many houses. It is perhaps worth remembering that the Roman *atrium*, the function of which was in part replaced by the peristyle, was not only a circulation and reception space but also used in cooking. It was not unusual for kitchens in Roman houses to be inserted into circulation areas also designed as reception space.

Tessellated pavements were commonly used in the portico, perhaps preferred as much for their durability as their quality. In the earlier part of the fourth century some porticoes were decorated with mosaic panels. This perhaps reflects the increased status of such areas in the reception activities of later Romano-British house. The best corridor pavements flanked the better rooms or were set into a central panel, such as the Orpheus mosaic at Brading (Price and Hilton Price 1881). Sarah Scott has observed (1994: 90–2) that corridor pavements had simple repetitive patterns not intended for lengthy scrutiny, and that these encouraged linear movement. The same has been said of corridors at Ostia and Pompeii (Clarke 1991: 16). As the Orpheus mosaic at Brading illustrates, this was not always the case. There were focal points within the corridors, which were not simply places of passage. Views obtained from corridors sometimes provided more important visual foci than the decorative features within them. A main purpose of the Italian portico was to afford a view, as in the Villa of the Mysteries at Pompeii (fig. 4). This suburban villa was built on a terrace overlooking the sea, and here the portico was the locus for an *ambulatio* that linked a bath suite in one wing and dining room in the other with a central *tablinum* and *atrium* (Clarke 1991: 19). The porticoes found in Romano-British houses offered a similar facility. The portico was heir to the Athenian stoa, by way of the Hellenistic gymnasium, providing a setting for movement, contemplation and philosophical thought. It presented an 'interplay of relay points and obstacles, reflections, references, mirrors and echoes'. This was gestural space, designed to embody ideology and bind it to practice (Lefebvre 1991: 216–17).

9

PRINCIPAL RECEPTION ROOMS

One of the purposes of the portico was to guide visitors to the main rooms of the house. The evidence of the mosaic floors presented in Chapter 7 indicates that some of the more important rooms may have been used in cult practice, an observation which can occasion little surprise given the importance attached to private mystery religions in late antiquity. This does not mean to say, however, that these houses should be viewed as religious rather than domestic buildings or that the cult activities required the complete reinvention of domestic space. Rather the needs of religious ritual involved an additional layering of activities. In most houses, regardless of the arrangements for worship, the main rooms were dining rooms and audience halls.

Such rooms can usually be recognised from both the scale of their design and the quality of their decoration. They could be found in different locations within the house, were laid out in different ways and served a variety of functions. Large reception rooms were commonly found at two principal locations: at the centre of the house or in a rear/end wing. They could also be found as free-standing buildings set apart from the house, and were sometimes placed inside ancillary buildings. There were several different forms that such rooms could take. There were large rectangular rooms, rooms with an apse at one end, bipartite rooms (a simple rectangle divided by a pair of responds), tripartite rooms and complex polygonal chambers. These differences were influenced in part by the date and location of the house, but can also reflect on the uses to which the rooms were put.

Central audience chambers

One of the most distinctive features of the Roman house, common to aristocratic houses throughout the empire, was the large central chamber set to command axial views across the peristyles and gardens. Such rooms were found in Roman Britain from the outset (fig. 62). In several villas such rooms were the largest and best decorated in the house, and sometimes the only reception room of note. End reception rooms were rare before the middle of the second century, and in this early period it seems likely that central reception rooms were used in their place. The villas at Fishbourne and Southwick were both built around central reception rooms before AD 100, as was Building D at Watling Court in London (Cunliffe 1971a, Winbolt 1932, Perring and Roskams 1991).

The central reception room at Dewlish not only had a large apse and a mosaic pavement showing hunting scenes but also was separated from the corridor end entrance porch by a complicated timber-framed division with folding doors. The room would not have been out of place in a courtyard house in Gaul or the Roman east, where dining rooms opened wide to the portico but could be closed off by folding doors (Deletang 1982, Ellis 1988). The mosaics in the apsidal-ended rooms at Lullingstone and Dewlish were both laid out in such a way that there was room for a dining couch from which the decorative panels could be admired (Witts 2000: 299–301).

The apsidal room of the Period 2 villa at Fishbourne was more likely to have been used as an audience hall (fig. 6). The mosaic stopped short of the apse wall, suggesting that a timber bench had been built here. Parallels can

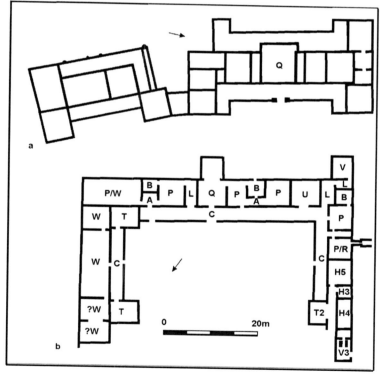

Figure 62 Central reception rooms (Q rooms). a: Gayton Thorpe (Q2) (Atkinson 1929). b: Spoonley Wood (Q3) (Middleton 1890).

be drawn with Domitian's Palace in Rome, where the audience chamber that measured 30 m by 37 m was apsidal ended (Cunliffe 1971a). Audience chambers, deriving inspiration from the architecture of public basilicas, have been identified in several of the more opulent private houses of the later empire (Ellis 2000: 170–4). Such rooms would have been suitable for gatherings of the family council (as Cicero *In Defence of Cluentius* 175–8), as well as being places for the head of the household to receive petitions and settle disputes (as Pliny, *Letters* 9,15).

The central reception room at Woodchester is likely to have been an audience room (Witts 2000). Some 14.4 m square, this is the largest reception room known from a Romano-British house (Clarke 1982). The elaborate mosaic pavement of Orpheus encircled by animals, supposedly the largest Roman mosaic known north of the Alps, was set over a hypocaust with flues 1.2 m high. Foundations for four central pillars may have supported an upper gallery and the room was built with one metre-thick walls, which suggest that it had been built to a greater height than the rest of the wing. It is probable that doorways had been set at the mid point of all four walls, an arrangement inappropriate for a dining room since it would have isolated diners in the middle or towards the corners of the room. Two heated rooms elsewhere within this villa were better suited to have been dining rooms.

The central location was an appropriate place for a principal reception room, axially arranged with the garden entrance. In some villas this room was probably used for dining but this may have been an unusual use once the fashion for placing heated dining rooms in a separate wing became widespread. There were several villas where the central reception room remained the larger and better room, but where a heated end reception room was also found. Similarly there were sites where a larger and better decorated room on the wing overshadowed the central reception room. The most common choice was to provide both types of room. This situation finds parallel in domestic space in imperial Ostia, where wall paintings and mosaics marked out two main reception rooms in most apartments (Meiggs 1973: 247). A larger and more accessible room suitable for use as an audience chamber (*tablinum*) was found near to the main entrance, whilst another reception room placed at the back of the apartment is likely to have been a dining room (*triclinium*). Centurions' quarters in Roman forts were also sometimes designed with two opposed reception rooms at either end (Hoffman 1995). A duality in reception requirements, between dining rooms and audience rooms, is also implied in the available literature by the distinction drawn between the *oecus* and *triclinium* on one part, and the *atrium* and *tablinum* on the other.

A separation of functions, involving audience halls and dining rooms, would account for the archaeological evidence from Roman Britain. It seems likely that the central reception rooms were used as audience halls offering facilities equivalent to those of the early Roman *tablinum*. Ellis (2000) describes late antique changes that relocated dining practice from the room adjacent to the *tablinum* to a main room on the far side of the peristyle, and describes this as a consequence of the desire to obtain views of the peristyle from the dining room. A similar philosophy might account for changes found in the design of Romano-British houses.

A similar room to the central reception rooms described above, but set at the front of the building, has been noted in some town houses. The southern part of House 28,1–2 at Verulamium provides illustration (fig. 63): a main reception room at the entrance overlooked a portico with a pavilion porch opposite (Rooms 1, 2 and 12). A narrow cross passage ran to one side of the reception room (Room 3). This entrance reception area was separated from

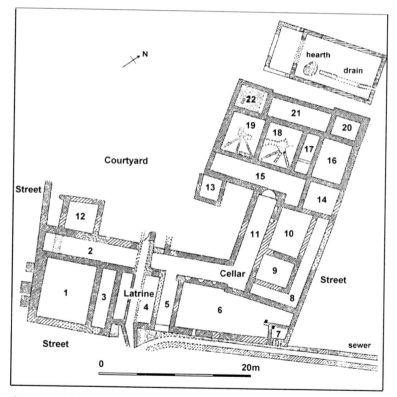

Figure 63 House 28, 1–2 at Verulamium (after Frere 1983). A reception suite by the front entrance to this building included a front room (Room 1) facing a porch (Room 12). This was separated from the probable living quarters (Rooms 8–10) by a group of lower status rooms (Rooms 4–7). Heated reception rooms and further living rooms were placed in a separate, rear, wing (Rooms 13–22). House 28,2, to the north, was appropriately located to have served as the stable block and workrooms of this property.

the other reception rooms by a series of low status rooms (Rooms 4–7). It seems likely that some of these front rooms were used in a similar way to the central rooms and may have been audience halls, perhaps used for a morning salutation. The distinguishing characteristics of these front rooms include their location, comparative size and relationship with circulation space. The provision of a front reception room rather than a central audience chamber would seem a natural design response to the different patterns of access prevailing in town. There are, however, several rooms at this critical location in the Romano-British town house of more uncertain type.

Central reception rooms were not a standard feature of the town house, and were infrequently decorated to high standard. This may reflect a greater reliance on public facilities for the reception activities for which these rooms were designed. In town less importance was attached to the provision of a second reception area, except in the most ostentatious houses.

End reception rooms

The importance of the end reception room in the design of the Romano-British house has already been emphasised at several points in this book (e.g. pp. 40 and 48). This feature emerges with striking clarity from the evidence of town houses, where the most lavishly decorated rooms were almost invariably located at the back of the house (fig. 59). This was evident as early as *c.* AD 100. Excavations at Gresham Street in London have recently uncovered a mosaic-floored reception room of this date set at the back of a timber-framed house and over looking an adjacent courtyard. Similar rear reception rooms made their first appearance in Verulamium in this period (Frere 1983: 10). It seems likely that the large heated wing rooms found at many villas were the rural equivalent of these back reception rooms.

The late first-century villa at Farningham was amongst the first villas to have been built to this design, with its best room placed in a side wing. Similar rooms were found in some other late first- and early second-century villas although this was an unusual arrangement for the period. In the first period of Romano-British domestic architecture the main room was more likely to have been located at the centre of the house. End reception rooms were not common until after *c.* AD 100. This emphasis on a large reception room placed in a side or rear wing may have taken inspiration from army housing. The Tribunes' houses at Inchtuthil, built in the 80s, provides an early Romano-British examples of the type (fig. 15) and centurions' houses were usually built with a main reception room at the back.

In both town and country there was a preference for placing end reception rooms in projecting wings that could be illuminated from several sides, especially where they could exploit the southeast aspect of the house. In villas this was more commonly the right-hand end of the building as viewed from the courtyard, where it was often placed in opposition to a bath-block in the left-hand wing. The walls of these end rooms were sometimes reinforced in a fashion that suggests that they had towered above other parts of the house, as described in Chapter 6. The importance of such rooms was marked by the use of hypocausts, mosaic floors and wall paintings, and sometimes by service corridors. They were also the most common targets of programmes of reconstruction and rebuilding within the Romano-British house, resulting in their frequent enlargement and improvement. The social importance of having such rooms increased through time.

In the earlier part of the second century the end reception rooms were generally of simple design, but more complex forms were soon developed. Many of the rooms were significantly longer than they were wide: a feature sometimes achieved by an arched opening linking two adjacent chambers. These bi-partite rooms were generally laid out to a 3:2 ratio, and were most commonly between 9–12 m long and 4–6 m wide. Apsidal-ended rooms were built in houses at Silchester before the end of the second century (Boon 1974: 194). Unusually deep horseshoe-apses were a particular feature of these houses; the one placed at the end of the reception room in House 1,2 at Silchester was an impressive 7.25 m across (Fox and St John Hope 1890: 735–8).

One of the earliest wing rooms to dominate domestic arrangements was an early second-century apse-ended room at the south end of the villa at Gorhambury. The equivalent room in the later villa here (c. AD 160–80) was also one of the first to be heated with a hypocaust (fig. 7). By the end of the century villas such as those at Faversham and Boughspring illustrate the wide diffusion of heated-room suites set in wings at the southernmost extremity of the building. The heated rooms in the west range of House 4,8 at Verulamium were considered by the Wheelers (1936) to have formed a bath suite but the design was wholly of a type with the suites of heated reception rooms described here (fig. 21). The west wing was occupied by three interconnecting chambers with a combined internal length of 23.6 m. Two smaller rooms were attached to this suite which had a total area of some 187.5 m square. These rooms were separated from the main range of living rooms to the north by a large furnace room which probably also served as a kitchen. Building 1 at Colliton Park, Dorchester, was a town house of competing ambition (fig. 20). The west range of this building contained a complex of lavishly decorated chambers in which a fairly typical extended reception suite had been enlarged by the addition of a further block of three rooms reached by a hall to the rear of the main room. In total the suite had a floor area of 155 m square.

The most complex arrangements were found in fourth-century courtyard villas. Impressive reception suites, including rooms containing ornamental water basins (piscina), have been found at Chedworth and Bignor. The use of ornamental basins was not a common fashion in Roman Britain, but was widespread elsewhere in the empire (Ellis 2000: 141). Several houses at Stobi in Italy had polygonal water basins in their dining rooms (Wiseman 1973), and considerable emphasis was placed on aquatic furniture in the design of *triclinia* at Pompeii. A similar approach has been noted in the design of villas around Trier (Slofstra 1995: 84–6).

Romano-British end reception rooms were often richly decorated, especially in the fourth century. The Hinton St Mary mosaic showing Christ came from a bipartite end reception room, as did the Frampton mosaic described in detail in Chapter 7. The Tyche mosaic and figurative painted wall plaster at Brantingham were from a similar architectural context (Liversidge *et al.* 1973), as was the Medusa mosaic in the apsidal room at Dalton Parlours. Sculptures were used to frame views into and from these rooms. Statues of Fortuna and Bonus Eventus flanked the reception room at Llantwit Major and a statue had been set into a niche facing the main room at Chedworth (Ellis 2000: 136, Fox 1887).

It is usually assumed that the finest reception rooms were dining rooms. Feasting had been an important way of demonstrating status throughout the Celtic world (as *Diodorus Siculus* V, 28.3–4). The conquest of Britain reinforced a tendency towards the Romanisation of dining practice witnessed by changing dietary preference and the large-scale importation of table wares and foods (Cunliffe 1988: 147–52). These changing tastes were no doubt the spur to Tacitus' reference to the seduction of Britons to the well-appointed dinner table (*Agricola* 21). The Roman feast was an occasion for entertainment. It demanded an appropriately large and well-decorated space. From Greek times the *andron* or *oecus*, used as a dining room, was likely to be the largest and best decorated room in the house. Such rooms were usually placed at the corner of the house so that they could be lit from two sides. References in classical sources indicate that it was common practice to locate principal dining rooms at the end of a colonnade, in locations that could be illuminated from several sides. Pliny, describing his villa in Tuscany, wrote that 'from the end of the colonnade (*porticus*) projects a dining room (*triclinium*): through its folding doors it looks on to the end of the terrace' (*Letters* 5,6). Ammianus Marcellinus describes guests passing the columns of a portico to reach the dining room (*Historiae* 28:4, 10–13). Gregory of Nyssa visiting a villa in Anatolia in the late fourth century dined in a hall (*oecus*) that was 'high roofed and well lit from all sides' and 'decorated with colourful pictures', which he reached by means of a colonnade (*stoa*) around an inner courtyard (*propylaeon*) (*Letters* 20, Rossiter 1989: 107). These authors were writing at different times about very different parts of the empire, but their descriptions show remarkable consistency. In the Roman world a guest normally reached a dining room by way of a colonnade, and having done so would expect to arrive in a large decorated room of open aspect.

The supper party was an occasion for the whole household to gather, including women and children (Thébert 1987: 366). At parties of the early empire the preferred gathering was of nine guests, accommodated three to a couch on three sides of the room, leaving the fourth side for the entertainers and servants. The arrangement of space suggests that smaller dinner parties, of six and eight, may have been more usual in some of the Romano-British houses described here (Witts 2000). The clearest evidence for the installation of a fixed dining couch in a Romano-British house comes from excavations of a courtyard house in the fort at South Shields (Hodgson 1996). A dining room was located to the rear of the building at the furthest end of the portico from the entrance, and overlooking a central courtyard. It was the largest room in the house, measuring an impressive 10 m by 6.6 m. Flagstones set into the *opus signinum* floor of this room marked the position of three couches opposite the room's entrance.

The typical late Roman dining room consisted of a large rectangular room, set opposite a peristyle, with a large apse at the back (Rebuffat 1969, Dunbabin 1991, Ellis 1995: 169). In such rooms the diners reclined on a semicircular couch or *stibadium* within the apse (Dunbabin 1991), whilst the larger room to the front was for entertainers and slaves to serve the guests. An illustration of this arrangement is shown in the Vienna Genesis, whilst its use in Britain is suggested in the representations of funeral banquets shown on tombstones from South Shields and Chester (Liversidge 1955). These depict the deceased reclining on a standard form of Roman couch, with curved head and foot rests, set within the backdrop of an apse surmounted by a cupola (fig. 64). Since this style of dining room is not supposed to have become popular until the fourth century (Ellis 2000: 67) it is interesting to note the diffusion in Britain of apsidal-ended reception rooms from the late first century. Apses do not always mark dining rooms, and some of the apses identified in the end rooms of late Romano-British houses were too small to have housed held *stibadium* couches (Witts 2000). This does not necessarily mean that these rooms were not used for dining, but simply that the diners could not have reclined on a couch set within the apse. Some rooms normally identified as dining rooms, such as Room 3 at Bignor, could not have been used as such if the expensive mosaic designs were intended to have been on display during the meal. These rooms were designed with other uses in mind.

The mosaic floors in bipartite and tripartite rooms can be divided into two groups on the basis of their decoration (Witts 2000). In some of these rooms emphasis was given to the decoration of one of the chambers and a comparative static arrangement would have suited the needs of seated diners. Chedworth offers a good example. The arrangement of mosaics and heated areas in these end rooms supports the notion that the larger central space was open and to be admired. A mosaic design faced the head table, whilst the smaller chambers were heated for comfort but had lesser pavements with wide borders where couches and tables could be placed. There are some instances where pillar hypocausts in the small rooms might have allowed a more intense heat than comfortable for dining. One wonders whether these

Figure 64 Tombstone of Julia Velva showing the deceased reclining on a couch framed by an apse. Courtesy of the Yorkshire Museum.

rooms were perhaps fired-up ahead of the meal, generating a residual heat for subsequent use.

The pavements and paintings would have complemented the readings and recitals that took place in these rooms as part of the *symposium* following the meal (Pliny, *Letters* 8,12). Many Romano-British mosaics offer appropriate literary and cultural allusions. Water, used both for washing and to mix with wine, also played an important part in the social ritual attached to the use of dining rooms for the *symposium* (Dunbabin 1993, Slofstra 1995: 81).

In other multi-chambered rooms, like those at Brading, Frampton and Hinton St Mary, all areas of the floor were closely ornamented, affording little space for couches. These designs were arranged to be viewed from a variety of different positions and favoured a processional use of the space that was both axial and climactic (Witts 2000). This reinforces the suggestion made in Chapter 7 that some pavements may have been designed against the needs of the Eucharist: a commemoration of the meal Jesus is said to have shared with his apostles and celebrated as Holy Mass. The division of these rooms into different chambers, separated one from the other by arches where curtains are likely to have hung, might have facilitated the need to separate catechumens from those celebrating the Eucharist. These modes of worship were essentially derived from pre-existing Roman social practice and other cults of this time are likely to have structured their worship around similar gatherings. This ritual meal can be viewed as an extension of the Roman *symposium* (Slofstra 1995: 89). This does not preclude the use of such rooms as dining rooms, indeed in the first centuries of Christian worship most rites would have taken place in private dining rooms. It is, however, possible to imagine situations in which the importance of the celebration of the Eucharist became so great that the needs of normal dining were relegated to lesser reception rooms. The different approaches to the arrangements of the mosaics described by Witts suggest that some end rooms were designed principally as dining rooms, but where other activities no doubt also took place. Whilst a minority of the grander rooms were decorated with the needs of worship foremost, these may also have been used as dining rooms. These late antique reception rooms, with their lofty halls and apses, provided a setting for early Christian gatherings. There is good reason to believe that this style of basilical architecture exercised a direct influence on contemporary developments in metropolitan church architecture.

Reception in aisled and strip buildings

Reception rooms, distinguished by the use of mortar floors and painted wall decorations, were added to the rear of strip buildings in the closing decades of the first century (fig. 12). There is a distinct possibility that this practice, influenced in part by the constraints of the narrow urban plots and in part by the design of centurions' houses, contributed to the fashion for the end reception rooms that came to characterise the design of Romano-British town houses in the second century. By the fourth century these reception rooms set behind commercial properties had been improved to include apses, hypocaust floors and mosaic pavements, as for example in the civilian settlement at Malton (Mitchelson 1964).

Reception rooms were also built within aisled buildings, usually within the central nave at the far end of the structure exploiting the higher roofed area. Where the aisled building was part of a larger complex this reception room was placed at the end closest to the main house (normally the north). It is likely that the rooms in aisled buildings were dining rooms, and that the fashion for larger and taller rooms had been met by locating these rooms within the aisled structures, where lofty internal spaces could easily be achieved. These rooms were frequently decorated to high standards, and sometimes heated with hypocaust floors. Smaller reception rooms in the adjacent aisles could also be heated and decorated with mosaic pavements. At Chilgrove the equivalent room was notable for the unusual nature of the mosaic decoration, involving a series of wheel or circle motifs possibly of ritual significance (Down 1979).

Where an aisled building equipped with a major reception room was set beside a main villa house, this house did not usually contain an end reception room. One of the most startling examples, both because of the quality of the mosaic pavement and the architectural complexity of the building, is the fourth-century trichoncal room at Littlecote (dated to c. AD 360). This consisted of two main chambers separated by a wide arched opening, with apses placed around all three remaining sides of the inner chamber. A well-executed mosaic of Orpheus surrounded by animals was laid on the floor, and incorporated a variety of other decorative elements: including the figures of other deities (perhaps Aphrodite, Nemesis, Demeter and Persephone representing the ages of man), and wine vessels and vine scrolls (Walters 1984). The possible use of this room in cult activity has already been considered in Chapter 7. Elsewhere in the Roman world triconch and multi-apsed halls were a common element in fourth- and fifth-century domestic architecture, and were primarily used as dining rooms (Lavin 1962). The form is thought to have its origins in late third-century Gaul. Here too it seems likely that the room could have been both a dining room and a cult room. The use of dining rooms in cult practice was not unusual. For instance meetings of the arval acta, a brotherhood dedicated to fertility rituals, took place around the supper table in the house of the master of the order (Beard 1985: 114–62) and we have already noted that early Christian gatherings focused on the ritual sharing of bread in the Eucharist. The origins of such use can be traced back to the first century. Perhaps the best known example is that of the Villa of the Mysteries at Pompeii (fig. 4: Room 25). The end reception room here was decorated against cult practice but was also used as a dining room (Ling 1997). It may not be so much that the Littlecote room looks like a church, but that the first churches were copies of dining rooms.

This suggestion is perhaps supported by the evidence of a fourth-century mosaic pavement in the principal reception room of the aisled building at Thruxton, figuring the god Bacchus, with a dedication to 'qvintvs natalivs natalinivs et bodeni'. The significance of this text has been much discussed, but perhaps the most convincing suggestion is that of Henig and Soffe (1993, for alternatives see Birley 1993: 239 and Black 1987). They suggest that the Bodeni, perhaps father and son but possibly a more extended family group, were the clients of Natalinus, and that the logical context for this collective dedication would be in the context of a religious cult or guild. The high status Natalinus with his Roman tri-nomina would have been the patron and the Bodeni clients or dependants who dined and shared in the religious practices undertaken here

It is also worth considering the possible role that villas may have had as meeting places for burial clubs, collegia and guilds. We know virtually nothing about such associations in Roman Britain, but it is likely that they existed and unlikely that they would have operated without the patronage of the land-owning classes. The communal nature of such activities might explain why these expensively decorated principal reception rooms were sometimes placed in aisled buildings rather than as part of the main house, as was the case at Littlecote. These aisled buildings were in any case generally designed as high-ceilinged buildings, set wing-like to one side of the main house, and equipped with kitchens and ovens. These characteristics would have made these attractive locations for a dining room.

Nor should it be assumed that the construction of a dining or cult room testifies directly to the wealth or status of the occupants of the building. Elsewhere in the Roman world reception activities took place at properties where the owner was not resident: feast days, rent-collection and a variety of administrative and social activities required gatherings in an audience or dinner hall. Even on estates run exclusively by an absentee landlord the bailiff could: 'confer distinction on any slave... by inviting him to dinner on a festival day. . . [but] not receive anyone as a guest unless he is an *amicus* or close relative of the master' (Columella 1,8).

Outside halls

Reception rooms were sometimes placed in purpose-built halls next to the main house. In the villa at Darenth a free-standing building set to one end of the main wing of the villa measured 14.6×4.6 m internally, with a central doorway nearly 3.7 m (fig. 27). Features that suggest that this had not been a simple barn include the fine painted wall plaster found within the room. Opposite the doorway a rectangular addition to the back of the main wall, slightly over 1 m deep and nearly 4.6 m long, may have been a buttress, but seems more likely to have supported a recessed podium. A free-standing room of similar proportions at Whittington Court (13.2×5 m internally) was even more clearly an important reception room (O'Neill 1952). This had a mosaic pavement and was linked with the main house by a mosaic-paved covered way. At Gargrave (Kirk Sink) a monumental square building with painted walls had also been linked to the main house by a covered walk (Hartley and Fitts 1988: 81).

Several classes of octagonal and circular buildings are known: these include small shrines, cold and dry hot rooms attached to bath suites. Further to these can be counted a small number of circular and octagonal heated and unheated rooms found on villa sites, which defy easy classification but are likely to have been used as principal reception rooms. Such rooms were usually set to one side of a main villa house with a view across a villa forecourt. The favoured location for these rooms was just beyond and slightly to the front of, the wing of the main house. At both Stroud and Great Casterton no main villa house has been found and rooms of this type were instead added outside aisled buildings (fig. 10). The rooms concerned could be either free-standing or attached to an end wing of the main house. The excavators of these structures have tended to prefer functional explanations. Those at Ditchley and Langton were described as threshing floors (Radford 1936: 45–6), and the heated room at Great Casterton was thought to be a corn dryer (Corder 1954). This interpretation was achieved by ignoring the quarter-round moulding around the edge of the floor and the coloured painted wall plaster in the destruction debris. This room was similar to the circular heated room with a channel hypocaust in the baths at Fontaines-Salées near Vézelay (Yegul 1995: 386), and it is possible that these rooms were free-standing sweat baths although, this seems unlikely.

The use of octagonal and irregular spaces had been introduced to Roman domestic architecture in houses such as Nero's Golden House at Rome, and the rooms associated with the more complex bath-houses described below (p. 175) illustrate the use of such forms in a Romano-British context. The unusual apse-ended octagonal room at Great Witcombe and the similar room at Walton-on-the-Hill may have had similar use to these free-standing octagonal rooms (Lowther 1950, Clifford 1954, Neal 1977). These occupied central locations towards the rear of their houses, and were similar in many respects to the central reception rooms but for their location and shape. The large heated octagonal room at Maidstone was supported by substantial buttresses and is likely to have towered above the rest of the house (Roach Smith 1876).

This chapter has been largely concerned with the architecture of patronage in the Romano-British house. This also is the theme of Chapter 10, where we look at other ways in which the buildings were used to entertain and impress guests and clients. In all significant respects the social approach to space appears consistent with Roman aristocratic practice. The evidence may lend itself to alternative interpretations, but on this reading it suggests that the houses were modelled around the needs of the audience with clients, the supper party with friends and the increasingly important needs of worship. These main rooms were given vital articulation by porticoes and corridors that drew inspiration from stoa and peristyle. Despite the fact that the houses of Roman Britain differed in appearance to the buildings of the Roman Mediterranean, this outward declaration of local identity was not at the cost of a close conformity with elite social practice.

10

ARCHITECTURES OF ABUNDANCE

The baths

The baths came second only to the dinner table as a place of regular social gathering, and the construction of urban baths was a key act of public benefaction. The taste would appear to have been acquired from early Greek practice, with origin in the Greek gymnasium, and developed from mid fourth century BC onwards. The main typological and technical developments took place in central Italy in the period *c*.100 BC (Fabbricotti 1976). The heated baths remained a central aspect of urban life in the Byzantine east, and outlived the empire to become the Turkish baths of today.

Roman baths were first built in Britain in military and public facilities. In Britain, as elsewhere, the baths were more of an urban than a domestic habit. Early public baths, of Neronian date, have been found at Silchester and Exeter. The modest nature of public baths in Britain has been attributed to the influence of the simpler, military, bath-house: in which the main rooms were arranged in a single row progressing from changing and cold rooms towards warm and hot ones.

Private bath suites were more likely to be found in the countryside, influenced by the desire to introduce urban amenities to rural life. The earliest known examples from Romano-British villas, as at Angmering and Eccles, are likely to be of Neronian date and sufficiently early for it to be unlikely that they were built in imitation of British urban practice. It is more likely that the builders of these early houses were influenced by contemporary practice in neighbouring provinces. The suites found in Romano-British villas find close parallel in the villa baths at continental sites, such as the villa Arianna in Varano, Stabiae (Yegul 1995: 63–4).

Roman baths were normally laid out in such a way that the bather would advance from cold rooms at the entrance, through ascending degrees of heat to the furthest and hottest room. The basic pattern of the Romano-British domestic bathing suite consisted of one unheated entrance room (*apodytrium*) that provided access to the rooms beyond. The character of this room differed according to circumstance: in the better baths it was likely to be larger than any of the other rooms in the suite and was often at least twice as long as wide. In more cramped circumstances, however, it could be little more than a corridor. This room was frequently decorated with a mosaic pavement, usually with aquatic references. At Beadlam the room had benches built around the sides, supporting its identification as a changing room (Neal 1996). These entrances chambers were commonly located in one of the projecting corner pavilions of the villa facade, at the opposite end of the portico to the end reception rooms (fig. 67: Room H1). Where this was the case the portico led directly to the main doorway to the baths. A common alternative to this, where the baths were set at the back of the house rather than to one side, was to approach the baths through a cross passage. In other cases the baths were built as a free-standing structure at a short distance from the main house.

In the more sophisticated bath suites the entrance room provided access to another unheated room, the cold room (*frigidarium*). This usually contained a cold plunge bath: sometimes in the middle of the room, sometimes to one side. These ranged from simple square basins to D-shaped and octagonal pools, and although some were large enough for shared use (like the bath at Dewlish, which was 3.6 m wide), they were not swimming pools. The large size of the pool at Halstock, which measured 7.93 × 4.5 m, was exceptional (Lucas 1993).

The simplest bath-suites did not have a separate cold room, and were instead more likely to contain a small plunge bath within the entrance room, where the functions of cold room and changing room were conflated (e.g. Chilgrove, Down 1979). In most cases the hot rooms were reached directly from the cold ones. In some instances, however, the cold room with the plunge bath was not in a series with these other rooms. In this arrangement the bather visiting the cold room had to return to the entrance chamber where the warm and hot rooms were reached by passing through a different door. The heated baths were smaller than most other rooms found in the Romano-British house, and were usually made D-shaped by the addition of an apse at one end. In a minority of cases apses were added to both ends of the room. These rooms were vaulted. Hollow brick voussoirs used to form the barrel-vaults have been found at sites such as Sparsholt (Brodribb 1979). Fragments of window glass indicate that many heated baths had glazed windows.

Commonly two, and sometimes three, of these small barrel-vaulted chambers were arranged in sequence (fig. 67: Rooms H3–H4b). The first of these spaces, furthest from the furnace, would have been a warm room rather than a hot one (*tepidarium*), and was less frequently built with an apse than the hot rooms beyond. Some warm rooms were also equipped with small plunge baths. This warm room was dispensed with in the simplest, utility, arrangements. The final two chambers were usually opened together to form a single hot room with a double barrel-vault (*caldarium*). A hot plunge bath was frequently placed next to the innermost, hottest, part of this room. In some arrangements, as at Chedworth, the final hot room was a single- rather than double-vaulted chamber. Beyond these rooms lay the furnace, over which was placed the vat of water which provided the hot steam that characterised these 'Turkish' baths.

In a few baths a fourth and slightly larger heated room was separately reached from the cold room. This was probably a dry-heated room rather than a steam one. In two early baths, at Ashtead and Eccles, particular emphasis was given to the dry-heat rooms. These were large circular structures reached from the entrance room by a separate corridor. The Eccles baths are likely to have been of Neronian date, whilst those at Ashtead were probably built early in the second century (Black 1987: 105–16). The use of round rooms for sweat bathing was of Greek origin, and gained particular popularity in military contexts where such rooms often stood independently of the rest of the bath suite.

A further sophistication involved the addition of a couple of large rooms to one end of the bath wing. Although these mosaic-paved rooms could have been used in much the same way as any other large reception room, their close association with the baths may indicate a more specific function. Small latrines were attached to some of the larger baths complexes although this was a less common practice than one might expect.

The evidence described above permits the identification of several different types of baths. The smallest suites consisted of no more than a cold room at the front with a single or double barrel-vaulted hot room behind. Several examples of this 'utility' type have been identified in a survey of the villas of Hampshire, where the form was widely adopted (Johnston 1978: 78–80). The 'standard' baths involved the addition of a changing room and warm room to form a row of rooms through which the bather would have to pass.

Two more complex types of baths are also found. In the first of these a dry-heat room, entered from the cold room, was added to an otherwise standard suite of rooms. In the second the cold room did not form part of a progression of rooms, but was separately entered from a larger changing room, and contained an ornamental plunge bath.

These cold rooms deserve some further attention. They were sometimes designed to reflect the shape of the central pool: the most impressive example of this was at Lufton, with its elaborate buttressed octagonal room (fig. 65, Hayward 1952). This room finds close parallel in the octagonal *frigidarium* with a central pool at Viterbo (Yegul 1995: 387–9). The presence of similar arrangements at Holcombe and Dewlish shows this to have been a fashion favoured in southwest Britain in the late third and fourth centuries (Walters 1996). These octagonal cold rooms with a large central plunge bath were given unusual architectural emphasis and the design may in part have been influenced by the contemporary interest in octagonal reception rooms in the same area. Connections between these Durotrigan villas are also suggested by the common use of 'Lindinis Group' mosaics at Keynsham, Lufton and Holcombe (P. Johnson 1983). This leaves open the question as to why these

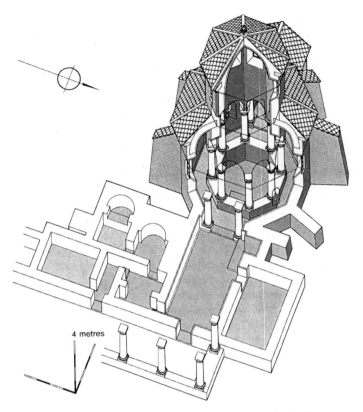

Figure 65 The cold bath and surrounding rooms of the villa at Lufton in Somerset. Axonometric reconstruction by Luigi Thompson (after Walters 1996).

rooms containing cold plunge baths were treated as the equal of the contemporary dining rooms. The design of the entrance to the cold plunge at Lufton suggests this to have been a much more important part of the baths than the small heated rooms tucked to one side. The case has already been made that some houses in this region may have seen Gnostic-Christian use. The villas at Lufton and Dewlish contained mosaics of the same stylistic group ('Durnovarian') as those found with Christian motifs at Hinton St Mary and Frampton. Baptism played a significant part in Gnostic ritual (Rudolph 1983: 226–8). If this religion had been practised in these houses, then the cold plunge baths here would almost certainly have been used in the baptismal rite (Thomas 1981: 221–5). Whilst the case cannot be proved it does provide a coherent explanation for what would otherwise be a rather curious architectural preference. These octagonal cold rooms preceded, and appear to have influenced, the design of octagonal church baptisteries, such

176

as that built by St Ambrose at Santa Tecla, Milan in AD 375/85. The original inspiration for this building type is likely to have derived from funerary architecture, and in particular from the mausolea built for the Tetrarchs at the end of the previous century. The baptistery was a place where the old life gave way to the new, in a ritual death leading to re-birth in Christ. It therefore made sense to draw on the architecture of death in the location and design of such rooms. For St Ambrose the octagonal form was also significant, the eighth day being that of resurrection (Roberti 1984: 115).

The earliest domestic baths were set in detached buildings on one side or the other of the forecourt area, or at Ashtead in a rather dominant position in front of the building. This structural isolation of the baths made sense when the main villa was built of timber, or thatch-roofed. Baths were often the first part of the house to be stone-built. The construction of stone-built bath blocks, set some distance from the associated timber villa, may be one of the reasons that in several cases baths have been discovered without trace of an attached house.

The early integration of baths into the domestic accommodation, as at Fishbourne and Southwick, was therefore an unusual feature. In the earlier period it was also the case that baths were frequently better decorated than the rest of the house. These features combine to suggest that the baths were given particular emphasis in the reception activities of the period. The integration of baths into the main houses was essentially a feature of the second century, at which time baths were added onto the back of existing villas. Villas newly built in this period were provided with baths from the outset. As has already been mentioned, these bath blocks were generally built either on the wing, or to the rear, of the building. The addition of such baths was frequently undertaken at the same time as the addition of a portico. One of the most notable features of the programme of second-century and later villa improvement, was the construction of more than one bath block at the same house. In most such cases one of the baths was clearly a lavishly decorated public suite laid out to one of the more complex plans described above. The second baths were smaller and more private, tucked behind or to one side of the house. This was the situation at both Ashtead in the late second century and Bignor in the fourth (fig. 28). The larger baths were often in a separate building and could be reached without having to go through the main house. Exceptionally there were a few sites, as North Leigh, where three baths were been built (Taylor 1939, 316–18). David Neal has suggested (1974–6) that at Gadebridge the second baths may have been built for the benefit of estate workers (as Columella, *Res Rusticae* 1.620). Separate bath facilities may sometimes have been needed to provide for both sexes, although this is unlikely to have been a pressing need in domestic contexts. The villa baths seem to have provided a public facility. This would make sense of the scale, location and duplication of such facilities.

Small baths were also sometimes built within aisled buildings. Examples include the well-decorated baths at Combley, Isle of Wight, and at Sparsholt. The typology and chronology of such constructions showed no significant differences to the other baths, and it seems likely that these too were for public use.

Baths were seldom found in town houses. Individual excavators have often been reluctant to interpret urban bath houses as private domestic structures, preferring to see them as facilities attached to inns and public buildings, but most of the smaller bath complexes from London were probably attached to private houses (Perring 1991b: 73). At Pudding Lane a masonry building put up *c.* AD 125/130 contained a small bath block with a mosaic-lined apsidal plunge bath and a room with a latrine. The heated room with a vaulted ceiling and underfloor heating found in the excavations at Winchester Palace in Southwark, also dated to the second century, is likely to have been part of a baths. An early third-century bath suite, from a town house in London near Billingsgate (Marsden 1980: 151–5), was also of a simple if rather unusual form. It was entered from a vestibule to either side of which were apsidal-ended heated rooms, and beyond which was a cold room with a water-tank against one wall. Unusually a small baths may also have been added to the rear of one of the strip buildings at One Poultry, where a heated room and small plunge bath were added in the early fourth century. Several other cold-plunges have been recorded in London and probably indicate the location of other baths. The evidence from other Romano-British towns is broadly similar, with most private baths suites built during the second and third centuries (Hull 1958: 208, Jones 1981, Blockley *et al.* 1995, Wheeler and Wheeler 1936: 100–10, Atkinson 1932). At Cirencester part of an unusual late Roman octagonal heated building was attached to a small bath suite and was seemingly associated with a private house (Rennie 1986). A room from the palatial building complex at Winchester Palace, Southwark was perhaps of a similar type.

As has already been mentioned, townsfolk were more likely to use public facilities than build private baths. The public nature of the baths was one of its social attractions. Private baths were rare in town houses in most parts of the empire, although the baths at the House of the Menander in Pompeii illustrate the occasional presence of such facilities from fairly early times, and Petronius (14, 73) puts private baths in the fictional house of Trimalchio. In North Africa the provision of private baths has been suggested to be a fairly late feature, and a sign of social distancing as the richer townsfolk no longer felt it appropriate to mix in public baths (Thébert 1987: 377). It is therefore interesting to note that there is no evidence for any greater preference for private bath-houses in later Romano-British houses, and if anything the fashion for the construction and equipment of such facilities was on the wane in the fourth century.

Gardens

Gardens were also important to the design of Romano-British houses, more so than one might suspect from references found in the archaeological literature. The dominance of man over nature is a recurring theme in Roman literature and art, and is reflected in Romano-British villas by some of the themes exploited in mosaics. This is also evident in the emphasis placed on the arrangement of porticoes and porches to exploit garden views. The popularity of pastoral and garden scenes framed by architectural fantasies in the paintings of Pompeii indicates something of the importance of these views. There was a dialogue between Roman artifice and the natural world, in which gardens played an important role. These open spaces not only offered light and focus, but also offered a representation of the natural world made subject to Roman order (Purcell 1987). Landscape features such as fishponds, canals, contrived views and towers were all exploited to establish the status of the proprietor. Gardens were therefore conceived of as part of the public reception space and not a place of private retreat.

Our ignorance about gardens in Romano-British towns is a matter of concern, and the situation in villa studies is little better. Only one garden can be reconstructed in detail, and this the unusual example of Fishbourne (fig. 66, Cunliffe 1971a: 120–33). The absence of evidence for early gardens in Romano-British towns is particularly frustrating. The character of modern urban rescue archaeology is ill-suited to advance this area of study, and the more recently excavated fragments of city gardens are likely to reach publication as a form of 'dark earth', if at all. These layers of grey and brown silty soil are commonly found in late antique and early medieval contexts in British towns, and although there are many different views as to how they formed it seems reasonably certain that they indicate the presence of open space. Some dark earth horizons may have owed their origin to the digging-over and enriching of gardens, although it is not possible to draw a distinction between market gardens and domestic ones. It was certainly the case that much open space in Pompeii was given over to orchards, market gardens and vineyards (Jashemski 1979: 43–8), and some of the root and stake-holes found beneath the dark earth in London were of similar character.

The evidence of the close-packed town houses in Flavian London suggests that gardens were rare during the early phases of settlement. It is also likely that those towns converted from military sites, as Colchester, would have had little by way of open space. It is therefore possible that the fashion for gardens in Romano-British cities was slow to develop. From the second century onwards, however, most Romano-British houses overlooked an enclosed garden or yard. The views obtained from the house were given both frame and focus by the built surroundings. There was considerable variation in the shape, size and proportions of these gardens and yards, the

Figure 66 Bedding trenches for hedges lining the central path of the garden of the villa at Fishbourne, Sussex (see fig. 6). Photograph by David Baker (Cunliffe 1971a). Reproduced by kind permission of the Society of Antiquaries of London.

definition of which is in many cases complicated by the poverty of the archaeological evidence.

Inevitably the larger open areas were most frequently found on rural properties, whilst irregular courtyards and yards were more frequently found in towns. Some of the houses treated here as peristyle courtyards are rather irregular examples of the form, in particular because of the fashion for building projecting porches, and putting emphasis on rooms at the corner of the courtyard. This design feature was derived from the use of projecting corner pavilions in winged-corridor buildings. Some early villa sites, notably Gorhambury and possibly Rivenhall, shared a Gallic preference for a symmetrical layout with a series of rectangular and trapezoidal courtyards set along a central axis (Rodwell and Rodwell 1985, Blagg 1990c: 198). This was not, however, the norm and most of the enclosures were surprisingly irregular. A simple bank and ditch frequently marked villa enclosures, although it seems likely that hedges would have been planted at these sites. Walled enclosures were also built at some sites, especially in the upper Thames valley.

Paths bisected several villa courtyards and gardens. At Frocester turf verges flanked the entrance with garden beds beyond (Gracie 1970). A 20 m wide avenue of trees or shrubs, at 4–6 m intervals, had been planted at Gorhambury (Neal et al. 1990). Many classical courtyards were crossed by pathways and these were usually garden features rather than principal routes of access. It is probably inappropriate to view the courtyard as a thorough-fare. The example of Fishbourne is instructive (fig. 6). Here the path crossing the courtyard garden was essentially a decorative feature and visitors to this property were more likely to use the peristyle portico that circumnavigated the open area. The courtyard was laid out as a formal garden of herbs and evergreens planted in bedding trenches laid out in geometric patterns of the type popular in Italy from Augustan times (Jashemski 1979). Species thought likely to have been used at Fishbourne include box hedges and flowering fruit trees. Box clippings and the seeds of ornamental plants have also been found in Roman contexts at Silchester, York and London (Dark and Dark 1997: 101). An ornamental pond and other features associated with a villa at Rectory Farm, Godmanchester, produced macrofossils of spruce, box and yew amongst a variety of plant remains (Murphy in Going 1997: 42). This preference for perennial species reflected Italian fashion where evergreens symbolised fertility and renewal (Knights 1994: 141).

The formal design of the Fishbourne garden was almost certainly an extreme example, but we cannot reconstruct detailed garden layouts at many other sites. The courtyards attached to many smaller villas appear to have been more functional in character, and some courtyards were laid out with hard surfaces (as at Turkdean where the yard was cobbled). The areas immediately in front of the later Roman town houses excavated in Winchester and Cirencester were also cobbled, and areas of planting were in some cases restricted to borders. Architectural features found in the open spaces surrounding villas and town houses, including pools, shrines and towers, illustrate a concern with landscape design.

Fountains and pools

A focal feature in many Roman courtyard gardens was the central piscina. The presence of water, or some visual references to the presence of water, was a common element to many garden vistas. As has already been mentioned (p. 145), some Romano-British villas were designed to exploit river or sea views. Further to this several gardens were adorned with pools and springs to match Italian and Gallic fashion (Slofstra 1995). The large pool dominating the facade of the first-century villa at Eccles is the most extreme instance of this form of landscape architecture (Detsicas 1964 and 1974). In the later villa at Darenth the pool (fig. 27) had taken the place of the axial approach road, and was set perpendicular to the principal villa facade, along the central axis of the villa forecourt (D.J. Smith 1978: 122). At the end of this pool stood a small structure covering a well, which in turn was located in front of a monumental gateway, apparently a decorative feature rather than a significant entrance. Viewed from the house the small building standing at the end of the stretch of water would have been framed by the gateway behind. Similar small, free-standing structures, both open-fronted and apsidal-ended, were also built over springs at Chedworth and Rapsley, although not in such focal positions (Fox 1887, Hanworth 1968). The 'Nymphaeum' at Chedworth might possibly have been used as a baptistery (Thomas 1981: 220). A spring-fed octagonal basin here had been decorated with Christian symbols, and the late fourth-century dismantling of this basin perhaps represents the decommissioning of an unauthorised baptismal font. Parallels can be drawn with fourth-century cold baths found at other villas in the area.

Rectangular pools or cisterns were also found in front of the villas at Bancroft, Gadebridge and Fishbourne, whilst the well at Ditchley and the fishponds at Shakenoak were visible from their respective buildings (Brodribb *et al.* 1968–78). The possibility that a room at Great Witcombe housed a fountain or nymphaeum has already been mentioned (p. 154), and a lead-lined basin at Downton may have been part of a water feature set in axial position in front of the main reception room (Rahtz 1963). The well in the forecourt of the house at Wroxeter was also placed to command views from the garden porch (fig. 58: Room 31)

It seems likely that the foundations of the smaller water basins of the type found in the gardens of some Pompeiian houses would not always leave recognisable archaeological trace, and features set at some distance from the villa houses may escape notice. It is consequently likely that the examples mentioned above do not represent the full extent of this fashion. Town house gardens do not provide such a rich variety of water-related features, and this may partly reflect an inadequacy in the water supply to many Romano-British towns.

Granaries and towers

Although there is little published evidence for pools and fountains in town house gardens, some small free-standing structures may have been designed as garden features similar to the Darenth structure just described. Most of the relevant evidence derives from the excavations at Silchester. The most substantial garden structure here was Block I, built next to House 23,2. This measured 5.5×5.2 m externally with walls 0.75 m thick (Fox and St John

Hope 1901: 232). These substantial foundations suggest that it had been a tall structure, perhaps a tower. Two stone blocks likely to have supported columns flanked a doorway into the east of the structure, and a rectangular 'porch' was added here in a later phase. The inside face of the wall footings had been rebated to take timbers, presumably part of a timber floor over an underfloor void or pit. This building formed a significant focal point within the garden, and it would have been clearly visible from the house's main reception rooms, if not also from the street. The excavators were of the view that this was a small shrine. Gardens are appropriate locations for small outdoor shrines, in which the dialogue between nature and order, established in the layout of peristyle and garden, could sensibly be extended.

A similar but less elaborate structure in the garden of House 1,2 at Silchester had walls approximately 600 mm thick. These too were much wider than those of the adjacent house. Here it was suggested in the original excavation report that this was a raised water-tank, as was also proposed for Room 28 of House 19,2, another structure with unusually thick walls, in this case about 900 mm across (Fox and St John Hope 1890: 735–8 and 1899: 235–6). Such buildings are not common in the other Romano-British towns to have been studied in detail. A building in the garden of House 4,1 at Verulamium and another associated with House 13S at Caerwent offers rare parallels (Wheeler and Wheeler 1936: 96–8, Ashby 1905: 307–9). A small buttressed building found in the excavations at Culver Street in Colchester was also probably of this type, and has been interpreted as a tower granary (Crummy 1992: 108–9). It was probably built in the second century and measured about 7 m across.

Similar structures found at villas merit mention. A buttressed masonry building opposite the end reception room of the villa at Gorhambury has been interpreted as a tower granary. This measured 6.4×6.8 m externally, with footings 750 mm wide, with a 2 metre wide porch suggested by footings for flanking masonry piers. An apsed outbuilding outside the Preston Court villa at Beddingham, an altogether much slighter construction, has instead been interpreted as a shrine (Esmonde-Cleary 1993: 307). These masonry towers, whether built as granaries or shrines, were distinctive landmarks. The emphasis placed on such features in Romano-British gardens can be compared to the importance accorded free-standing Egyptian-style towers in the sacro-idyllic landscapes of early imperial wall paintings of Italy.

Cellars

Cellars were built beneath end reception rooms in several town houses and villas (Perring 1989). The fashion for their use was largely restricted to the period c. AD 70–155 and to the territories surrounding London, Colchester and Verulamium, as well as villas in the upper Thames and Cotswolds (fig. 71). This distribution suggests that the spatial practices represented by these cellars were only adopted by some of the communities of Roman Britain (e.g. the Dobunni, Corieltauvi, Cantii and Catuvellauni/Trinovantes). These rooms were usually entered from the main portico or corridor by means of descending ramps or stairs, sometimes along an unnecessarily protracted corridor. The rooms were usually rectangular, although there were also several 'corridor' cellars (less than 3.6 m wide but 7–13 m long), and a few unusually large rooms (3.8–7.0 m wide). Cellar walls were often white- or yellow-painted, and more complex schemes were rare. The decoration of the villa at Lullingstone included palm trees with dates, and coloured panels were used at Hartlip and Great Witcombe (Taylor 1932: 117–18, Liversidge 1987, Clifford 1954). Small niches arranged in groups punctuated the walls of some cellars. An apse was also found at the end of the corridor shrine at Verulamium and in the cellars at Gorhambury and Ridgeons Gardens, Cambridge (figs 7 and 63, Selkirk and Selkirk 1978). These various details suggest that cellars were sometimes used in reception activities, although some had been used to store grain and amphorae (Johnston 1972: 121–2).

Running water was channelled to many of the cellars, and features that may have been used as water containers have been noted in others. In some cases the provision of water seems likely to have been associated with ritual use. This has been suggested for both the Colchester 'Mithraeum' and the villa at Great Witcombe where an altar base was found inside the cellar. The most convincing evidence for ritual use derives from the cellar found beneath the house church at Lullingstone. A well stood in the centre of this room, and the niche on the opposite wall was decorated with water divinities. An altar was subsequently built in one corner of the room, where marble busts had been set over a low platform. A cellar at Cambridge is also supposed to have been used as a shrine: an interpretation based on the evidence of a series of votive burials. A series of ritual shafts containing dog and infant burials had been dug after the cellar had been backfilled. Small pots had been set into the walls or floors of at least four other cellars, probably for votive purposes, and infant burials were found in a cellar at Colchester. Odd assemblages of finds from within some of these cellars might also be explained as the votive offerings characteristics of fertility cults (Perring 1989: 286–7, Wait 1985: 262–3).

Romano-British cellars were inspired by ideas introduced from cellar-using parts of Gaul (Cortet 1971). Since their distribution was limited, it seems that these ideas did not spread widely. There is a distinct possibility that cellars served as both cult rooms and stores; these functions can be complementary since fertility cults were directly concerned with the harvesting of agricultural produce. Cellars in Italy and Gaul were used in the worship of mother goddesses (Packer 1971: 126, Le Gall 1963: 168–72, Boon 1983). The combination of underground chambers, running water, tutelary goddesses and votive offerings was particularly important in the worship of Isis. Purpose-built cellars were used in this cult, and were designed to be flooded by fresh water, a symbol of fertility and life beyond the grave (Wild 1981, Griffiths 1975: 296–307). The use of subterranean rooms was not restricted to the cult of Isis, and underground chambers had had a long history of use in other fertility and mystery cults (e.g. Vermaseren 1977: 30).

These cellars can also be viewed in the same light as the gardens, cellars, fishponds and fountains. These features all celebrated rural abundance, adorned the views obtained from the house, had religious connotations, and drew attention to the patron's command of nature and control of the landscape.

11

THE LIVING QUARTERS

Room suites

In this chapter we conclude our exploration of space in the Roman house with a review of the evidence for the sleeping quarters, service rooms and other more private household areas. Although these were the parts of the house where most of life was lived, they were usually the least architecturally imposing. Private rooms, where fewer guests were prone to stray, were of less concern to the Roman architect and therefore lack some of the diagnostic architectural features that characterise the more ostentatious public rooms. Such areas were still likely to have conveyed messages to those who used them, although symbol and gesture were accorded less importance. The organisation of domestic space provides important clues about family structure and private routines.

Some individual features, such as hearths and ovens, can help identify kitchens and workrooms. The choices about where to place such features can have implications about the ways in which spaces were used and perceived, and this in turn can have implications about the way in which society was organised. This evidence will be dealt with in more detail towards the end of the chapter, but such features are not always present. Where the individual rooms are anonymous it can sometimes be more fruitful to investigate common patterns of room suites and association. Various observers have attempted to identify room suites within the Romano-British house. In the most thorough of these studies Drury has suggested (1982) that there were six different room sets evident in the plans of *mansiones*. The typology omits patterns that occur frequently in town houses and the range of possibilities is actually greater. The chief problem encountered in any such analysis is that complete patterns of doorways cannot be reconstructed from the fragmentary evidence.

The most commonly repeated arrangement involved setting small rooms either side of a large central room, which small rooms were in turn flanked by large rooms at the ends of a principal block (figs 67–70). In smaller houses these larger rooms, at the ends and middle of the block, included the

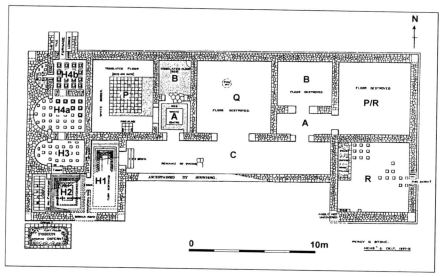

Figure 67 The Roman villa at Newport, Isle of Wight (after Stone 1929).

main reception rooms of the house. Buildings of this type contained two small domestic suites sandwiched between the reception rooms. A reduced version of the same arrangement involved omitting one of the end rooms and the adjacent small rooms or passageway. In these houses the principal wing consisted of two larger reception rooms flanking smaller rooms: usually an antechamber and rear chamber. This plan was rarely encountered in the countryside but was common in some towns, notably Caerwent. Although elements of this plan are sometimes evident in Gallo-Roman villas, it was essentially a Romano-British design and perhaps derived from local adaptations of military house types (Black 1994: 100).

Suites formed of groups of two to five rooms can be identified. Rooms of four main types were found within these suites: small antechambers (figs 68–70: A) were separated from square rear chambers (figs 68–70: B) by a party wall (an H-plan arrangement). These were commonly set alongside both larger living rooms (figs 68–70: P) and narrow passages (figs 68–70: L, transverse lobbies in the descriptive terminology proposed by J.T. Smith 1997). Four similar arrangements account for the majority of the evidence, and the main difference between these was whether they included one or two larger living rooms. The suggestion that these suites served as the main living and sleeping quarters of the house is supported by the limited evidence available (Nash-Williams 1951: 106). At Newport and Sparsholt similar suites were set either side of the central reception room: each of these included an antechamber and rear chamber with a larger room to one side (fig. 60). In both buildings the suite to the right of the central reception

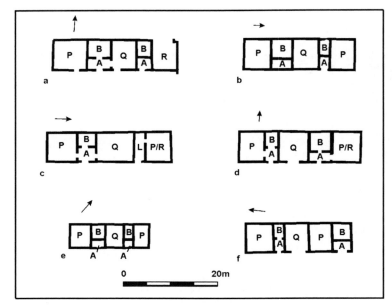

Figure 68 The most common arrangement of space in the main wings of Romano-British
houses (for letter codes see fig. 53). a: Silchester House 8,1; b: Silchester House
27,1; c: Caerwent, House 3S; d: Verulamium House 6,1; e: Newport; f: Sparsholt.

room took up more space than that to the left. It has been argued that the
presence of two or more room suites within the same house illustrates the
presence of an extended family (J.T. Smith 1997: 48). This seems unlikely. It
was unusual for the larger villas and town houses of Roman Italy not to have
several suites of bedrooms and reception rooms and there is little question
here of multiple ownership. The Villa of the Mysteries outside Pompeii
illustrates the point. Two three-room suites (fig. 4: Rooms 6–8 and 3–5),
show similarities to the Romano-British examples. There is ample evidence
for multiple suites in the houses of Pompeii and at Settefinestre three two-
roomed suites of bedrooms linked to reception rooms can easily be identified
(Wallace-Hadrill 1988: 90).

The archaeological evidence accords with the literary sources. In several
letters Pliny refers to rooms within his villas grouped into suites (*diaetae*). A
bedroom suite in his villas at Laurentum is described as containing a room
(*cubiculum*) for use at night which was heated by an adjacent furnace
(*hypocauston*), and associated with an ante-room (*procoeton*) and a second room
(*cubiculum*) (*Letters* 2,17). Another letter refers to a suite (*diaeta*) in which an
unlit bedroom (*dormitorium cubiculum*) was next to an informal dining room
(*cenatio*) for entertaining personal friends (Pliny, *Letters* 5,6). Such sources
make it clear that husband and wife often reigned separately over their own

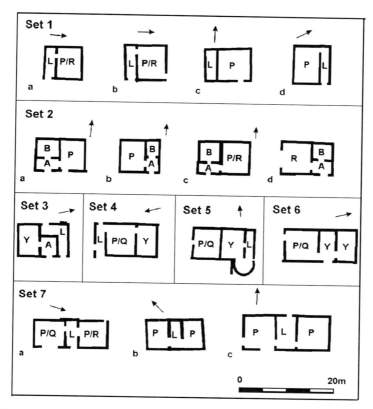

Figure 69 Room suites. Set 1 (L+P) a: Caerwent 3S; b: Silchester 24,2; c: Silchester 27,1; d:
Farningham. Set 2 (A+B+P/R) a and b: Newport; c: Silchester 27,1; d: Pitney. Set
3 (A+Y+L) Latimer (Branigan 1971). Set 4 (L+P+Y) Latimer. Set 5 (P+Y+L)
Brislington (Branigan 1972). Set 6 (Y+Y+P) Latimer. Set 7 (P+L+P) a: West
Park; b: Verulamium 1,1; c: Silchester 27,1.

domestic and sleeping quarters (Carcopino 1941: 184). Privileged guests and
senior relatives might also have found need to make use of extended private
quarters. These requirements, and the use of different suites in different
seasons or for different times of the day, readily account for the provision of
several suites in the houses of Roman Italy. Large houses were the consequence: the fictional house described by Petronius contained four dining
rooms and twenty bedrooms (*Satyricon* 14,77). The complex arrangements
found in palatial Romano-British houses can be accounted for by a less
excessive profligacy in the use of domestic space.

Most suites were accessed from small rectangular antechambers, usually
1.5–2.9 m deep by 2–5 m wide. In some instances all four walls of these rooms
were pierced by doorways (fig. 68: Room A). The pavements in these rooms

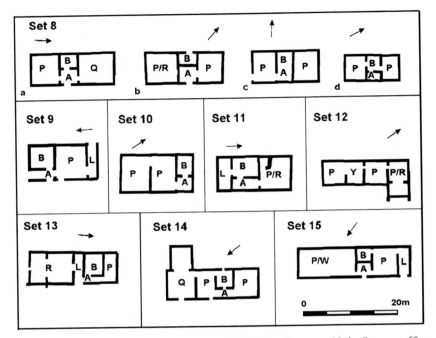

Figure 70 Room suites (continued). Set 8 (P+A+B+P/Q). a: Caerwent 3S; b: Caerwent 6S; c: Silchester 24,2; d: Silchester 15,B3 (St John Hope 1897). Set 9 (A+P+B+Y) Silchester 19,2. Set 10 (A+B+P+P) Farningham. Set 11 (L+A+B+P/R) Beadlam. Set 12 (P+Y+P+R) Chilgrove 2. Set 13 (R+L+A+B+P) Chedworth. Set 14 (P/Q+P+B+A+P) Spoonley Wood. Set 15 (P+A+P+B+L) at Spoonley Wood.

were not generally of high status, although tessellated floors were used in more luxurious houses. In some instances rooms at this location may alternatively or additionally have been used as a small kitchen and toilet. Ovens and a soakaway were found in an antechamber at Frocester, and at Box a drain in the equivalent room was supposed by the excavator to have been used for 'the necessary convenience' (Gracie 1970, Brakspear 1904). Furnaces and ovens were also sometimes found in rooms of this type (Lowther 1929, Zant 1993: 87).

Small rectangular rooms were set behind these antechambers (fig. 68: Room B). These generally measured about 1.55–3 m by 2–4.6 m, and were only slightly longer than they were broad. Several of these rear chambers were heated by hypocausts. This was more often the case in the countryside where more than one in four of the rooms of this type had underfloor heating, than in town where only 14 per cent of such rooms had this luxury. Only baths and end reception rooms were more likely to have had underfloor heating within the Romano-British house. Black has suggested (1994) that the main purpose of these rooms, when they were equipped with a hypocaust, was to heat the adjacent rooms. This may have been one collateral benefit of having a heated room at this central location within the residential quarters, but it is unlikely that this was the only or indeed the main purpose of such chambers. In some cases these rooms were also well decorated, although rarely to the standard of the main reception rooms, and in at least two cases foundation deposits were placed in pots set beneath the floors of rooms of this type (Meates 1973 and 1979). On balance it seems most likely that these rooms were most often used as bedchambers. The archaeological evidence is inconclusive, but it is consistent with what we know of the Roman house to find the main bedroom to be a heated and well-appointed room associated with a suite of rooms at the heart of the house. Bedrooms were places for conducting intimate business and had a role in the reception activities of the Roman patron (Pliny, *Letters* 2,20, Riggsby 1997). At Pompeii the main bedchamber was often attached to an important reception area, whilst small private bedrooms in north African houses were often dispersed with reception rooms around the peristyle (Thébert 1987). Even in the warmer circumstances of Roman Ostia bedrooms were sometimes heated, as was the case in the House of the Fortuna Annonaria (Boersma 1985). Sources suggest that the Roman bedchamber was sparsely furnished. Furniture included a couch, chest and chamber pot: the wicker chairs used for the morning toilet are shown on some Romano-British reliefs (Liversidge 1955).

Not all houses contained the standard arrangement of an antechamber with a square room behind. Sometimes a single slightly larger room occupied the equivalent part of the house. Examples were found at the villas at Boxmoor and Feltwell, where rooms of this type flanked central reception rooms (fig. 24b). The provision of doorways through two or three walls of the rooms of this type suggests that some were used in a similar way to the antechambers described above. In a minority of examples these rooms were more private, and had under floor heating, as in the villa at Atworth (Mellor and Goodchild 1942: Room 6). Rooms of this type perhaps stood in place of the antechamber and rear chamber arrangement where one or other of these rooms was not needed, or where the separation between these spaces was achieved by a lightweight screen or partition. Similarly proportioned rooms were sometimes found in other locations, most often at one end of the main wing of the building and might have provided further accommodation, perhaps of a lower status.

The larger rooms associated with domestic suites were typically about 4.6 m wide and 5.8 m long. This stands close comparison with the typical American-English living room of 4.6×5.5 m (Schlefen 1976: 195–7). Standards of decoration in these larger rooms varied according to the quality of the building, although they were often provided with mortar or tessellated floors and painted walls. These rooms were also a favoured location for fixed fireplaces (fig. 20 and fig. 67: Room P). It has already been noted that such rooms were sometimes found in the central and wing locations normally favoured by principal reception rooms and some overlap in function can be suggested. Many suites contained two rooms of this type (and some three).

Narrow rooms (transverse lobbies) were frequently found associated with both domestic suites and end reception rooms in both villas and town houses (figs 68–70: Room L). Such passages were also used to divide service quarters from living quarters. Excavators have diversely proposed that these rooms were used as corridors, antechambers, stairs, closets, kitchens, furnace chambers and shrines. Good arguments can be developed in support of all of these suggestions, which are not mutually contradictory. The use of portable furniture, such as chamber pots and braziers, means that there were few fixtures and fittings to help archaeologists describe the uses to which the service rooms were put. At Folkestone, however, the narrow room leading to the baths contained a stone basin and seems likely to have been a toilet. The use of some narrow rooms as kitchens is suggested in a strip buildings at Newgate Street in London, where this room contained a series of hearths and had been provided with a vent in the rear wall (fig.12: Building K, Room ii). Such rooms are closely paralleled in form, location and arrangement with a kitchen and closet in House IV, 10:11 at Herculaneum (Perring and Roskams 1991: fig. 90). At Pompeii kitchens were generally small and placed where they would not interfere with the rest of the building and often also served as closets (Jansen 1997: 128). Latrines had been set to the back of small narrow chambers leading off the entrance passage from at least the second century BC, as evident in the plans of Hellenistic houses at Delos. In the houses of Roman Italy the kitchen was also the principal focus for household religion: niche shrines were commonly placed here and the Lares, Penates and Genius were often painted on the wall next to the hearth (Clarke 1991: 9, Foss 1997). Some of the narrow Romano-British rooms considered here may similarly have had ritual use. Receptacles designed to receive votive deposits, as represented by pots sunk into the floor, were found in such rooms at Dewlish and Sparsholt. Infant burials were also commonly found in these locations and other kitchens (E. Scott 1991, and see below p. 198). More significantly Room 9 in House 14,2 at Silchester contained a rectangular structure which has credibly been interpreted as a *lararia*. This room may have been used as a kitchen before the insertion of the supposed shrine (Fox and St John Hope 1896: 219–33). Hearths, thresholds and burials were all associated with Roman fertility ritual (Rykwert 1976).

It is difficult to establish whether these cross passages also contained stairs to upper floors as has sometimes been suggested. At Building K from the Newgate Street site in London a row of postholes down one side of the room might have supported a timber stair but this could alternatively have supported a scaffold during a phase of repair to the roof. Similar rows of post holes in the narrow rooms of the villas at Gadebridge and Boughspring are open to similar interpretation (Neal 1974–6, Neal and Walker 1988). An understair can sometimes be a convenient site for a kitchen and latrine (for examples from Roman Italy see Boersma 1985 and Foss 1997: 206). Generalising from this evidence it is possible to suggest an association between passages, cooking and ritual activities in some Romano-British houses.

Bed-sitting rooms

The use of suites of living rooms was confined to the rich. Most people would have lived and slept in and above the barns, workrooms and shops where they worked. Such accommodation is difficult to recognise from the archaeological evidence. There is, however, evidence for the living conditions of one particular group of urban poor. Rows of small rectangular rooms, heated by a fixed fireplace, were a characteristic of the densely populated quarters of early Roman London. Typically these rooms measured 3–4 m square, and were reached from a corridor alongside the building. It seems likely that these were one-roomed lodgings: small bed-sitting rooms designed for rental income. A row of narrow single storey buildings, separated by narrow alleys, was squeezed together behind the early forum at London (fig. 13b, Milne and Wardle 1995). Since these buildings lay in an area later used for public buildings it is possible that they had always been on public property and provided the city with rents. Similar rooms for rent may also have been set to the back of one of the workshops found in excavations at Newgate Street. Here a row of three small square rooms measuring 2.9–3.0 m by 3.3–3.44 m, each with a fireplace built against one wall, were set off a corridor (fig. 12: Building K, Rooms iv-vi). These rooms were of a similar size and character to the rooms within the barracks at some fort sites, as at Wallsend where the rooms were approximately 3.6 m square (Goodburn 1976: 306–7). This evidence is similar to that obtained from the crowded cities of Roman Italy, such as Ostia, where families rented single rooms in long corridor houses (Casey 1985: 44). Similar rows of self-contained rooms may have accommodated slaves in patrician houses like the House of the Menander at Pompeii and the villa at Settefinestre (George 1997).

Halls

Several villas were laid out around a large central hall. Unlike the Germanic parallels for the type, the Romano-British halls were notably longer than they were wide and were typically less than 7 m wide (Oelmann 1921: 64–73, J.T. Smith 1997: 23–45). In a survey of such buildings by J.T. Smith architectural distinctions can be drawn between wide-nave halls and ridge-post halls. Such rooms made up the bulk of the domestic space in the buildings within which they were located. They were not only larger than the audience rooms described above (p. 160), but were usually undecorated and more likely to contain hearths, hypocaust furnaces, ovens and other domestic features. At Chiddingfold, a tank had been placed near the centre of the room (Black 1987: fig. 13). Crudely paved floors at villas such as Littleton, Cherington and Colerne suggest that these rooms were subjected to heavy use (Haverfield 1906: 323–4, Lysons 1817: 117, Godwin 1856). In the buildings at Cox Green and Wraxall these central rooms were sub-divided into smaller rooms (Bennett 1963, Sykes and Brown 1961), and there is a possibility that slightly built timber screens and partitions may sometimes have escaped recognition in other rooms of the type.

Outbuildings containing a large front room and smaller rear room were common at both Silchester and Verulamium (e.g. fig. 63). The workrooms inside aisled and strip buildings generally stretched the full width of the building and much of its length. Ovens and hearths were commonly found in these areas. These barn-like structures were sometimes provided with an exceptionally wide entrance, as House 19,2 at Silchester which building also contained a water tank (Fox and St John Hope 1899: 235–6). The large aisled outbuilding to the rear of House 22,1 at Cirencester (which measured 13.5×6 m internally) was provided with foundations nearly 1 m across (McWhirr 1986). These were much wider than those of the adjacent house and it seems likely that this was a taller structure. Finds from this building included an iron coulter and bone weaving tablets. It is tempting to see these buildings as barns of a similar type to that attached to the House of the Menander at Pompeii (Ling 1983).

In several villas the halls opened onto the main corridors. The design of the villa at Kingsweston was unusual and deserves further consideration (Boon 1950). It had a large central room, 6.5 m by 16.6 m, which was divided from the facade corridor by an arcade in which stone Tuscan columns set at 1.6–1.8 m intervals supported a series of arches formed of white-painted voussoirs. This architectural detail suggests that the room was a public part of the building. The provision of rooms of this type was essentially a late Roman phenomenon, with little evidence for their presence in villas in Britain prior to the late third century.

It has frequently been assumed that these Romano-British halls were places of social gathering, along the lines of the medieval hall, and might have been suitable for the assembly of kin-groups. Attempts to define and describe the social arrangements represented by halls are, however, open to dispute (see J.T. Smith 1985 and Webster and Smith 1987 on contradictory interpretations of the villa at Barnsley Park). On the assumption that halls were used as reception rooms the locations of hearths and doorways have been used to reconstruct social arrangements (J.T. Smith 1997). Centrally located hearths might suggest a community not overly concerned with distinctions of rank. This was a characteristic of some broad halls of the Mayen type, but is rarely found in the main houses at Romano-British sites. More normally the hearths were placed closer to one end of the room than the other, and in these situations might possibly have distinguished an inferior lower-end, from a superior upper-end. Alternatively hearths were displaced to one corner or side of the room, where they were unable to provide a clear focus for social activity.

These interpretations are predicated on an assumed reception function, but in several Romano-British hall buildings it is clear that the main reception activities took place elsewhere. Reception activities were often directed towards rooms that flanked the hall. Good examples of this arrangement include the villas at Langton and Dalton Parlours (Corder and Kirk 1932, Sumpter 1988). It is probable that many Romano-British halls were workrooms, barns and kitchens. Only in the simplest buildings, where no better facilities existed, is it likely that these main rooms were also used as dining rooms. The Romano-British hall finds parallel not only in the Gallo-Germanic building traditions represented by the broader halls typified by the villa at Mayen (Oelman 1921: 64–73), but also in the Roman *atrium*: a central hall that could be used as a kitchen and workroom as much as a reception room.

Kitchens and workrooms

Most service facilities were tucked into corridors or antechambers adjacent to the rooms that they served. The likely use of some of these transverse lobbies as kitchens has already been described in our consideration of room suites. Such small corridor-conveniences provided facilities for basic food pre-paration and the toilet. The more serious kitchen work: baking and butchering and the like, probably took place in the outbuildings. In town commercial bakeries and taverns would also have been used. Some kitchens have, however, been identified in larger establishments. These were commonly set close to the angle between the two main wings of the house and were often adjacent to end reception rooms (e.g. fig. 21).

Lean-to corridors with earthen or low-status floors, often partitioned-off to form small rooms, were commonly built at the back of houses. These were often used as service corridors and storage areas. In House 23,1 at Winchester, an unusually wide rear corridor extended the full length of the house and terminated in a small room that may have served as a kitchen (Zant 1993: 142). One of the earlier urban examples of a rear corridor comes from the early Flavian Building D at Watling Court. Infant burials were found beneath the floors of these rooms in several houses. This was sufficiently frequently the case for it to be suggested that there was a positive preference for disposing of such remains in kitchens and service areas (Scott 1991).

Smaller workrooms and shops were set at the front of some town houses. Rooms 1 to 4 at Colchester Lion Walk, Building 20, could possibly have been small shop units (Crummy 1984: 62–3). The best of these was entered across a Purbeck marble threshold for a door 2.5 m across and had painted walls.

Latrines flushed by running water were rarely provided, but are easily recognised (e.g. fig. 63: Room 4). The masonry drainage channels supported a timber framework with seats. Such facilities were most frequently associated with baths, although latrines were also found attached to some larger town houses. Small outhouses, set over latrine pits some distance from the main house, are likely to have been common on rural sites.

Hearths and ovens

Hearths and ovens were standard fixtures in most houses, although their importance was reduced by the adoption of hypocaust floors and portable braziers. The simplest hearths were small affairs set directly over the ground or on a small clay base. These were usually circular between 300–500 mm in diameter and set in a shallow hollow. The provision of a tile base was a common sophistication. It has been suggested that the use of floor-level hearths, rather than raised features, might have facilitated the use of heavy hanging cauldrons (Casey and Hoffman 1998: 118). These were most common in the workshops and halls and were often set towards the middle of such rooms (Green 1982).

Hearths built in the residential quarters were often a little more elaborate with small tile or stone platforms set against a wall (Johnston 1978: 82–8). The platforms were sometimes recessed into the wall against which they were built, and cheek-walls could be built to either side. In more complex examples the hearth was set within a semicircular breastwork up to 800 mm across. These structures were built either in similar fashion to the walls against which they were set, or were built of tile and coated with plaster or daub. These structures might have supported horizontal bars from which cooking pots could have been hung, and may also have supported corbelled hoods to funnel smoke out of the building, although most fireplaces vented under the eaves rather than through chimneys. Such fireplaces were not common in Roman Italy but were frequently found in Romano-Gallic houses (Degbomont 1984: 17–18, Adam 1994: 59).

The furnaces that heated the baths were used as boilers to supply steam and hot water and might also have been used as domestic ovens. Tile or stone platforms were therefore built to support water tanks that were suspended on iron beams (Wacher 1971). Kitchens, workrooms and other service areas were provided with ovens: usually rectangular structures enclosing a narrow flue or keyhole-shaped central furnace, typically 300–500 mm deep and 1.0–1.5 m long. These were usually tile-built with wattle and daub superstructures. Fittings associated with the hearths and ovens include fuel boxes and ash pits (Frere 1972: 17). A more complex form of oven, with a drying floor and T-shaped flue, was built on a range of rural sites (Morris 1979). These 'corn driers' may have been used in both the parching of grain for storage and as malting ovens (van der Veen 1989). Although most evidently associated with the processing of agricultural surplus there may have been social or functional aspects to the use of these ovens that resulted in them being built within the residential wings of some late Romano-British houses. They were widely found in porticoes and corridors, suggesting that the use of these rooms changed during the course of the fourth century.

Other fixtures and furnishing

Boon (1983) has described a group of small structures that may have been used as domestic shrines (*lararia*). Some were built like cupboards with side walls and an open front that could be closed by a wooden door (type A), others were low platforms (type B), stone plinths (type C), or recessed niches (type D). Niches were widely used to contain sacred images. At Lullingstone three female figures painted at the back of a niche, one with water spurting from her nipples and another pouring water from a jug, have been identified as water nymphs (Liversidge 1987). There are too few examples to establish a chronology for the use of these features, which were located in a variety of different kinds of rooms, and their identification as *lararia* cannot be confirmed from the archaeological evidence.

There were few other permanent household fittings although upright storage jars were fixtures in some houses (Crummy 1984: 63). Small vessels let into the floors of some rooms may have been placed as votive deposits. At Fishbourne a group of pots was found crushed in fire debris from a late third-century conflagration. The disturbed character of the assemblage and some iron angle brackets found at the same location, suggests that the pots had sat on a wooden tray or box above the floor (Cunliffe 1971a: 188). In second-century fire horizons at London and Verulamium groups of pots have been found where they originally stood on the ground (Frere 1972: 17–18, Perring and Roskams 1991:15). A more substantial storage feature is represented by the sunken strong box found in the room next to the hall at Brislington (Barker 1900).

Char marks on the structural timbers from the framed building reused at Cannon Street shows that lamps had been mounted on brackets nailed to the sides of the exposed timbers (Goodburn 1992). One of these mountings had been 1.15 m above floor level, and another, perhaps for a bedside or working light, was placed only 560 mm high. Such wall mountings are likely to have been common, but the archaeological record is reticent on such matters.

Stone and timber benches were built along the sides of some larger rooms. The bench around the 'audience' chamber at Fishbourne is the most notable and a similar row of postholes supporting a bench was recorded at Boughspring (Neal and Walker 1988). Stone benches were also built in some outbuildings attached to both villas and town houses. Although stone steps were commonly employed to address minor changes of level, timber stairs are more likely to have been used to reach upper floors and lofts. Evidence for one of these was preserved in the plaster rendering of the cellar in the villa at Piddington (Selkirk and Selkirk 1996).

After the hearths referred to in the above section, the most common fixtures were those associated with water supply and drainage. Outside of the baths, where fountains and pools were found in the better houses, few domestic buildings were supplied with running water.

Foundation offerings and infant burials

Animal carcasses were buried during the construction of numerous Romano-British houses. Dogs were interred beneath houses at London and Winchester (Perring and Roskams 1991: 69–70, Cunliffe 1964: 43, Zant 1993: 61), and sheep beneath a building at Leadenhall Court in London and in the villa at Kingsweston (Milne 1992: 15, Boon 1950). A wild boar was used in the construction of a conquest-period fort at Chelmsford (Goodburn 1976: 342), and at Bourton Grounds Temple, Buckingham, a horse's skull was found under a late Roman threshold (Luff n.d.). A foundation offering of pots containing fish bones and shells was associated with the construction of a hypocaust floor at Winchester (Zant 1993: 113). Various small pots found under the floors of Romano-British houses may have contained further votive deposits of this nature.

Neo-natal burials have been found in service areas inside or immediately adjacent to several villas and town houses (Scott 1991). Contrary to some suggestions this burial practice was not 'remarkably un-Roman' (Hingley 1997). Pliny mentioned the Roman practice of burying infants under the eaves of the house (*Natural History* 7,15), and the implication of other ancient sources is that it was thought fonder to keep these unfortunates at home than to dispatch them to a cemetery (Fulgentius, *Sermones Antiqui* 7). Domestic infant burial was a significant act. The arrival of a new child marked an important moment in the ritual life of the Roman household, especially during the first nine days of life before the infant was named. Varro describes the Roman custom of celebrating the arrival of a baby with a nocturnal attack on the domestic threshold to dispatch evil spirits. Death in its turn demanded the ceremonial purification of the house (Ogilvie 1969: 13, 102–3). Given the importance of both childbirth and death it is inconceivable that the choice of where to bury the dead infant was casual or insignificant. Although these observations are drawn from our knowledge of Roman social practice it is difficult to believe that things were otherwise in Britain, although we lack the supporting testimony of written sources.

Infant burials are most frequently found in service areas, especially in kitchens and other areas where agricultural products were processed, although corridors were also used to this end (Scott 1991). Roman kitchens were normally closely associated with the household gods; fertility and prosperity sprang from this focal point and this was where household shrines were most usually located. The underworld also held enormous significance in Roman fertility ritual, and it seems likely that infant graves were placed where the spirits could contribute most effectively to the prosperity and care of the living.

12

THE ROMANO-BRITISH HOUSEHOLD

One of the opening points made in this book is that it should be possible to reconstruct social arrangements from the evidence of the plans of Roman houses. In order to do so it has been necessary to speculate about the different ways in which the rooms were used and were articulated within the house. Through the identification of common patterns of arrangement it has been possible to identify and describe domestic and reception suites. It has also been possible to recognise more popular arrangements of such suites of rooms, most notably in the way in which a rear reception wing was often separated from a main wing containing the residential quarters. Most previous descriptions of the Roman house have provided typologies of the different ways in which these principal wings could be arranged, rather than explore the meaning that could be extracted from a comparison of the different preferences in room design.

Two issues, in particular, merit further attention. In the first place we need to review the evidence of the accommodation in order to describe the likely composition of the Romano-British household. It will be argued that the Romano-British domestic arrangements were not evidently different to those found in the Roman Italy and that we are not therefore able to conclude that different patterns of family structure and tenure applied in Britain. Finally our attention can turn to the critical issue of how power and status were expressed in Roman Britain. Here it is concluded that Romano-British houses provided a setting for a society that subscribed to the Roman ideal and drew on Roman architectural tradition in the display of rank and power. In both areas of study the evidence of house design has an important contribution to make, but also needs to be set into its broader context.

Household size

It is difficult to make any reliable estimate as to the size of population likely to have been found in the different classes of building described here. Large households were not uncommon in the Roman world (Treggiari 1975: 48–77). Further to the problems of establishing whether or not extended

200

families were found in Romano-British houses, there is also the issue of domestic servants and slaves to address. The epigraphic record leaves little doubt that slaves were commonly present. The evidence of urban cemeteries, where males often outnumbered females by two or three to one, might reflect the predominant use of male slaves in urban households (Harris 1980: 119).

Three different approaches to estimating population size have commonly been employed: density per cubic metre of living space, density per room, and capita average per house. Hingley (1989) has estimated that the aisled building at Lodge Farm, North Warnborough might have housed some 30–60 residents (a population density of one person for every square 10 m, following ratios described by Cook and Heizer 1968). Packer, in his survey of Ostia (1971), instead assumes the presence of one person for each *cubiculum*: a figure that Meiggs (1973) has doubled. A more useful figure for Roman urban population density derives from the work of Wallace-Hadrill at Pompeii (1994), which suggests an average number of six to eight inhabitants per house and a density of one person per 35–45 m square (with an average house size of 271 m square). As a rule of thumb Wallace-Hadrill settles on an average figure of one inhabitant per room.

There was considerable variety in house size in Roman Britain and the available sample is almost certainly biased towards larger properties. Smaller town houses measuring less than 100 m square and containing fewer than five rooms are likely to have been the most common. Better houses containing reception facilities more usually contained 8–10 rooms with an average size of slightly less than 250 m square. Houses of this scale, which compare closely with the average Pompeiian houses described by Wallace-Hadrill, were common throughout all of the towns described here, and many of the more modest villas were similarly proportioned. Centurions' quarters were typically 230–59 m square, and were normally occupied by well-off men, who may have had families and slaves living with them (Hoffman 1995: 111).

Larger houses could contain more than 40 rooms, extending over an area in excess of 1700 m square, but these were in the minority. At Silchester, for instance, only eight houses had more than 25 rooms (i.e. about 6 per cent of the total). The evidence from Romano-British towns, most of which is of the later period (i.e. later than the middle of the second century), is similar to that described by Wallace-Hadrill in his study of Pompeii (1994). Although late Romano-British urban households had similar demands on space to their earlier Italian equivalents, and illustrate a similar ranking of scale, it is not possible to conclude that society was similarly structured. Romano-British towns were generally smaller than their Italian equivalents, and to make up magisterial numbers curial office may have extended much further down the scale. The style of life that Wallace-Hadrill attributes to a Pompeiian *plebs media*, admittedly one which was modelled on that of the aristocratic villa and involved the display of wealth in luxurious domestic architecture, would in Britain have been enjoyed by an urban class of higher rank. In Britain as in Italy the place for wealth display *par excellence* was the villa. In later Roman Britain the largest villas were commonly twice the size of the largest houses in the nearest important town.

Family structure

There have been several attempts to reconstruct social arrangements in Roman Britain from the archaeological evidence, and much attention has been given to the contextual information provided by both classical and Celtic sources. Unfortunately the sources are indirect and the archaeological evidence inconclusive. In the light of the subsequent history of the province it is reasonable to conclude that there were parts of Roman Britain where social custom remained British (Stevens 1966: 108–28). Welsh law, the codification of which has traditionally been ascribed to the tenth century, describes systems of landholding of likely Celtic descent (Jones 1972: 320–39). In these systems the extended family, which could include all male descendants of a common great-grandfather, numbering also wives and unmarried children (rich individuals might exceptionally have had more than one wife), was of greater social importance than the nuclear one (Herlihy 1985). Such families are likely to have given rise to large and complex households, or groups of related households. Additionally partible inheritance encouraged the generational subdivision of ever-smaller parcels of land between more and more descendants of an estate's founder. It has been suggested that some Romano-British houses might present evidence for social arrangements influenced by these native traditions of family and tribal structure (Charles-Edwards 1972, J.T. Smith 1978).

The Celtic sources come from a different region and a different period, and their relevance to Roman Britain has been questioned (Todd 1978: 198). The implication of Caesar's writings is that southern Britain had a stratified society with a developed patron-client system similar to that of Gaul (Caesar, *DBG* 1,4; 1,17–18; 6,11–13; 8, 40). Unfortunately this source is equally problematic since Caesar's terms of reference were so profoundly Romano-centric.

J.T. Smith has suggested that villas in Britain, Germany and Gaul flouted basic standards of classical architecture in order to accommodate the joint occupancy of settlements, that in turn derived from the joint ownership of land (J.T. Smith 1997). In his view this may have been a consequence of the continued primacy of extended family kin groups: the outward form of the buildings was Roman but the nature of the family structure and life within had retained a different and local form. The main evidence presented for a deviation from the classical ideal is a lack of evident symmetry in building facades. This is the wrong place to start from: the symmetrical house facade was an invention of the seventeenth-century classical revival and not a standard element of Roman house design. But the argument still merits close attention.

In several villas different suites of rooms were set to either side of a principal room at the central axes of the building. At Boxted in each of two three-cell units two subdivided rooms flank a middle room. These suites typically included an antechamber, bedroom and reception room. Smith sees the presence of two or more suites within the same house as evidence for the permanent residence of two family groups and draws parallels with the 'unit-system' house, where the division of an inheritance would result in two households being established on a single site. This may have been the case, but such suites were common throughout the Roman world (fig. 4), where they may have provided separate private quarters for the master and mistress of the house, for guests and for use in different seasons. This might also have been the case in Britain (and this is the argument presented in Chapter 11). The presence of replicated room suites can not really be used as evidence for or against the presence of extended families.

At other Romano-British sites the presence of two or more bath-houses has been seen as possible proof of the existence of two households, although here it is instead possible to argue that different baths were provided for different social groups within the community of dependants reliant on the villa. It is consistent with Roman social practice for patrons to have provided facilities for the separate entertainment of different groups of relatives, guests, clients and dependants.

Villa complexes based on two adjacent houses, one of which contained superior reception facilities, present more compelling evidence for the presence of separate family units, although here too the evidence can be challenged. Relevant sites include the villas at Newton St Loe, Halstock, Gayton Thorpe, Marshfield, Paulton and Beadlam. Smith cites several other examples and provides a range of continental parallels from the northern parts of Gaul. It has been argued, however, that in many of these sites these separate buildings may have provided separate facilities rather than parallel residences. Rippengal (1993) has noted the very different arrangements of space found inside some of the adjacent buildings usually described as paired unit-system houses. He sees them providing supplementary rather than parallel facilities. In several instances the two adjacent buildings could have functioned as two wings of a single property. At Beadlam, for instance, the west house contained a bath suite and a residential suite, whilst the north wing included a series of larger reception rooms (Neal 1996). This spatial arrangement comfortably duplicates the facilities found in the wings of contemporary town houses. The fact that some establishments had been spread over two separate blocks has no necessary significance.

Two other strands of evidence have also been drawn on to support the suggestion that extended families were a feature of villa society in Roman Britain. The first of these is that similar arrangements are also evident in the arrangement of some high status pre-Roman settlements, such as Glastonbury. The evidence from Glastonbury has, however, been reassessed and can no longer be used to support this argument (Barrett 1987). The second is the text found on the mosaic at Thruxton. This inscription, sometimes taken to represent the presence of a kinship group (Black 1987: 81), also lends itself to alternative explanations, as discussed above p. 170. In sum there is no convincing evidence that Romano-British villas were unit houses.

The argument is in any case based on a misunderstanding of the differences between Roman and British social arrangements. There is a surprising assumption made in some studies that the division of inheritance was some kind of Celtic peculiarity, rather than standard practice within ancient society (as Esmonde-Cleary 1989: 114). Unless otherwise directed, Roman property passed to all children in equal proportions on the death of a father, although such inheritance was not automatic from the mother until the late second century AD. References in the Code of Justinian witness various problems associated with this inheritance law (see Gardner and Wiedemann 1991: 117–42), and by the classical period most Romans left wills.

Notwithstanding this pattern of partible inheritance, the literary evidence indicates that in Italy the Roman household was based on a small family unit of father, mother and dependant children, 'next comes the relationship between brothers, between cousin's . . . since these relatives cannot be contained within one household, they leave to found other households.' (Cicero, De Beneficiis 1, 54). It was exceptional for adult sons to live with their fathers and for adult brothers and sisters to share a common household. Roman families were consequently smaller than has sometimes been imagined. The combination of a high death-rate and low rate of social reproduction (with an average age gap between father and child of as much as forty years), also meant that many families were short-lived. Indeed it has been suggested that a high number of Roman parents, perhaps 60 per cent, were not survived by a male heir (Hopkins 1983: ix, Garnsey and Saller 1987: 129).

It has also been argued that the evidence of tombstone dedications suggests that in the western provinces the nuclear family was the focus of familial obligation, and that members of the extended family were comparatively unimportant (Saller and Shaw 1984: 124–56). Sibling and extended family dedications are rarer than dedications from outside the family. This pattern extended to Roman Britain where, from 98 relationships described, 80 per cent were from within the nuclear family, 6 per cent from extended family relationships, 11 per cent from other heirs and 3 per cent servile. The validity of the inferences drawn from this evidence has been challenged because the measure is of relationships between pairs of people not family structures (Martin 1996). It is also difficult to draw a sharp distinction between nuclear and extended family structures when no such clear distinction is found in the terminology used in classical sources. It remains the case, however, that when a person could not rely on a member of the nuclear family to provide a funerary dedication, then they were far more likely to turn to unrelated friends or dependants than to distant relatives (Saller and Shaw 1984). The tombstone evidence from Roman Britain is consistent with the broader pattern of dedications found in the western empire and supports the view that family units were generally small (Martin 1996: 53). The extended kinship group is not in evidence.

Partible inheritance does not automatically give rise to extended kinship groups, and such systems were generally alien to the Roman experience. Although the unit-system can sometimes illustrate the workings of partible inheritance this is not always the case. The unit-system house may also reflect the need to keep an elder son at his father's side after his marriage without causing friction between the separate households (Gresham 1971: 175). As Millett has noted the construction of two adjacent houses at some sites could witness the presence of the separate but adjacent nuclear households of a proprietor and his heir (Millett 1990b: 198–9).

If the houses described by J.T. Smith had been extended and subdivided to accommodate separate units of an extended family (in equal or unequal relationship), it is surprising that this process of subdivision did not continue. Villas would have become villages, as each new generation witnessed a further fragmentation of the property. This did not occur to any significant scale. Stevens (1947) suggested that the Celtic kinship structure might have extended throughout the less overtly Romanised parts of Britain, which he defined as those areas without patterned mosaics. This convenient division of the country between Roman and Celtic spheres is difficult to put to the test, but the examples presented by J.T. Smith awkwardly include many higher status sites in lowland areas where Roman models of land-ownership are more likely to have applied. The urban evidence is also unhelpful to those who would see Celtic patterns of ownership. Several larger town houses include two or more different and asymmetrical suites of rooms that conform to the pattern described by J.T. Smith (1987: 110). These, however, are found in the richest and most Romanised town houses, whilst in the lower-status roadside settlements the workshops and houses show no evidence for plot or building division along unit-system lines. This is perhaps the reverse of what would be expected.

Despite the concerted arguments of Smith and others on this matter, it remains possible to understand Romano-British houses through reference to the classical evidence. Notwithstanding pronounced regional differences, the domestic architecture in Britain is consistent with the picture that derives from Roman documentary sources. Property law in Britain, like elsewhere in the empire, could have been based on partible inheritance and individual ownership, and the main social unit could have been the nuclear family. There may have been important distinctions between family structure in

Britain and other parts of the Roman world, but these are not illustrated by the architecture or supported by any other direct source of evidence.

Inheritance and land-ownership

Citizenship, in Britain as elsewhere, was subject to Roman law. Caracalla's edict of 212, which extended citizenship to all, was, according to Dio, aimed at increasing revenue from estate duties. It could only have been effective in this purpose if property could be bequeathed and inherited in accordance with Roman law: in the context of which the alienability of property would have been a constant corrective to any 'native' tendency towards clan-based ownership. The evidence of legal disputes and the discretionary powers open to local administrations suggest that conflicts between Roman and local law were not always resolved, but that this was exceptional (as Stevens 1947).

Evidence for Roman land-ownership is clear enough, and references to the sale and transfer of title other than through inheritance are common (e.g. Pliny, *Letters* 2,15; 6,3; 1, 24; Juvenal, *Satires* 3, 223). The ideal of the ancient city-state was for citizens to have sufficient economic independence to play a full part in public life, and this relied on the ownership of land. Roman law therefore recognised a freedom to sell or testate land, although some restrictions were placed on this to limit the social consequences of disinheritance (as the *Lex Falcidia* of 40 BC that established that heirs had a right to not less than one-quarter of the estate). Although Roman law could accommodate joint land holding, it encouraged the private ownership of land and gave considerable powers over inheritance to the testator. In a Roman will of AD 108, part of an estate was left jointly to a group of freedmen: '[since] however [I have divided the ground] into so many parts and they all [cannot equally] possess the whole that is left [to them. . . . I appoint as curators' (Gardner and Wiedemann 1991). This was an unusual circumstance.

It has been argued that effective private control of land was established in Britain before the Roman conquest (Gregson 1982). According to Tacitus (*Annales* 14, 31), the Icenian king Prasutagus left a will naming his two daughters and Nero as co-heirs, although the source cannot be relied upon to have understood the legal framework within which this took place. Land grants would have accompanied the foundation of the coloniae at Colchester, Lincoln, Gloucester and York, whilst the confiscations which preceded the Icenian revolt are also described by Tacitus. The imperial family would have owned extensive estates in Britain as they did throughout the empire, and the life of Saint Melania the younger refers to her ownership of land in various provinces including Britain (Applebaum 1972: 23). A writing tablet discovered in reclamation dumps beside the river Walbrook in London preserved part of the text of a legal document of the 14th of March AD 114, concerning a dispute over the ownership of a wood in *civitate Cantiacorum*

(Kent). It refers to the previous purchase of the wood for 40 denarii, the ownership of which was claimed by Lucius Iulius Betucus (*RIB* 2446, Hassall and Tomlin 1994: 302–3). A wooden tablet that was found in a well at Chew Park villa also seems to record the sale of land (Turner 1956: 117–18). At least in some parts of Britain land was owned, sold and bequeathed in the same fashion as elsewhere in the Roman world.

Bailiffs and tenants

Classical sources debate the respective merits of using tenant farmers or stewards to manage estates, reflecting the dispersed nature of landholdings in Roman Italy (as Pliny, *Letters* 3,19; Columella 1,7; Pliny, *Letters* 9,36). We do not know if this also applied in Britain since the documentation does not exist (Reece 1988: 67–71). We know, however, that at least some property in Britain was owned from abroad and therefore farmed by tenants. Imperial estates, which it has been estimated formed 15 per cent of the total land within the empire, would have been worked by tenants. An inscription from the villa at Combe Down, near Bath, refers to Naevius (Aug. lib. adiutor procc.), a freeman and assistant to the procurators, who restored a principia. This building was perhaps part of an imperial estate of which Naevius was the administrator (*RIB* 179, Birley 1979: 147). We also know that the late Roman system of tied tenants or coloni applied in Britain (Jones 1973: 795–808). It is not necessarily the case that these forms of landholding would have generated different patterns of housing, although it is held more likely that tenant farmers were less likely to invest in status display than owner farmers. The classical sources suggest that bailiffs' residences could also have competed for opulence with the houses occupied by landowners (Millett 1990b: 189).

Bailiff-run estates on the Italian model required separate 'urban' quarters for the owner and for the day-to-day administration of the estate. As a consequence it has been suggested that the lesser buildings found on some Gallic villa estates may have housed bailiffs (Wightman 1985: 114). This could equally apply to some of the Romano-British sites laid out with two related houses, although in the absence of epigraphic support this remains a matter of speculation.

The role of rented housing is similarly uncertain. Rented housing may have provided for all but a small proportion of the urban population in antiquity (Casey 1985: 43) and even the wealthy sometimes preferred to rent in town (Juvenal, *Satires* 3, 223). Investment in urban property was therefore a significant economic activity: 'town property brings good returns but it is terribly risky. If there were any way of stopping houses perpetually burning down at Rome I would sell my farms and buy town property every time' (Aulus Gellus, *Noctes Atticae* xv.1.1–3). London's comparatively large urban population may have encouraged land-owners to become landlords and several houses of *c.* AD 100 could have been designed for multiple occupancy. This may well have been the case in the rows of small 'bed-sitting rooms' found attached to strip buildings at Newgate Street and Leadenhall Court.

In the late republic the speculative redevelopment of run-down urban property was clearly profitable, attracting investment from the likes of Crassus and Cicero (Plutarch, *Crassus* 2.2–4, Cicero, *Letters to Atticus* 14.9). Subsequently the emphasis of legislation is on repair and maintenance, with speculative housing redevelopment only permitted as a result of fire, collapse or resale (Laurence 1994b: 76, Strabo, 5.3.7). Third-century legislation implies instead that by this date the profit motive was no longer adequate to guarantee urban renewal.

Gender in the Romano-British house

The evidence of room suites implies that in better houses more than one member of the household had private rooms into which guests could be received. The architectural evidence compares closely to that of Roman Italy, where sources indicate that the lady of the house frequently had her own rooms. Since it has been proposed that women in Roman Britain had a stronger position in law than in Rome itself (Allason-Jones 1990), similar arrangements would not have been out of place in Romano-British houses.

This involved the parallel, but not necessarily equal, exercise of social patronage. It is much harder to find evidence for more systematic division by gender. Much has been made of the absence of any evident differences of age or gender in the *atrium*-peristyle houses of Roman Campania. The segregation of womenfolk within the house was seen as a Greek habit, and had little place in contemporary writings on Roman households and society (Wallace-Hadrill 1988: 50–1). It has, in any case, already been noted (p. 15) that the archaeological evidence for the presence of separate quarters for men and women in the Greek house is unconvincing (Jameson 1990: 104). A few references do, however, infer that some parts of the house were more readily associated with one sex than the other. These include Plutarch's account of affairs in the 'women's quarter' (*gynaikonitis*) of Cato's household (*Cato the Younger*, 24–5). According to Procopius (*Histories* 5, 2.6–15), a sixth-century Ostrogothic prince of Italy 'started howling and went off to the men's part of the palace'. Ray Laurence has proposed that 'gender divisions which are spatially indistinct were emphasised temporally' (1994b: 131). It does indeed seem likely that the different sexes would have exploited houses differently according to prescribed social roles.

The arrangements that prevailed in Roman Britain may have been different where the extended family was the norm. A division into distinct male and female sections may have occurred where extended families formed large communal groups. An attempt has been made to identify such divisions from the evidence of finds' distributions in the aisled house at

Lodge Farm, North Warnborough. Since certain classes of finds that are more readily associated with the domestic activities of one sex or the other do not distribute evenly across the site it has been concluded that gender divisions were evident (Hingley 1989: 45, based on Liddell 1931 and Applebaum 1972). Since rubbish is not usually left in primary working areas there is a suspicion that these finds were not associated with the use of the building but its abandonment. The classification of artefacts into male/female is also not entirely convincing since the 'male' objects such as knives, spears and ironmongery may have been used in outdoor/workshop environments whilst the 'female' combs, shuttles and spindle-whorls may dominate in domestic environments. The North Warnborough evidence might instead illustrate the presence of a large 'workshop' and a series of smaller living rooms with no particular emphasis on gender.

Private and public

In a society where rank was indicated by and reinforced by social patronage the house was necessarily a public place (Wallace-Hadrill 1988: 46). The exercise of power relied on direct social contact; Rome knew of no institutional surrogates for human interaction. The Roman aristocracy therefore needed ample space for the exercise of its public duties, and the higher the rank the greater the number of visitors received. The obligations of the host, the burdens of *hospitium* and *amicitiae*, were considerable. House guests were commonly entertained (Fronto, *Letters to his Friends* 1,3), and since the upper classes could travel with a significant entourage private houses could be crowded with visitors. Roman domestic space was designed to accommodate the interplay of social relationships within complex households that could include several powerful figures within the same family, as well as important and less important guests. Such a model can perhaps explain the evidence of those houses in Roman Britain that contained several 'private' suites of living rooms. Separate spatial domains could be established within a single household in order to define separately functioning private worlds (Grahame 1997). Privacy permitted the avoidance of power, and the design of the Roman house appears to have acknowledged this need.

Vitruvius gives a full description of the way in which domestic space could be both private and public:

> Those rooms no one is allowed to enter are considered 'private': bedrooms, dining rooms, bathrooms and so on. But the public rooms are those which people have a right to go into without being invited: entrance halls, courtyards, porticoes and so on. It follows that men of average wealth do not need entrance courts, tablina, or atriums built in grand style because such men are more apt to discharge their social obligations by going round to others than

have others come to them. . . . Those engaged in oratory or public speaking need larger and finer houses with room for those who come to hear them. And those of the highest status, who are involved in politics and the struggle for office and have to appear in public, must have high and impressive entrance-halls, wide courtyards and wide porticoes . . . to show off visibly how important they are.

(*On Architecture* 6, 5.1–2)

Pliny's descriptions of his domestic routine suggest a distinction between morning and evening reception activities. Spaces clustered around the entrance to the house were for morning use, whilst areas of private entertainment were reached through the peristyle and were for evening use. The front part of the house consisted of more austere halls (*atria*), with greater luxury on show in the inner reception rooms. A hierarchy of social interaction is evident, from the public *salutatio* to the private *cena* and the intimacies of the bedroom (see Tacitus, *Dialogues* 3.1, 14.7; Seneca, *de Ira* 3.8.6; Pliny, *Letters* 5,3; Cicero, *Verr.* 3.133). A similar hierarchy can be reconstructed from the Romano-British evidence. This is evident in the way in which audience chambers might be found near the front porch, but the main reception rooms were instead found in a separate wing to the rear of the house. The importance of the processional route through the Romano-British house has already been described (p. 147). As in Italy distinction between private and public space within the house were made evident by both scale and allusion. Larger reception rooms could be very public, explicitly basilical, in their design (e.g. the Casa dell'Atrio a mosaico, Wallace-Hadrill 1988: 60–1). Many details of domestic design, as in the use of apses, pediments, peristyles and columns, were imported to Roman houses from public contexts. The apse was particularly potent in this context, because of the common use of the semi-cupula as a frame in various public contexts (e.g. recess of *caldarium* in baths, cult image recess, tribunal in basilica, etc.). These were the areas that were favoured for building improvement in Romano British houses. The most commonly documented household improvements made were the addition of a portico or corridor, the enlargement or improvement of an end reception room, the construction of baths and the insertion of mosaics and hypocausts.

The Roman house was the centre of many public functions but few of these could be divorced from the other parts of the building: areas where guests, friends and clients were received were usually linked to the service quarters and the intimate parts of the house. The social activities that were most readily separated from the patron's residence were bathing and worship: hence the public baths and temples that characterised so many Roman towns. The second century witnessed a growing preference to locate such facilities within the private realm. The arrangements of many villa baths suggests that they were for public use, and it is just as likely that facilities for public worship would have been attached to private houses. There are many social advantages to the patron in making clear his superior position in the religious affairs of a community. It is possible to argue that the social rituals attached to the use of the baths, porticoes and dining rooms provided a focus for the development of systems of worship, and that these in turn reinforced the importance of such space. This provides a social context for some of the architectural changes described in this book.

13

CULTURE AND SOCIETY IN ROMAN BRITAIN

Romanisation

There is a school of thought that views the adoption of Roman fashion in Britain as unconvincing and shallow: a veneer applied to unreformed native culture. A distinction has therefore been proposed between a Romanised cultural superstructure and a native social substructure (Reece 1990). This permits the view that change was superficial, whilst spatial concepts remained unchanged (Hingley 1990: 139). Following from this some studies of the evidence from Roman Britain have also sought evidence for resistance, involving the cultural rejection of Roman impositions (Hingley 1997). Since power emanated from Rome and gave privilege to the owners of property, architectural design is perhaps one of the last places where we should expect to see resistance to Roman cultural patterns. The term resistance is, in any case, unhelpful. It implies a clear divide between value systems that could be either accepted or rejected. But the competing interests of class and community are invariably more complex. Neither Rome nor Britain stood as discrete concepts that could be placed in opposition. Roman hegemony inspired something approaching a global culture. Rome was so diversely interpreted and constantly evolving that it eventually survived without the benefit of Roman people, Italian territory or Latin language. On the other hand Britain had no identity and no meaning except within terms defined by Rome. Britannia appears to have been a Graeco-Roman invention used for the purposes of contrast, conquest and government. Other realities – the horizons of ownership, community and knowledge – generated more profound contrasts within Romano-British society. These different realities found expression in the architecture, and are at issue here.

The Roman conquest brought about a wholesale change in building fashion on elite sites throughout most of lowland Britain. This was not just a matter of outward appearance, but was evident in form, fabric and meaning. The arrangement of space, both with regard to the hierarchy of reception activities and in the space set aside for private quarters, can be described in Roman terms. The central argument of this book is that houses in Roman

Britain were designed to provide a setting for social behaviour that followed Roman practice. An instructive contrast can be drawn with the very different impact of British colonialism in India. Here a distinct form of native housing, with traditional courtyard houses for extended multi-generational families, existed separately from civil station architecture of bungalows for westernised nuclear families (King 1976). No equivalent distinctions can be found in Roman Britain. We can see differences between rich and poor, town and country, military and civilian, but not between Roman and native.

In all areas amenable to archaeological study the Romano-British house testifies to the integration of Britain into the Romano-Hellenistic world. Where conflicting cultural preferences can be suggested, as in the choice of round houses as opposed to rectangular ones, these can be explained as internal to Romano-British power systems. Roman houses in Britain were not slavishly copied from the houses of Roman Italy or Gaul but incorporated new variations on established themes. This creative adaptation shows an active involvement in the cultural arguments and social practices of empire. Approaches to the use of decorative motif, particularly in the field of mosaic design and in the applied arts, imply a ready understanding of the classical message and a close engagement in the intellectual arguments that absorbed educated classes throughout the empire.

There is currently some debate as to the extent to which this process of Romanisation was a product of internal forces, an indigenous impulse to copy and adapt (Millett 1990b), or was actively promoted by the imperial administration (Whittaker 1997, Hanson 1997). Both forces are likely to have been at work. Tacitus, in a widely quoted reference to Roman Britain, claimed that his uncle, Agricola 'encouraged individuals and assisted communities to build temples, fora and private houses. . . . Competition for honour took the place of compulsion' (*Agricola* 21). The changes represented in the architecture were not only willed by the administration but also the consequence of elective affiliation, reinforced by peer-group competition. The impact of imperial policy on the progress of Romanisation was most evident in public fashion. For instance the vigorous development in London's architecture in the early Flavian period, under Hadrian and again *c.* AD 200 seems likely to have been consequent on the political attention given by the administration to British affairs at these times (Perring 1991b). Public architecture had a significant impact on private fashion. New ideas were often introduced in this sphere and ushered from public to private by imperial and local patronage (Stahl and Stahl 1976).

Romano-British domestic architecture was the outcome of developments that started *c.* AD 50 and were not complete until after AD 155, although innovation was greatest in the period AD 75–125. This, therefore, was not the product of a moment of imperial will, but a dynamic process with its own creative momentum. It generated a recognisably British form of Romano-Hellenistic culture. This process relied on the active involvement of elite society. The thesis advanced by Millett, that the emulation of Roman models played a critical part in the acculturation process, has seen modification but remains the current orthodoxy (1990a). In this view the administration depended on a native elite grouped in 'city-state' communities that governed on Rome's behalf. Elite power remained in traditional hands, now reinforced by its identification with Rome. Emulation of Roman fashion set the elite apart from the rest of society and contributed to the maintenance of power (Trow 1990, Haselgrove 1987).

The adoption of Roman modes of display was in part a response to the post-conquest redundancy of previous cultural patterns. Chief amongst the disruptions to previous patterns of social display was the suppression of warfare: a vital conduit for pre-conquest elite competition. Similarly a flood of new imports devalued status display based on prestige goods, whilst changes in the control of trade and the increased social mobility of mercantile classes challenged the existing status quo. New ways of establishing and defining a social hierarchy were required in these unsettled circumstances. In this context investment in property became an important outlet for competition once it was clear that Rome offered a secure environment for such practice. This change in elite behaviour in Britain can be dated to the period after c. AD 65. New building forms developed rapidly over the following century in a period of competitive improvement accompanied by an increasing ability to command wealth represented by property. The main changes took place approximately one generation after conquest, following a pattern similar to that observed in the Romanisation of Spain and Gaul (Woolf 1995).

Cultural adaptation was not simply a dialogue between Roman and native, involving the rejection of one cultural system in preference for another (G. Woolf 1998: 7–11). Practices and objects became Roman because they were located within systems of power that defined themselves as Roman. This definition required that the components could be conceived of in a Roman fashion, and involved absorbing and internalising attributes that could be taken to manifest the cultural language of the wider empire. But there was no single concept of what being Roman meant, and there was no unique source of Roman civilisation. The need to pursue such fashion was a function of the competitive display inherent in the arrangements of patronage and clientage on which ancient society relied. This did not involve mere imitation so much as participating in a system characterised by both difference and agreement (G. Woolf 1998).

Romans deployed rank in almost all forms of social activity, and the Hellenising tastes of the Roman aristocracy provided the shared cultural language for structured engagement (Garnsey and Saller 1987: 116–17). Houses were a critical part of this process. The writings of Petronius provide explicit testimony to the Roman awareness of the social function of domestic architecture and decoration. Leading citizens invested in *luxuria* to reinforce social position (Plutarch, *Cato maior* 18.4). Fashion was driven by the need to search out new means of displaying status in order to retain a distinction between superior behaviour and the imitative aspirations of inferior classes (Cicero, *de Legibus* 3.30–1). This process was most evident in periods of social change, which explains why the house of Lepidus could be one of Rome's finest in 78 BC but fail to rank as one of the best hundred in the city a generation later (Pliny, *Natural History* 36,110).

Architecture defined status and demonstrated power. It spoke of the favourable relations with power held by an elite whose authority derived from Rome, and articulated the relationship between power and the surplus that ensured prosperity and underpinned the lordly largess needed in the exercise of patron–client relations. Wealth was pumped into property, the ownership of which was the principal direction for surplus capital and a vehicle for status display. The design of Romano-British houses was a consequence of such competitive expenditure, involving investment in buildings, mosaics and wall paintings. These vehicles for expression were explicitly Roman, and established or celebrated the owner's dominance over land and nature. The symbols were employed to illustrate affiliation and to mark status within the evolving social hierarchy (Grahame 1998).

Power systems in Roman Britain depended on the patronage networks that permeated Roman society. The congregation of clients at a patron's home provided a visual demonstration of social hierarchy (e.g. Ammianus Marcellinus, *Historiae* 28:4, 10–3), and the public representation of success in both buildings and ceremonies reinforced social order. It can be argued that the development of urban society in the northwest provinces accompanied the assimilation of tribal relations into Roman patronage systems and the attendant development of peer-group competition operating to Roman social rules (Slofstra 1983: 95, G. Woolf 1998: 156).

The formation of identity

The main sources of Roman ideas in Britain were themselves of provincial origin. The systems of patronage that operated in Britain gave greater potency to Romano-Gallic models than to those derived from Italy or the eastern Mediterranean (Reece 1988: 9). The evidence presented here suggests that civilian housing in Britain had been much influenced by the architecture of the army. Millett (1999) has observed that army life contributed to the development of a distinct form of elite culture. Service involved a complex range of social ties and obligations, but soldiers were drawn from a range of communities with divergent experiences of being Roman. The army transformed these different perceptions into coherent form, in the elaboration of a shared language of power that clarified the rules of social engagement. The army created its own form of identity from the dynamic of military life. This was the filter through which British society first came into regular contact with Rome, and had a formative influence on the development of Romano-British culture. For instance the evidence of diet has been used to show how high status sites in Britain adopted a military pattern of consumption, rather than a Mediterranean one (King 1984). This military pattern, involving a high consumption of beef, had developed to the north of the Alps in the course of the first century AD. The evidence of the architecture conforms to this model. The reduction of the peristyle to a winged-corridor facade, and the preference for housing commercial ventures within free-standing strip buildings, marked out a particular form of Roman architecture that had been developed north of the Alps.

Although the army may have inspired certain architectural preferences it was not uniquely important, and elite society in Britain had access to a range of other ideas and practices. These were elaborated differently by the various communities of the province, and there were marked differences between the Roman styles adopted in the different regions of Britain. The richest and most powerful families of Roman Silchester, for example, were more concerned to own a house that conformed to local ideas of sophistication than to copy directly from Rome, Trier or London. This urban society retained a local focus. Regional styles are most evident in aspects of decoration and design. Mosaics, in particular, have been used to identify regional preferences. But similar distinctions can also be found in the other aspects of decoration, such as the types of roof finial used and in the use of unusual architectural features such as cellars and octagonal rooms. When these features are plotted they show clear patterning. The fourth century distribution of regional mosaic styles reflects pre-Roman patterns of coin distributions (fig. 71). This is no coincidence. Both patterns reflect the distribution of high status sites within the landscape, and the different styles/coins represent different social affiliations. What this shows is that the networks of affiliation that applied in the fourth century had been inherited from the pre-Roman period. Change had occurred mainly in the ways in which those affiliations were described. Where once the members of a tribal aristocracy held coinage of a local king, they now used mosaics that drew on a shared repertoire of signs, symbols and meanings. Notwithstanding the considerable differences in the way in which power was expressed between the first and fourth centuries and in the systems of allegiance that underpinned that power, the pattern illustrates remarkable continuity. This shows that the adoption of decorative styles in the Roman period was influenced by these pre-established factors of regional identity. Beyond the better integration of some peripheral areas, the boundaries that Rome inherited, Rome kept. In some cases two or three different civilian administrations appear to have remained part of the same social and cultural network, such that it is difficult to spot any significant differences between the Atrebates and the Regni, or between the Trinovantes and the Catevellauni.

The regions that had not exploited pre-Roman coinage were least likely to

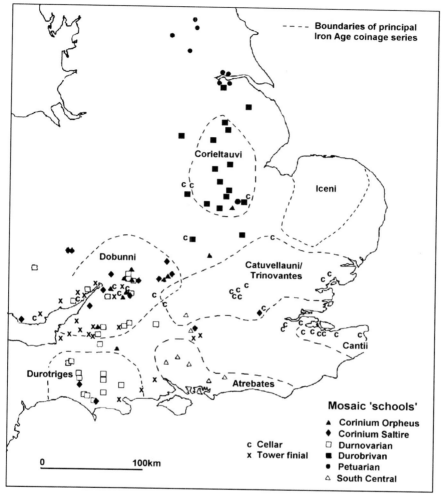

Figure 71 Distribution of styles of mosaics and some other features illustrative of regional
architectural traditions, showing also the abiding influence of pre-Roman tribal
identities on elite cultural groupings.

adopt Roman styles of architecture. The ability to participate in Roman
social life depended on the presence of a social hierarchy that was supported
by the private ownership of land and could command economic surplus. The
need to participate in Roman life, in the patronage networks for which the
architecture was designed, was driven by the desire to maintain this privileged
social position. The fact that villa society flourished amongst those communities that had previously made use of Iron Age coin supports the
suggestion that these areas had already developed the social structures

required. The communities that made use of Rome were those predisposed to do so. But even after three centuries of Roman rule, villa society had made little headway in many areas that had not used pre-Roman coin. Here we have not so much rejection as indifference.

Greg Woolf's study of Roman Gaul (1998) makes the important point that most studies of the Roman world have over-stressed the homogenising effects of Roman hegemony. Participation in complex systems promotes diversity. There was more than one route to power, and communities and individuals were faced with strategic choices about how best to align themselves. The different communities of power in Roman Britian included networks of land-owning aristocrats based on pre-Roman tribal affiliations, colonial cities, the imperial administration and army, and attendant communities of merchants and craftsmen. These groups elaborated different kinds of Roman house, but used shared spatial concepts.

By the fourth century, however, different interpretations of Romano-Hellenistic culture may have taken elite society to the point of conflict. Disagreement over belief systems, as perhaps illustrated by the growth and suppression of Gnosticism, may have exposed tensions between town and country, empire and community, state and citizen. If this were the case then it can be argued that Britain's problem was not that it had failed to absorb the culture of Rome, but that it had done so too well.

Town and country

Towns and villas were the scene of social life, but the relationship between the two is uncertain (Blagg 1990c). Rivet (1964), working from the writings of Varro, Virgil and Columella, saw the Roman villa as the country estate of a town-dweller. It is now more widely believed that town life in Roman Britain remained subordinate to the countryside (Drinkwater 1983). The town houses and villas described here were probably the property of an elite that was resident in both town and country. Just as the town house gave the rural gentry access to the social and economic benefits of civic life, so the villa took urban values into the countryside. Participation in Roman civic life depended on the ownership of urban property. For instance at Tarentum it was a requirement to maintain a house in town or within a mile of it. The size of house was specified as 1500 tiles, which has been seen as approximately equivalent to 140 m square (Hassall 1979: 243). Some town houses were perhaps designed for seasonal use, when the head of the household and his or her entourage attended on civic business and the social round (Esmonde-Cleary 1989: 80). Such arrangements might account for the design of some of the smaller town houses, better suited as occasional lodgings.

In the first Romano-British towns there is little evidence that status was demonstrated through rituals attached to the private houses. These were transient communities of merchants and officials. Most buildings were not built to last and the elite does not appear to have planned against permanent residence. Status may instead have been represented in other forms of consumption and display. This is suggested by the presence of high status goods and jewellery in early finds, assemblages. Improvements in urban architecture in the early second century witness the greater social ambitions of a property-owning class. It is not clear if this was the consequence of increased urban prosperity, or whether the faltering fortunes of urban merchants had made it easier for a landed aristocracy to assert their social primacy. The evidence from the larger towns suggests the latter (Perring 1991b). Patterns of dedications from Roman Britain show an emphasis on corporate bodies at the expense of the individual, perhaps indicating an absence of serious competition for power in this forum (Blagg 1990a, Millett 1990b: 82–4).

Notwithstanding the rural basis for the generation of wealth and power in provincial Roman Britain, villa distribution reflected urban influence. Expenditure on villa decoration is more evident in areas that had seen greater investment in urban facilities (Millett 1990b: 195). Administratively important centres also had a shallow fall-off in density of villas around them, while centres without administrative status had a more rapid fall-off (Hodder and Millett 1980). Villas were built in imitation of towns and provided urban facilities within the countryside. The villa, with its baths and walls, was in some respects a more important symbol of the Roman urban order than the town house. In towns status and power could be declared through public buildings and facilities. In town the private house only became important in the later period, when public facilities were no longer given equivalent architectural emphasis. In the countryside status more directly attached to the individual landowner from the outset. The constraints and limitations of crowded urban sites may also have added to the tendency to treat the villa as a more important site for the display of status.

In the later period the local elite remained responsible for raising taxes, now generally collected in kind rather than cash, but civic office had for many become more of a burden than an honour. Those who could do so gained exemption from the duties of magistracy. By the end of the third century military officers and administrators had largely replaced the traditional aristocracy at the head of the empire and were dominant in those cities that retained an administrative role. Provincial aristocracies were still made up of land-owning families but these were increasingly able to direct their affairs from the countryside. The political and social life of later Roman cities may have come to involve no more than a handful of leading families and state officials. The later Romano-British urban habit was arguably little more than an affectation of the rich, built on a variety of administrative rituals of increasingly peripheral importance.

Partly as a consequence of this elite domination, but also reflecting patterns that were common throughout the empire, Romano-British cities appear to have been comparatively well integrated. Only in the very first towns can it be argued that there was any zoning of class and function and even here the evidence is inconclusive. For the most part Romano-British cities were simply not large enough to have generated a segmentary society, beyond the fact that the main arterial roads leading into towns and flanking the main public buildings were liable to be more attractive to commercial uses.

Social change

The purpose of the architecture described here was not to demonstrate token loyalty to some remote imperial authority, but to enhance the standing of local magnates within a community of peers and to consolidate power over a circle of dependants. Property ownership was restricted, and villa owners were able to maintain social status through reference to traditional architectural forms. Changing fashion might allow certain forms to become redundant, but in the Romano-British countryside models that became fashionable in the second century AD were still being copied in the fourth. The contrast with the rapid change evident in Britain in the century following the conquest is striking. From the late second century until the early fourth the picture appears to be one of a small and comparatively secure elite, competing within itself. Decorative elements, such as wall paintings and mosaics, saw more rapid stylistic development.

The changes evident in second-century Roman Britain can be compared to developments in architectural formality in early imperial Italy. The shift of emphasis from *atrium* to peristyle in the Pompeiian house and the tendency towards a more formalised organisation of space, as in the layout of gardens, reflected changing social attitudes in the Augustan period (Jashemski 1979: 43–8). The more hierarchical and formalised use of space implies an increased concern for social distinctions. At Ostia a clear change in the nature of the housing – from a mix of rich and poor, commercial and residential in the early imperial *insulae*, to a city dominated by the *domus* houses of the rich in the later empire – was the product of second century changes. Epigraphic evidence illuminates the social context of these architectural changes; the social fluidity and commercial vigour of the early empire was followed by a widening gulf between rich and poor (Meiggs 1973: 235–62).

Something similar may have taken place in Roman Britain. Eleanor Scott (1990) has suggested that the development of winged-corridor facades and gateways in Romano-British villas might reflect social changes brought about by vulnerability to threat of market forces, in which the purpose of winged-corridor facades and courtyards was to provide a buffer between private rooms and the outside world. A different view of the social function of the portico has, however, been described here (p. 145). This was an architectural feature that closely reflected the prevailing social rituals of Rome and was intended more as a statement about elite affiliation and less about privacy. The layering of social encounters achieved by the portico was part of the Roman norm and conveys no particular message about the vulnerability or otherwise of the Romano-British elite.

Urban commerce appears to have become less important and more subordinate to the interests of the landed classes. Where wealth and good taste were previously expressed in the public sphere, with the consequent emphasis on public architecture, later Roman society placed greater importance on the individual. The increase in wealth and social complexity that came with empire contributed to the development of an increasingly segmentary society in which the aristocracy was less able to integrate all parts of the population (Nicolet 1980: 390). Earlier ideas of community, built from the social structures of the city-state, were increasingly irrelevant (Brown 1971: 66). Private houses and palaces became more important than public buildings. Later Romano-British houses followed patterns established in the earlier period, although increased emphasis was placed on ritual and ceremony. Extravagant reception suites dominated these houses. Wealth came to be used to define the social divide rather than bridge it; this was not just evident in the buildings of the period but also in social custom, dress and literature (MacMullen 1976: 72–3). Leone, in a discussion of Georgian domestic architecture which seems equally appropriate to the Roman house, points out that the regimented architecture created the inhibitions and isolation needed to prevent attack on the established order (Leone 1984: 27, see also Isaac 1982).

Cultural knowledge played an important role in defining rank, and however interpreted the mosaics of fourth-century Britain were clearly deployed to establish a distinction of taste and learning (Brown 1971, Scott 2000: 126–7). The Roman ruling class had long seen its role in the context of a civilising mission built on enlightened culture, on the values of *humanitas* (G. Woolf 1998: 55–7). Learning and understanding were what set the ruling classes apart, and this emphasis on educated culture (*otium*) undoubtedly contributed to the development of both the decorative arts of later Roman Britain and the philosophical ideas that inspired them. Roman culture and social practice not only represented the contingent as universal, but in some cases also appear to have offered a vision of eternal life. The biggest promise of all that was found in the Romano-British house was that of knowledge. For instance Gnostics were 'people who knew', and their knowledge at once constituted them a superior class of beings, whose present and future status was essentially different from that of those who, for whatever reason, did not know (Schaff 1889). The messages found here reinforced the values of an aristocratic society that was facing a series of threats to it status.

Concluding remarks

I have tried to show how elite society in Britain embraced the architecture, ideas and practices of Rome and made them its own. This was transparently the case in matters of construction technique and interior design, and a strong argument can be advanced to suggest that it was also the case in matters of social and household arrangements. The communities of Britain did not simply copy. They adapted and elaborated Roman architectural form against local needs, but were no less Roman as a consequence. A regional variation of Roman culture had developed around the army and its agents, and this contributed to differences that can be seen between Britain and the Mediterranean provinces. The emphasis given to the baths, porticoes and dining rooms suggests, however, that the social practices in Britain can be placed within the Hellenistic architectural tradition. The late development of Romano-British architecture, essentially a product of the early second century, may also have contributed to some of its individual characteristics. Towns were less central to social life in this period. One of the chief purposes of reception space in the late Romano-British house may have been to provide a setting for the rituals and arguments that in earlier periods would have been directed into the public sphere. Gnostic and kindred cosmographies can be used to explain many features of the private house. Given what we know of the beliefs of the time it is probable that dining rooms were used for Eucharistic worship, and that some plunge baths witnessed the occasional baptism. It should therefore be no surprise to find that some houses were configured and designed to provide an appropriate setting for such activities. It must be stressed that ritual and ceremony were always important in domestic life, and the elaborate celebration of religious mystery simply placed greater emphasis on such uses. There is no need to draw exaggerated distinctions between dining rooms and cult rooms or between private life and public activities.

One of the arguments presented here is that the Romano-British house was a departure that owed little to earlier British domestic architecture and which had little influence on what came after. This was manifestly the case in terms of building technology, spatial order, and interior design. The nature of the changes that accompanied the emergence and disappearance of the Roman house in Britain appears to sustain the view of Lefebvre (1991), who argued that spatial revolutions can be related to changes in the nature of the economic structure of power. In his view the creation of new types of space was a consequence of shifts from one system of economic control (ancient, feudal and capitalist) to another. This supposes that spatial identities were created by the forces and relations of production, and not by ideologies (Lefebvre 1991: 210). Marxist models hold that the transformations that accompanied the creation and destruction of ancient society were economic and attached to the changing modes of production. Fundamental to this was a shift in power relations from systems articulated through the control of people to ones articulated through the control of land (A. Woolf 1998: 113).

But the argument developed here is a different one. It is my view that the spatial identities and visual patterns created by Romano-British houses were essentially ideological. Houses were designed to declare cultural affiliations defined by shared social practices and beliefs. Although such ideologies are built to serve the interests of economic systems, and therefore reproduce them, the relationship is an indirect one. Roman architecture was the product of a particular understanding of space, and contributed to the replication of a power that was differently conceived to that which came before and after.

But do different spatial concepts and expressions of identity relate to modes of production? Roman architecture, as Rome itself, depended on modes of production based on the ownership of land and the extraction of surplus in the form of taxes and rents. Roman approaches to space could not be developed without certain preconditions being met, but its evolution was not an inevitable corollary of the imposition of Roman administration.

Elite society was better able to extract surplus and accumulate wealth under Rome than previously. Intensification was evident. But power had probably been based on the ownership of land for some time prior to the introduction of Roman building styles. The architectural choices may have reflected changes in the manifestation of power rather than its economic structure. The way in which power was represented changed as a consequence of changing social allegiances. The acceptance of Roman social models can be treated simply as a changed means of expression of power. Some of elite society embraced the Roman argument because they believed in it. The importance of this architecture goes beyond the need to impress clients and establish the status of individual patrons. Social cohesion was also reinforced by a shared world-view, an ideology. In the Roman world power resided in ownership and knowledge. Investment in property followed from choices made about affiliation to the power structures of Rome and had a positive feedback, since landscape improvement could both improve the ability to generate and replicate surplus.

The houses that have been described here owed their architectural complexity to their social context. They were designed as monuments to the prosperity that flowed from the established social order, and as theatres for regulated social interaction. These were very Roman buildings, used in ways that would have been familiar to elite society throughout the Roman world, but which had no place in defining social order where the Rome was not accepted. The messages that these buildings conveyed, and the social practices that they housed, were of Rome. When Britain no longer belonged to that world, and with the rejection of the Roman urban model of social life, these structures were inevitably redundant. The particular patterns of social life that Rome introduced to Britain were never revived.

BIBLIOGRAPHY

Abramson, P., 1999, 'The Major Trenches: Excavations of the Vicus, 1974 and 1980–82', in
C. Philo and S. Wrathmell (eds), *Roman Castleford 2: Excavations 1974–85. The Structural
and Environmental Evidence*, Yorkshire Archaeology 5, 126–51.

Adam, J.P., 1994, *Roman Building: Materials and Techniques* (transl. A. Mathews), London.

Agache, R., 1975, 'La Campagne à l'époque Romaine dans les grandes plaines du Nord de la
France', in H. Temporini (ed.), *Aufstieg und Niedergang der Romische Welt* 2.4, Berlin/New
York, 658–713.

Allason-Jones, L., 1990, *Women in Roman Britain*, London.

Allison, P., 1993, 'How do we Identify the use of Space in Roman Housing', in E.M.
Moorman (ed.), *Functional and Spatial Analysis of Wall Painting. Procs 5th International
Congress on Ancient Wall Painting*, Leiden, 1–8.

Alston, R., 1997, 'Houses and Households in Roman Egypt', in R. Laurence and A. Wallace-
Hadrill (eds), *Domestic Space in the Roman World: Pompeii and Beyond*, Journ. Roman
Archaeol. Suppl. Ser. 22, Michigan, 25–40.

Anderson, A.S. and Wacher, J.S., 1980, 'Excavations at Wanborough, Wiltshire: An Interim
Report', *Britannia* 11, 115–26.

André, N. 1976, 'Maisons en abside d'époque Grecque archaique de la Monedière à Bessan
(Herrault)', *Gallia* 34, 95–128.

Applebaum, S. 1972, 'Roman Britain', in H.P.R. Finberg (ed.), *The Agrarian History of
England and Wales* 1.2, Cambridge, 3–277.

Ashby, T., 1905, 'Excavations at Caerwent Monmouthshire on the Site of the Romano-British
City of Venta Silurum in 1904', *Archaeologia* 59, 289–310.

—— 1906, 'Excavations at Caerwent Monmouthshire on the Site of the Romano-British
City of Venta Silurum in 1905', *Archaeologia* 60, 111–30.

Ashby, T., Hudd, A.E. and King, F., 1910, 'Excavations at Caerwent Monmouthshire on the
site of the Romano-British City of Venta Silurum in the year 1908', *Archaeologia* 62.1, 1–20.

—— 1911, 'Excavations at Caerwent, Monmouthshire on the site of the Romano-British City
of Venta Silurum in the years 1909 and 1910', *Archaeologia* 62.2, 405–48.

Ashby, T., Hudd, A.E. and Martin, A.T., 1901, 'Excavations at Caerwent Monmouthshire on
the Site of the Romano-British City of Venta Silurum', *Archaeologia* 57, 295ff.

—— 1902, 'Excavations at Caerwent Monmouthshire on the Site of the Romano-British City
of Venta Silurum in 1901', *Archaeologia* 58, 1ff.

—— 1903, 'Excavations at Caerwent Monmouthshire on the site of the Romano-British City
of Venta Silurum in 1902', *Archaeologia* 58, 391–406.

—— 1904, 'Excavations at Caerwent Monmouthshire on the Site of the Romano-British City of Venta Silurum in 1901–3', *Archaeologia* 59, 1ff.

Atkinson, D., 1929, 'The Roman Villa of Gayton Thorpe', *Norfolk Arch.* 23, 166–209.

—— 1932, 'Caistor Excavations 1929', *Norfolk Arch.* 24, 93–133.

Baldwin Smith, F., 1956, *Architectural Symbolism of Imperial Rome and the Middle Ages*, Princeton.

Barker, P., 1975, 'Excavations on the Site of the Baths Basilica at Wroxeter 1966–1974: An Interim Report', *Britannia* 6, 106–17.

Barker, W.R., 1900, 'Remains of a Roman Villa Discovered at Brislington, Bristol, December, 1899', *Trans. Bristol and Glos. Archaeol. Soc.* 23, 289–308.

Barrett, A.A., 1978, 'Literary Classics in Roman Britain', *Britannia* 9, 307–14.

Barrett, J.C., 1987, 'The Glastonbury Lake Village: Models and Source Criticism', *Archaeol. Journ.* 144, 409–23.

Bateman, N., 1986, 'Bridgehead Revisited', *London Archaeol.* 5.9, 233–41.

Beard, M., 1985, 'Writing and Ritual. A Study of Diversity and Expansion in the Arval Acta', *Papers British School at Rome* 53 (NS40), 114–62.

Bek, L., 1983, 'Questiones Convivales: The Idea of the Triclinium and the Staging of Convivial Ceremony from Rome to Byzantium', *Analecta romana Instituti danici* 12, 81–107.

Bell, M., 1990, *Brean Down: Excavations 1983–1987*, London.

Bennett, C.M., 1963, 'Cox Green Roman Villa', *Berks. Arch. Journ.* 60, 62–91.

Bergmann, B., 1995, 'Visualizing Pliny's villas', *Journ. Roman Archaeol.* 8, 406–20.

Berry, C.A.F., 1951, 'The Dating of Romano-British Houses', *Journ. Roman Studies* 41, 25–31.

Bidwell, P.T., 1979, *The Legionary Bath-House and Basilica and Forum at Exeter*, Exeter.

—— 1985, *The Roman Fort of Vindolanda*, HBMC Archaeol. Rep. 1, London.

—— 1996, 'The Exterior Decoration of Roman Buildings in Britain', in P. Johnson with I. Hayes (eds), *Architecture in Roman Britain*, CBA Res. Rep. 94, York, 19–32.

Bietti Sestieri, A.M., de Grossi Mazzorin, J. and De Santis, A., 1990, 'Fidenae: La struttura dell'età del ferro', *Archeologia Laziale* 10, 115–20.

Birley, A.R., 1979, *The People of Roman Britain*, London.

—— 1993, 'Review of R.G. Collingwood and R.P. Wright: *RIB*, Vol. 2, Instrumentum Domesticum (Personal Belongings and the Like)', *Journ. Roman Studies* 83, 237–9.

Birley, R., 1977, *Vindolanda: A Roman Frontier Post on Hadrian's Wall*, London.

Bishop, M.C. and Dore, J.N., 1988, *Corbridge. Excavations of the Roman Fort and Town, 1947–1980*, HBMCE Archaeol. Rep. 8, London.

Black, E.W., 1985, 'Hypocaust Heating in Domestic Rooms in Roman Britain', *Oxford Journ. Archaeol.* 4.1, 77–92.

—— 1987, *The Roman Villas of South East England*, BAR Brit. Ser. 171, Oxford.

—— 1994, 'Villa-owners: Romano British Gentlemen and Officers', *Britannia* 25, 99–110.

Blagg, T.F.C., 1976, 'Tools and Techniques of the Roman Stonemason in Britain', *Britannia* 7, 152–72.

—— 1977, 'Schools of Stonemasons in Britain', in J. Munby and M. Henig (eds.), *Roman Life and Art in Britain*, BAR Brit. Ser. 41.1, Oxford, 51–74.

—— 1979, 'The Use of Terra-Cotta for Architectural Ornament in Italy and the Western Provinces', in A. McWhirr (ed.), *Roman Brick and Tile*, BAR Int. Ser. 68, Oxford, 267–84.

—— 1980, 'Roman Civil and Military Architecture in the Province of Britain', *World Archaeol.* 12.1, 27–42.

—— 1982, 'Reconstruction of Roman Decorated Architecture: Proportions, Prescriptions, and Practices', in P.J. Drury (ed.), *Structural Reconstruction. Approaches to the Interpretation of the Excavated Remains of Buildings*, BAR British Ser. 110, Oxford, 131–52.

225

—— 1984, 'An Examination of the Connections Between Military and Civilian Architecture in Roman Britain', in T.F.C. Blagg and A.C. King (eds), *Military and Civilian in Roman Britain*, BAR Brit. Ser. 136, Oxford, 249–63.

—— 1990a, 'Architectural Munificence in Britain: The Evidence of Inscriptions', *Britannia* 21, 13–32.

—— 1990b, 'Building Stone in Roman Britain', in D. Parsons (ed.), *Stone: Quarrying and Building in England AD 43–1525*, Phillimore, 33–50.

—— 1990c, 'First-century Roman Houses in Gaul and Britain', in T.F.C. Blagg and M. Millett (eds), *The Early Roman Empire in the West*, Oxford, 194–209.

—— 1991, 'Buildings', in R.F.J. Jones (ed.), *Roman Britain: Recent Trends*, Sheffield, 3–14.

—— 1996, 'The External Decoration of Romano-British Buildings', in P. Johnson with I. Hayes (eds), *Architecture in Roman Britain*, CBA Res. Rep. 94, York, 9–18.

Blanchard-Lemeé, M., Olivier, A. and Rebourg, A., 1986, 'Deux maisons à pavements d'Augustodunum (Autun, Saône et Loire)', *Gallia* 44, 120–49.

Blockley, K., 1985, *Marshfield, Ironmongers Piece, Excavations 1982–3: An Iron Age and Romano-British Settlement in the South Cotswolds*, BAR Brit. Ser. 141, Oxford.

Blockley, K. and Day, M., 1979, 'Marlowe Car Park Excavations', in 'Interim Report on Excavations in 1980 by the Canterbury Archaeological Trust', *Arch. Cant.* 95, 265–78.

Blockley, K., Blockley, M., Blockley, P., Frere, S.S. and Stow, S., 1995, *Excavations in the Marlowe Car Park and Surrounding Areas*, Archaeol. Canterbury 5, Canterbury.

Bloemers, J.H.F., 1985, 'Le Nord-Ouest de l'empire: Le bassins de l'Escaut, de la Meuse et du Rhin', in J. Lasfargues (ed.), *Architectures de terre et de bois*, Documents D'Archéologie Française 2, Paris, 131–42.

Boddington, A. and Marsden, P., 1987, '160–162 Fenchurch Street, 1976', in P. Marsden (ed.), *The Roman Forum Site in London: Discoveries before 1985*, London, 92–100.

Bodel, J., 1997, 'Monumental Villas and Villa Monuments', *Journ. Roman Archaeol.* 10, 5–35.

Boersma, J.A., 1985, Amoenissima Civitas. *Block V.ii at Ostia: Description and Analysis of its Visible Remains*, Assen.

Boethius, A., 1960, *The Golden House of Nero. Some Aspects of Roman Architecture*, Ann Arbor.

—— 1978, *Etruscan and Early Roman Architecture* (revised by R. Ling and T. Rasmussen), Harmondsworth.

Boon, G.C., 1950, 'The Roman Villa in Kingsweston Park (Lawrence Weston Estate) Gloucestershire', *Trans. Bristol and Glos. Archaeol. Soc.* 69, 5–39.

—— 1974, *Silchester: The Roman Town of Calleva*, Newton Abbot.

—— 1983, 'Some Romano-British Domestic Shrines and their Inhabitants', in B. Hartley and J. Wacher (eds), *Rome and her Northern Provinces*, Gloucester, 33–55.

Brakspear, H., 1904, 'The Roman Villa at Box, Wiltshire', *Archaeol. Journ.* 61, 1–32.

Branigan, K., 1971, *Latimer*, Bristol.

—— 1972, 'The Romano-British Villa at Brislington', *Procs Somersetshire Archaeol. and Nat. Hist. Soc.* 116, 79–85.

—— 1976, *The Roman Villa in South-West England*, Bradford-on-Avon.

Brigham, T., 1990, 'The Late Roman Waterfront in London', *Britannia* 21, 99–184.

Brigham, T. and Watson, B., 1996, 'Current Archaeological Work at Regis House in the City of London, *London Archaeol.* 8, 31–7.

Brigham, T., Goodburn, D. and Tyres, I., with Dillon, J., 1995, 'A Roman Timber Building on the Southwark Waterfront, London', *Archaeol. Journ.* 152, 1–72.

Brinson, J., 1963, 'Chesterford, Great', in M.R. Hull (ed.), 'Roman Gazeteer', *The Victoria History of the Counties of England: A History of Essex* 3, 72–88.

Brodribb, G., 1979, 'Tile from the Roman Bath House at Beauport Park', *Britannia* 10, 139–56.

Brodribb, G. and Cleere, H., 1988, 'The *Classis Britannica* Bath-house at Beauport Park, East Sussex', *Britannia* 19, 217–74.

Brodribb, A.C.C., Hands, A.R. and Walker, D.R., 1968–78, *Excavations at Shakenoak Farm, Near Wilcote, Oxon*, Parts 1–5, Oxford.

Brown, F.E., 1974–5, 'La protostoria della Regia', *Atti della Ponteficia Accademia Romana di Archeologia*.

—— 1990, 'Comment on Chapman: Some Cautionary Notes on the Application of Spatial Measures to Prehistoric Settlements', in R. Samson (ed.), *The Social Archaeology of Houses*, Edinburgh, 93–109

Brown, P., 1971, *The World of Late Antiquity*, London.

Bruneau, P., 1978, 'Deliaca, II', *Bulletin de Correspondance Hellénique* 102.1, 109–45

Buckland, P.C., 1988, 'The Stones of York, Building Materials from Roman Yorkshire', in J. Price and P.R. Wilson (eds), *Recent Research in Roman Yorkshire. Studies in Honour of Mary Kitson Clark*, BAR Brit. Ser. 193, Oxford, 267–75.

Bulleid, A., and St George Gray, H., 1911, *The Glastonbury Lake Village*, Vol. 1, Taunton.

Burch, M., Lees, D., Hill, J., Rowsome, P., Jones, S. and Treveil, P., 1997, 'Number 1 Poultry – the Main Excavation: Roman Sequence', *London Archaeol.* 8, 127–36.

Burnham, B. and Burnham, H., 1991, 'A Burnt Timber Building from within the Fort at Pumsaint', *Britannia* 22, 203–7.

Burnham, B.C. and Wacher, J., 1990, *The 'Small Towns' of Roman Britain*, London.

Bushe-Fox, J.P., 1913, *Excavations on the Site of the Roman Town at Wroxeter, Shropshire, in 1912*, Soc. of Antiqs Res. Rep. 1, Oxford.

—— 1916, *Excavations on the Site of the Roman Town at Wroxeter, Shropshire, in 1914*, Soc. of Antiqs Res. Rep. 4, Oxford.

Carandini, A., 1990, 'Il palatino e le aree residenziali', *La Grande Roma dei Tarquini, Roma: Palazzo delle Espozioni, Catalogo della Mostra*, Rome, 97–9.

Carandini, A. and Ricci, A. (eds), 1985, *Settefinestre: una villa schiavistica nell' Etruria Romana: 1, La villa nel suo insieme*, Modena.

Carcopino, J., 1941, *Daily Life in Ancient Rome* (transl. E.O. Lorimer), Harmondsworth.

Casey, J., 1985, 'The Roman Housing Market', in F.O. Grew and B. Hobley (eds), *Roman Urban Topography in Britain and the Western Empire*, CBA, Res. Rep. 59, London, 43–8.

Casey, J. and Hoffman, B., 1998, 'Rescue Excavations in the Vicus of the Fort at Greta Bridge, Co. Durham 1972–4', *Britannia* 29, 111–83.

Chapman, H., 1979, 'A Roman Mitre and Try Square from Canterbury', *Antiq. Journ.* 59, 403–7.

—— 1981, 'Two Ceramic Representations of Roman Buildings from the City of London', in A.C. Anderson and A.S. Anderson (eds), *Roman Pottery Research in Britain and North-West Europe*, BAR Int. Ser. 123, Oxford, 511–16.

Charles, F.W.B., 1982, 'The Construction of Buildings with Irregularly-Spaced Posts', in P.J. Drury (ed.), *Structural Reconstruction: Approaches to the Interpretation of the Excavated Remains of the Buildings*, BAR Brit. Ser. 110, Oxford, 101–12.

Charles-Edwards, T.M., 1972, 'Kinship, Status and the Origin of the Hide', *Past and Present* 56, 3–33.

Choisy, A., 1873, *L'art de batir chez les romaines*, Paris.

Clarke, D.L., 1972, 'A Provisional Model of an Iron Age Society and its Settlement System', in D.L. Clarke (ed.), *Models in Archaeology*, London, 801–85.

Clarke, G., 1982, 'The Roman Villa at Woodchester', *Britannia* 13, 197–228.

Clarke, J.R., 1991, *The Houses of Roman Italy, 100 BC – AD 250*, Oxford.

Clifford, E.M., 1954, 'The Roman Villa, Witcombe', *Trans. Bristol and Glos. Arch. Soc.* 73, 5–69.

Cocks, A., 1921, 'A Romano-British Homestead, in the Hambledon Valley, Bucks.', *Archaeologia* 71, 141–57.

Coles, J.M., Heal, S.V.E. and Orme, B.J., 1978, 'The Use and Character of Wood in Prehistoric Britain and Ireland', *Procs Prehistoric Soc.* 44, 1–46.

Collingwood, R.G. and Richmond, I.A., 1969, *The Archaeology of Roman Britain*, 2nd edn, London.

Cook, S.F. and Heizer, R.F., 1968, 'Relationships among Houses, Settlement Areas and Population in Aboriginal California', in K.C. Chang (ed.), *Settlement Archaeology*, California, 79–116.

Corder, P., 1954, *The Roman Town and Villa at Great Casterton, Rutland. 2nd Interim Report for the Years 1951–1953*, Oxford.

Corder, P. and Kirk, J.L., 1932, *A Roman Villa at Langton, near Malton, East Yorkshire*, Oxford.

Cortet, O., 1971, *Sous-sols caves dans l'habitat gallo-romaine (Cote d'Or, excepte' Alesia)*, Dijon.

Cotton, M.A., 1947, 'Excavations at Silchester 1938–9', *Archaeologia* 92, 120–67.

Coulon, G. and Joly, D., 1985, 'La Gaule Intérieure: Le Centre', in J. Lasfargues (ed.), *Architectures de terre et de bois*, Documents D'Archéologie Française 2, Paris, 93–102.

Cowan, C., 1995 (for 1992), 'A Possible Mansio in Roman Southwark: Excavations at 15–23 Southwark Street, 1980–6', *Trans. London and Middx Archaeol. Soc.* 43, 3–191.

Crummy, P., 1980, 'Mosaics from Middleborough, Colchester', *Mosaic* 2, 5–9.

—— 1984, *Excavations at Lion Walk, Balkerne Lane, and Middleborough, Colchester, Essex*, Colchester Archaeol. Rep. 3, Colchester.

——1988, 'Colchester (Camulodunum/Colonia Victriciensis)', in G. Webster (ed.), *Fortress into City. The Consolidation of Roman Britain, First Century AD*, London, 24–47.

—— 1992, *Excavations at Culver Street, the Gilberd School, and Other Sites in Colchester 1971–85*, Colchester Archaeol. Rep. 6, Colchester.

Cunliffe, B.W., 1964, *Winchester Excavations 1949–60, Vol. 1*, Winchester.

—— 1971a, *Excavations at Fishbourne 1961–69 Vol. 1*, Soc. of Antiqs Res. Rep. 26, Leeds.

—— 1971b, *Excavations at Fishbourne 1961–69 Vol. 2*, Soc. of Antiqs Res. Rep. 26, Leeds.

—— 1978, *Iron Age Communities in Britain*, London.

—— 1988, *Greeks, Romans and Barbarians. Spheres of Interaction*, London.

D'Arms, J., 1970, *Romans on the Bay of Naples. Social and Cultural Studies of the Villas and their Owners from 150 BC to AD 400*, Cambridge, MA.

Dark, K. and Dark, P., 1997, *The Landscape of Roman Britain*, Stroud.

Darling, M.J., 1987, 'The Caistor-By-Norwich "Massacre' Reconsidered", *Britannia* 18, 263–72.

Davey, N., 1961, *A History of Building Materials*, London.

Davey, N. and Ling, R., 1982, *Wall Painting in Roman Britain*, Soc. Prom. Roman Studies, London.

De Boe, G., 1986, 'Het ontstaan en de ontwikkeling van de Romeinse "vicus" te Grobbendonk', *Acta Archaeologica Lovanensia* 25, 101–18.

de Chazelles, C.A., Fiches J.L. and Poupet, P., 1985, 'La Gaule Méridionale', in J. Lasfargues (ed.), *Architectures de terre et de bois*, Documents D'Archéologie Française 2, Paris, 61–72.

de la Bedoyere, G., 1991, *The Buildings of Roman Britain*, London.

Degbomont, J.-M., 1984, *Le Chauffage par hypocauste dans l'habitat privé. De la place St-Lambert à Liege à l'Aula Palatina de Trèves* (2nd edn), Etudes et Recherches Archéologiques de l'Université de Liège.

Deletang, H., 1982, 'Contribution de la photographie aerienne a l'etude typologique des villas Gallo-Romaines da sud de la beauce', in *La villa Romaine dans les provinces du nord-ouest*, Caesorodunum, 17.

Desbat, A., 1981, 'L'architecture de terre à Lyon à l'époque romaine', in S. Walker (ed.), *Récentes recherches en archéologie gallo-romaine et palaeochrétienne sur Lyon et sa région*, BAR, Int. Ser. 108, Oxford, 55–81.

—— 1985, 'La Gaule Intérieure: La région de Lyon et de Vienne', in J. Lasfargues (ed.), *Architectures de terre et de bois*, Documents D'Archéologie Française 2, Paris, 75–84.

—— 1992, 'Note sur l'apparition des constructiones à arases de briques dans la région lyonnaise', *Gallia* 49, 45–50.

Detsicas, A., 1964, 'Excavations at Eccles, 1963. Second Interim Report', *Arch. Cant.* 80, 121–35.

—— 1974, 'Excavations at Eccles, 1973. Twelfth Interim Report', *Arch. Cant.* 89, 119–34.

Dickmann, J.A., 1997, 'The Peristyle and the Transformation of Domestic Space in Hellenistic Pompeii', in R. Laurence and A. Wallace-Hadrill (eds), *Domestic Space in the Roman World: Pompeii and Beyond*, Journ. Roman Archaeol. Suppl. Ser. 22, Michigan, 121–36.

Dilke, O.A.W., 1985, 'Ground Survey and Measurement in Roman Towns', in F.O. Grew and B. Hobley (eds), *Roman Urban Topography in Britain and the Western Empire*, CBA Res. Rep. 59, London, 6–13.

Dixon, P., 1982, 'How Saxon is the Saxon house?', in P.J. Drury (ed.), *Structural Reconstruction: Approaches to the Interpretation of the Excavated Remains of the Buildings*, BAR Brit. Ser. 110, Oxford, 275–88.

Down, A., 1979, *Chichester Excavations 4: The Roman villas at Chilgrove and Upmarden*, Chichester.

Drew, C.D. and Selby K.C., 1937, 'First Interim Report on the Excavations at Colliton Park, Dorchester 1937–8', *Procs Dorset Nat. Hist. and Archaeol. Soc.* 59, 1–14.

Drinkwater, J.F., 1983, *Roman Gaul*, London.

Drury, P.J., 1975, 'Roman Chelmsford – Caesoromagus', in W. Rodwell and T. Rowley (eds), *The Small Towns of Roman Britain*, BAR Brit. Ser. 15, Oxford, 159–73.

—— 1982, 'Form, Function and the Interpretation of the Excavated Plans of some Large Secular Romano-British Buildings', in P.J. Drury (ed.), *Structural Reconstruction: Approaches to the Interpretation of the Excavated Remains of the Buildings*, BAR Brit. Ser. 110, Oxford, 289–308.

Dunbabin, K.M.D., 1978, *The Mosaics of Roman North Africa: Studies in Iconography and Patronage*, Oxford.

—— 1991, 'Triclinium and Stibadium', in W.J. Slater (ed.), *Dining in a Classical Context*, Ann Arbor, 121–48.

—— 1993, 'Wine and Water at the Roman Convivium', *Journ. Roman Archaeol.* 6, 116–41.

Dunnet, B.R.K., 1966, 'Excavations on North Hill, Colchester', *Archaeol. Journ.* 123, 27–61.

Ellis, S.P., 1988, 'The End of the Roman House', *American Journ. Archaeol.* 92, 565–76.

—— 1995, 'Classical Reception Rooms in Romano-British Houses', *Britannia* 26, 163–78.

—— 2000, *Roman Housing*, London.

Esmonde-Cleary, A.S., 1989, *The Ending of Roman Britain*, London.

—— 1993, 'Roman Britain in 1992, I Sites Explored: England', *Britannia* 24, 284–309.

—— 1997, 'Roman Britain in 1996, I Sites Explored: England', *Britannia* 28, 414–53.

—— 1998, 'Roman Britain in 1997, I Sites Explored: England', *Britannia* 29, 381–432.

Evans, E., 1994, 'Military Architects and Building Design in Roman Britain', *Britannia* 25, 143–64.

Fabbricotti, E., 1976, 'I bagni nelle prime ville romane', *Cronache Pompeiane* 11, 29–111.

Faulkner, N., 1997, 'Verulamium: Interpreting Decline', *Archaeol. Journ.* 153 (for 1996), 79–103.

—— 2000, *The Decline and Fall of Roman Britain*, Stroud.

Flitcroft, M. and Tester, A., 1994, 'Scole', *Current Archaeol.* 140, 322–5.

Foss, P., 1997, 'Househould Organization and the Rituals of Cooking and Eating', in R. Laurence and A. Wallace-Hadrill (eds), *Domestic Space in the Roman World: Pompeii and Beyond*, Journ. Roman Archaeol. Suppl. Ser. 22, Michigan, 196–218.

Foster, S.M., 1989, 'Analysis of Spatial Patterns in Buildings (Access Analysis) as an Insight into Social Structure: Examples from the Scottish Iron Age', *Antiquity* 63, 40–50.

Fouet, G., 1969, *La villa gallo-romaine de Montmaurin, Haute-Garonne*, Gallia Suppl., 20.

Fox, G.E., 1887, 'The Roman Villa at Chedworth, Gloucestershire', *Arch. Journ.* 44, 322–36.

—— 1895, 'Excavations on the Site of the Roman City at Silchester, Hants, in 1894', *Archaeologia* 54, 439ff.

Fox, G.E. and St John Hope, W.H., 1890, 'Excavations on the Site of the Roman City at Silchester, Hants', *Archaeologia* 52, 733ff.

—— 1894, 'Excavations on the Site of the Roman City at Silchester, Hants, in 1893', *Archaeologia* 54, 199–238.

—— 1896, 'Excavations on the Site of the Roman City at Silchester, Hants, in 1895', *Archaeologia* 55, 215–56.

—— 1898, 'Excavations on the Site of the Roman City at Silchester, Hants, in 1897', *Archaeologia* 56.1, 103ff.

—— 1899, 'Excavations on the Site of the Roman City at Silchester, Hants, in 1898', *Archaeologia* 56.2, 229–50.

—— 1901, 'Excavations on the Site of the Roman City at Silchester, Hants, in 1900', *Archaeologia* 57.2, 229–51.

Frend, W.H.C., 1992, 'Pagans, Christians, and "the Barbarian Conspiracy" of AD 367 in Roman Britain', *Britannia* 23, 121–31.

Frere, S.S., 1964 (for 1962), 'Excavations at Dorchester on Thames, 1962', *Archaeol. Journ.* 119, 114–49.

—— 1972, *Verulamium Excavations 1*, Soc. of Antiqs Res. Rep. 28, London.

—— 1982, 'The Bignor Villa', *Britannia* 13, 135–96.

—— 1983, *Verulamium Excavations 2*, Soc. of Antiqs Res. Rep. 41, London.

—— 1984, 'Roman Britain in 1983. I: Sites Explored', *Britannia* 15, 266–332.

—— 1985, 'Roman Britain in 1984. I: Sites Explored', *Britannia* 16, 251–316.

—— 1986, 'Roman Britain in 1985. I: Sites Explored', *Britannia* 17, 364–427.

—— 1987: *Britannia: A History of Roman Britain* (3rd edn), London.

—— 1991, 'Roman Britain in 1990. I: Sites Explored', *Britannia* 22, 222–92.

Frere, S.S. and Williams, A., 1948, 'Canterbury Excavations, Christmas 1945 and Easter, 1946', *Arch. Cantiana* 61, 1–44.

Frézouls, E., 1982, *Les Villes Antiques de la France I. Belgique*, Strasbourg.

Gallet de Santerre, H., 1978, *Ensérune*, Paris.

Gardner, J.F. and Wiedemann, T., 1991, *The Roman Household: A Sourcebook*, London and New York.

Garnsey, P.D.A. and Saller R.P., 1987, *The Roman Empire. Economy, Society and Culture*, London.

George, M., 1997, '*Servus* and *Domus*: The Slave in the Roman House', in R. Laurence and A. Wallace-Hadrill (eds), *Domestic Space in the Roman World: Pompeii and Beyond*, Journ. Roman Archaeol. Suppl. Ser. 22, Michigan, 15–24.

Giles, A.G., 1981, 'Interim Report on the Excavation of Barton Field, Tarrant Hinton, for 1980', *Procs Dorset Nat. Hist. and Arch. Soc.* 103, 90–1.

Glasbergen, W., 1972 (for 1967), *De Romeinse Castella te Valkenburg ZH. Cingula 1.*

Glassie, H., 1975, *Folk Housing in Middle Virginia: A Structural Analysis of Historic Artifacts,* Tennessee.

Godwin, E.W., 1856, 'Account of a Roman Villa Discovered at Colerne, in the County of Wilts.', *Archaeol. Journ.* 13, 328–32.

Going, C., 1997, 'Roman', in J. Glazebrook (ed.), *Research and Archaeology: A Framework for the Eastern Counties, 1. Resource Assessment,* East Anglian Archaeology Occasional Paper 3, Norwich, 35–46.

Goodburn, D., 1992 (for 1991) 'A Roman Timber Framed Building Tradition', *Archaeol. Journ.* 148, 182–204.

—— 1995, 'Beyond the Post-hole: Notes on Stratigraphy and Timber Buildings from a London Perspective', in E. Shepherd (ed.), *Interpreting Stratigraphy 5,* 43–52.

Goodburn, R., 1976, 'Roman Britain in 1975. I: Sites Explored', *Britannia* 7, 291–377.

Goudineau, C., 1979, *Les Fouilles de la Maison au Dauphin,* Paris: 37 suppl. à Gallia.

Gracie, H.S., 1970, 'Frocester Court Roman Villa: First Report', *Trans. Bristol and Glos. Arch. Soc.* 89, 15–86.

Graham, A.H., 1988, 'District Heating Scheme', in P. Hinton (ed.), *Excavations in Southwark 1973–76, Lambeth 1973–9,* London and Middx Archaeol. Soc. and Surrey Archaeol. Soc. Joint Publication 3, London, 27–54.

Grahame, M., 1997, 'Public and Private in the Roman House: the Casa del Fauno', in R. Laurence and A. Wallace-Hadrill (eds), *Domestic Space in the Roman World: Pompeii and Beyond,* Journ. Roman Archaeol. Suppl. Ser. 22, Michigan, 137–64.

—— 1998 'Material Culture and Roman Identity. The Spatial Layout of Pompeian Houses and the problem of Ethnicity', in R. Laurence and J. Berry (eds), *Cultural Identity in the Roman Empire,* London and New York, 156–78.

Green, C. and Draper, J., 1978, 'The Mileoak Roman Villa, Handley, Towcester, Northampton-shire. Report on the Excavations of 1955 and 1956', *Northants Archaeol.* 13, 28–66.

Green, H.J.M., 1982, 'The Origins and Development of Cruck Construction in Eastern England', in P.J. Drury (ed.), *Structural Reconstruction: Approaches to the Interpretation of the Excavated Remains of Buildings,* BAR Brit. Ser. 110, Oxford, 87–100.

Greene, K., 1986, *The Archaeology of the Roman Economy,* London.

Greenfield, E.D., 1959, 'A Note on the Villa at Great Staughton, Rutland', *Journ. Roman Studies* 49, 118.

Gregson, M., 1982, 'The Villa as Private Property', in K. Ray (ed.), *Young Archaeologist: Collected Unpublished Papers, Contributions to Archaeological Thinking and Practice,* Cambridge, 143–91.

Gresham, C.A., 1971 'Gravelkind and the Unit System', *Archaeol. Journ.* 128, 174–5.

Griffiths, J.G., 1975, *Apuleius of Madauros. The Isis Book (Metamorphoses, Book xi),* Etudes Preliminaire aux religiones orientales dans l'empire Romain 39, Leiden.

Grimal, P. and Woloch M., 1983, *Roman Cities,* Madison.

Grimes, W.F., 1968, *The Excavation of Roman and Mediaeval London,* London.

Gurney, D., 1986, *Settlement, Religion and Industry on the Fen-edge: Three Romano-British Sites in Norfolk,* Hunstanton.

Hadman, J., 1978, 'Aisled Buildings in Roman Britain', in M. Todd (ed.), *Studies in the Romano-British Villa,* Leicester, 187–96.

Hamerow, H., 1994, 'Migration Theory and the Migration Period', in B. Vyner (ed.), *Building on the Past. Papers Celebrating 150 Years of the Royal Archaeological Institute,* London.

Hammer, F., 1985, 'Early Roman Buildings in Fenchurch Street', *Popular Archaeol.* 6.12, 7–13.

Hanson, W.S., 1978, 'Roman Military Timber-Supply', *Britannia* 9, 293–305.

—— 1982, 'Roman Military Timber Buildings: Construction and Reconstruction', in S. McGrail (ed.), *Woodworking Techniques before AD 1500*, BAR Int. Ser. 129, Oxford, 169–86.

—— 1997, 'Forces of Change and Methods of Control', in D.J. Mattingly (ed.), *Dialogues in Roman Imperialism. Power, Discourse, and Discrepant Experience in the Roman Empire*, Journ. Roman Studies Suppl. 23, Portsmouth, Rhode Island, 67–80.

Hanworth, R., 1968, 'The Roman Villa at Rapsley, Ewehurst', *Surrey Arch. Colls.* 65, 1–70.

Harden, D., 1961, 'Domestic Window Glass, Roman, Saxon and Medieval', in E.M. Jope (ed.), *Studies in Building History: Essays in Recognition of the Work of Bryan O'Neil*, London, 44–52.

Harries, J., 1992, 'Christianity and the City in Gaul', in J. Rich (ed.), *The City in late Antiquity*, London, 77–98.

Harris, W.V., 1980, 'Towards a Study of the Roman Slave Trade', in J. D'Arms and E. Kopff, *Roman Seaborne Commerce*, Memoirs of the American Academy at Rome 36, 117–40.

Hartley, B. and Fitts, L., 1988, *The Brigantes*, Gloucester.

Haselberger, L., 1997, 'Architectural Likenesses: Models and Plans of Architecture in Classical Antiquity', *Journ. Roman Archaeol.* 10, 77–94.

Haselgrove, C., 1984, 'Romanisation before the Conquest: Gaulish Precedents and British Consequences', in T.F.C. Blagg and A.C. King (eds), *Military and Civilian in Roman Britain*, BAR Brit. Ser. 136, Oxford, 5–64.

—— 1987, 'Culture Process on the Periphery: Belgic Gaul and Rome during the Late Republic and Early Empire', in M. Rowlands, M. Larsen and K. Kristiansen (eds), *Centre and Periphery in the Ancient World*, Cambridge, 104–24.

—— 1995, 'Social and Symbolic Order in the Origins and Layout of Roman Villas in Northern Gaul', in J. Metzler, M. Millett, N. Roymans and J. Slofstra (eds), *Integration in the Early Roman West*, Dossier d'Archéologie du Musée National d'Histoire et d'Art 4, Luxembourg, 65–76.

Hassall, M.W.C., 1979, 'The Impact of Mediterranean Urbanism on Indigenous Nucleated Centres', in B.C. Burnham and H.B. Johnson (eds), *Invasion and Response: The Case of Roman Britain*, BAR Brit. Ser. 73, Oxford, 241–54.

Hassall, M.W.C. and Rhodes, J., 1975, 'Excavations at the new Market Hall, Gloucester, 1966–7', *Trans. Bristol and Glos. Archaeol. Soc.* 93, 15ff.

Hassall, M.W.C. and Tomlin, R.S.O., 1994, 'Roman Britain in 1993: II. Inscriptions', *Britannia* 25, 293–314.

Haverfield, F.J., 1900, 'Romano-British Remains', in H.A. Doubleday (ed.), *The Victoria History of the Counties of England: A History of Hampshire and the Isle of Wight*, 265–349.

—— 1906, 'Romano-British Somerset', in *The Victoria History of the Counties of England. A History of Somerset 1*, 207–372.

Hayward, L.C., 1952, 'The Roman Villa at Lufton, near Yeovil', *Procs Somersetshire Archaeol. and Nat. Hist. Soc.* 97, 91–112.

Heighway, C. and Garrod, P., 1980, 'Excavations at Nos. 1 and 30 Westgate Street, Gloucester', *Britannia* 11, 73–114.

Hemsoll, D., 1990, 'The Architecture of Nero's Golden House', in M. Henig (ed.), *Architecture and Architectural Sculpture in the Roman Empire*, Oxford, 10–38.

Henig, M., 1995, *The Art of Roman Britain*, London.

—— 1997, 'The Lullingstone Mosaic: Art, Religion and Letters in a Fourth-century Villa', *Mosaic* 24, 4–7.

Henig, M. and Soffe, G., 1993, 'The Thruxton Roman Villa and its Mosaic Pavement', *Journ. British Archaeol. Assoc.* 146, 1–28.

Herlihy, D., 1985, *Medieval Households*, London.

Hill, P.R., 1981, 'Stonework and the Archaeologist, Including a Stonemason's View of Hadrian's Wall', *Archaeolgia Aeliana* 5.9, 1–22.

Hillier, B. and Hanson, J., 1984, *The Social Logic of Space*, Cambridge.

Hingley, R., 1989, *Rural Settlement in Roman Britain*, London.

—— 1990, 'Domestic Organisation and Gender Relations in Iron Age and Romano-British Households', in R. Samson (ed.), *The Social Archaeology of Houses*, Edinburgh, 125–48.

—— 1997, 'Resistance and Domination: Social Change in Roman Britain', in D.J. Mattingly (ed.), *Dialogues in Roman Imperialism. Power, Discourse, and Discrepant Experience in the Roman Empire*, Journ. Roman Studies Suppl. 23, Portsmouth, Rhode Island, 81–102.

Hodder, I. and Millett M., 1980, 'Romano-British Villas and Towns: A Systematic Analysis', *World Archaeol.* 12, 69–76.

Hodge, A.T., 1960, *The Woodwork of Greek Roofs*, London and New York.

Hodgson, N., 1996, 'A Late Roman Courtyard House at South Shields and its Parallels', in P. Johnson with I. Hayes (eds), *Architecture in Roman Britain*, CBA Res. Rep. 94, York, 135–51.

Hoffman, A., 1980, 'L'architettura', in *Pompeii 79*, 111–15.

Hoffman, B., 1995, 'The Quarters of the Legionary Centurions of the Principate', *Britannia* 26, 107–51.

Holloway, R.R., 1994, *The Archaeology of Early Rome and Latium*, London.

Hopkins, K., 1983, *Death and Renewal*, Cambridge.

Hull, M.R., 1958, *Roman Colchester*, Soc. of Antiqs Res. Rep. 20, Oxford.

Hunter, A.G., 1981, 'Building-Excavations at the Cross, Gloucester, 1960', *Trans. Bristol and Glos. Archaeol. Soc.* 99, 79ff.

Hurst, H., 1999, 'Topography and identity in *Glevum colonia*', in H. Hurst (ed.), *The Coloniae of Roman Britain: New Studies and a Review*, JRA Monograph Ser. 36, 113–35.

Isaac, R., 1982, *The Transformation of Virginia 1740–1790*, Chapel Hill.

Jackson, D.A., 1973, 'A Roman Lime Kiln at Weekley, Northants', *Britannia* 4, 128–40.

James, S., Marshall, A. and Millett, M., 1984, 'An Early Medieval Building Tradition', *Archaeol. Journ.* 141, 182–215.

Jameson, M.H., 1990, 'Domestic Space in the Greek City State', in S. Kent, (ed.), *Domestic Architecture and the Use of Space: An Interdisciplinary Cross Cultural Study*, Cambridge, 92–113.

Jansen, G., 1997, 'Private Toilets at Pompeii: Appearance and Operation', in S. Bon and R. Jones (eds), *Sequence and Space in Pompeii*, Oxford, 121–34.

Jashemski, W., 1979, *The Gardens of Pompeii*, New Rochelle, NY.

Jessupp, R.F., 1958, 'The "Temple of Mithras" at Burham', *Archaeologia Cantiana* 70, 168–71.

Johnson, A., 1983, *Roman Forts of the 1st and 2nd centuries* AD *in Britain and the German Provinces*, London.

Johnson, P., 1983, 'The Ilchester Lindinis Officina', *Mosaic* 8, 5–8.

Johnson, P. and Hayes, I. (eds), 1996, *Architecture in Roman Britain*, CBA Res. Rep. 94, York.

Johnston, D.E., 1969, 'Sparsholt', *Current Archaeol.* 12, 14–18.

—— 1972, 'A Roman Building at Chalk, near Gravesend', *Britannia* 3, 112–48.

—— 1978, 'Villas of Hampshire and the Isle of Wight', in M. Todd (ed.), *Studies in the Romano-British Villa*, Leicester.

Jonas, H., 1958, *Gnostic Religion*, Boston.

Jones, A.H.M., 1973, *The Later Roman Empire* AD *284–602: A Social, Economic and Administrative Survey* (2nd edn), Oxford.

Jones, G.R.J., 1972, 'Post-Roman Wales', in H.R.P. Finberg (ed.), *The Agrarian History of England and Wales. 1.2. AD 43–1042*, Cambridge, 281–382.

Jones, M.J. (ed.), 1981, 'Excavations at Lincoln. Third Interim Report: Sites Outside the Walled City 1972–1977', *Antiqs Journ.* 61.1, 83–114.

Jung, C.G., 1955, 'Transformation Symbolism in the Mass', in *Eranos Yearbooks 2: The Mysteries*, New York.

Keevill, G.D., 1995, 'Processes of Collapse in Romano-British Buildings: A Review of the Evidence', in E. Shepherd (ed.), *Interpreting Stratigraphy 5*, 26–37.

—— 1996, 'The Reconstruction of the Romano-British Villa at Redlands Farm, Northamptonshire', in P. Johnson with I. Hayes (eds), *Architecture in Roman Britain*, CBA Res. Rep. 94, York, 44–55.

Keevill, G.D. and Booth, P., 1997, 'Settlement, Sequence and Structure: Romano-British Stone-built Roundhouses at Redlands Farm, Stanwick (Northants), and Alchester (Oxon)', in R.M. and D.E. Friendship-Taylor (eds), *From Roundhouse to Villa*, Northants, 19–45.

Kimmig, W., 1983, *Die Heuneburg an der oberen Donau*, Stuttgart.

King, A.C., 1984, 'Animal Bones and the Dietary Identity of Military and Civilian Groups in Roman Britain, Germany and Gaul', in T.F.C. Blagg and A.C. King (eds), *Military and Civilian in Roman Britain*, BAR Brit. Ser. 136, Oxford, 187–218.

King, A.C. and Potter, T.W., 1990, 'A New Domestic Building Facade from Roman Britain', *Journ. Roman Archaeol.* 3, 195–204.

King, A.D., 1976, 'Cultural Pluralism and Urban Form: The Classical City as Laboratory for Cross-Cultural Research in Man-Environment Interaction', in A. Rapoport (ed.), *The Mutual Interaction of People and Their Built Environment*, The Hague, 51–76.

Knights, C., 1994, 'The Spatiality of the Roman Domestic Setting', in M. Parker Pearson and C. Richards (eds), *Architecture and Order. Approaches to Social Space*, London and New York, 113–46.

Kolling, A., 1972, 'Schwarzenacker an der Blies', *Bonner Jahrb.* 172, 238–57.

Kuttner, A., 1993, 'Vitruvius and the Second Style', *Journ. Roman Archaeol.* 6, 341–7.

Laurence, R., 1994a, *Roman Pompeii, Space and Society*, London and New York.

—— 1994b, 'Urban Renewal in Italy: The Limits to Change', in M. Locock (ed.), *Meaningful Architecture: Social Interpretations of Buildings*, Avebury, 66–85.

Lavin, J., 1962, 'The House of the Lord', *Art Bulletin* 44.1, 1–27.

Lawrence, A.W., 1973, *Greek Architecture* (3rd edn), Pelican History of Art Ser., Harmondsworth.

Le Gall, J., 1963, *Alesia: Archeologie et Histoire*, Paris.

Leach, E., 1978, 'Does Space Syntax really "Constitute the Social"?', in D. Green, C. Haslegrove and M. Spraggs (eds), *Social Organisation and Settlement: Contributions from Anthropology, Archaeology and Geography*, BAR Int. Ser. 47, Oxford, 385–402.

Leach, E.W., 1997, 'Oecus on Ibycus: Investigating the Vocabulary of the Roman House', in S. Bon and R. Jones (eds), *Sequence and Space in Pompeii*, Oxford, 50–72.

Leech, R., 1981, 'The Excavation of a Romano-British Farmstead and Cemetery on Bradley Hill, Somerton, Somerset', *Britannia* 12, 177–252.

Lefebvre, H., 1991, *The Production of Space* (transl. D. Nicholson Smith), Oxford.

Leone, M.P., 1984, 'Interpreting Ideology in Historical Archaeology: Using the Rules of Perspective in the William Paca Gardens in Annapolis, Maryland', in D. Miller and C. Tilley (eds), *Ideology, Power and Prehistory*, Cambridge, 25–36.

Liddell, D.M., 1931, 'Notes on Two Excavations in Hampshire', *Procs Hampshire Field Club* 10, 224–36.

Ling, R., 1976, 'Stuccowork', in D. Strong and D. Brown (eds), *Roman Crafts*, London, 209–22.

—— 1983, 'The Insula of the Menander at Pompeii, Interim Report', *Antiqs Journ.* 63, 34–57.

—— 1985, 'The Mechanics of the Building Trade', in F.O. Grew and B. Hobley (eds.), *Roman Urban Topography in Britain and the Western Empire*, CBA Res. Rep. 59, London, 14–27.

—— 1989, 'Lullingstone and the Study of Wall Painting in Britain', *Journ. Roman Archaeol.* 2, 378–84.

—— 1991, 'Brading, Brantingham and York: A New Look at Some Fourth-Century Mosaics', *Britannia* 22, 147–57.

—— 1992, 'A Collapsed Building Facade at Carsington, Derbyshire', *Britannia* 23, 233–6.

—— 1997, 'Mosaics in Roman Britain: Discoveries and Research since 1945', *Britannia* 28, 259–96.

Liversidge, J., 1955, *Furniture in Roman Britain*, London.

—— 1968, *Britain in the Roman Empire*, London.

—— 1987, 'The Wall Paintings', in G.W. Meates (ed.) *The Roman Villa at Lullingstone, Kent. Vol. 2: The Wall Paintings and Finds*, Kent Archaeol. Soc. Monograph 3, 5–46.

Liversidge, J., Smith, D.J. and Stead, I.M., 1973, 'Brantingham Roman Villa: Discoveries in 1962', *Britannia* 4, 84–106.

Lloyd, J.A., 1985, 'Some Aspects of Urban Development at Eusperides/Berenice', in G. Barker, J. Lloyd and J. Reynolds (eds), *Cyrenaica in Antiquity*, BAR Int. Ser. 236, Oxford, 49–66.

Lowther, A.W.G., 1929, 'Excavations at Ashtead, Surrey. Second Report (1928)', *Surrey Arch. Colls* 38.1, 1–17.

—— 1950, 'Roman Villa at Sandilands Road, Walton-on-the-Hill. Excavations of 1948–9', *Surrey Arch. Colls* 51, 65–81.

—— 1976, 'Romano-British Chimney Pots and Finials', *Antiqs Journ.* 56, 35ff.

Lucas, R.N., 1993, *The Romano-British Villa at Halstock, Dorset, Excavations 1967–1985*, Dorset Nat. Hist. and Archaeol. Soc., Monograph Ser. 13, Dorchester.

Luff, R. (n.d.) (unpublished), 'New Perspectives and Directions in the Zooarchaeology of East Anglia and Environs', Cambridge Faunal Remains Unit Report.

Lysons, S., 1797, *An Account of the Roman Antiquities Discovered at Woodchester*, London.

—— 1813, *Reliquiae Britannico-Romanae I*, London.

—— 1817, 'An Account of the Remains of Several Roman Buildings and other Roman Antiquities Discovered in the County of Gloucester', *Archaeologia* 18, 112–25.

McCarthy, M.R., 1991, *Roman Waterlogged Remains and Later Features at Castle Street, Carlisle*, Cumberland and Westmoreland Antiquarian and Archaeol. Soc. Res. Ser. 5, Stroud.

McCarthy, M.R., Padley, T.G. and Henig, M., 1982, 'Excavation and Finds from The Lanes, Carlisle', *Britannia* 13, 79–89.

MacDonald, W.L., 1965, *The Architecture of the Roman Empire I*, Publications in the History of Art 17, Yale.

—— 1986, *The Architecture of the Roman Empire II: An Urban Appraisal*, New Haven and London.

McGann, J., 1987, 'Is Clay Lump a Traditional Building Material?', *Vernacular Architecture* 18, 1–16.

Mackenna, S.A. and Ling, R., 1991, 'Wall Paintings from the Winchester Palace Site, Southwark', *Britannia* 22,159–72.

Mackreth, D.F., 1987, 'Roman Public Buildings', in J. Schofield and R. Leech (eds), *Urban Archaeology in Britain*, CBA Res. Rep. 61, London, 133–46.

MacMullen, R., 1974, *Roman Social Relations 50 BC to AD 284*, New Haven.

—— 1976, *Roman Governments Response to Crisis AD 235–337*, New Haven and London.

McWhirr, A. (ed.), 1979, *Roman Brick and Tile*, BAR Int. Ser. 68, Oxford.

—— 1986, *Houses in Roman Cirencester*, Cirencester Excavations 3, Gloucester.

—— 1988, 'Cirencester. Corinium Dobunnorum', in G. Webster (ed.), *Fortress into City. The Consolidation of Roman Britain, First Century AD*, London, 74–90

Marsden, P., 1980, *Roman London*, London.

Marsden, P. and West, B., 1992, 'Population Change in Roman London' *Britannia* 23, 133–40.

Martin, D.B., 1996, 'The Construction of the Ancient Family', *Journ. Roman Studies* 86, 40–60.

Mason, D.J.P., 1989, 'The Heronbridge Roman Site', *Archaeol. Journ.* 145 (for 1988), 123–57.

Massy, J.L., 1989, 'Fontoy, Moderweise', *Gallia Informations Préhistoire et Histoire 1989–2*, 107.

Meates, G.W., 1973, 'Farningham Roman Villa II', *Arch. Cant.* 88, 1–21.

—— 1979, *The Lullingstone Roman Villa. 1: The Site*, Kent Archaeol. Soc. Monograph 1, Maidstone.

Meiggs, R., 1973, *Roman Ostia* (2nd edn), Oxford.

Mellor, A.S., and Goodchild, R., 1942, 'The Roman Villa at Atworth, Wilts.', *Wilts. Archaeol. and Nat. Hist. Mag.* 49, 46–95.

Mellor, J.E. and Lucas, J., 1980, 'The Roman Villa at Norfolk St, Leicester', *Leic. Arch. and Hist. Soc. Trans* 59, 68–70.

Meyer, M.W., and Robinson, J.M., 1981, *The Nag Hammadi library in English* (2nd edn), San Francisco.

Middleton, J.H., 1890, 'On a Roman Villa in Spoonley Wood, Gloucestershire; and on Romano-British Houses Generally', *Archaeologia* 52, 651–68.

Miles, D., 1984, *Archaeology at Barton Court Farm, Abingdon, Oxon*, CBA Res. Rep. 50, Oxford.

Millett, M., 1982, 'Distinguishing Between the Pes Monetalis and the Pes Drusianus: Some Problems', *Britannia* 13, 315–20.

—— 1990a, 'Romanization: Historical Issues and Archaeological Interpretation', in T.F.C. Blagg and M. Millett (eds), *The Early Roman Empire in the West*, Oxford, 35–41.

—— 1990b, *The Romanization of Britain: An Essay in Archaeological Interpretation*, Cambridge.

—— 1994, 'Evaluating Roman London', *Archaeol. Journ.* 151, 427–34.

—— 1999, 'Coloniae and Romano-British studies', in H. Hurst (ed.) *The Coloniae of Roman Britain: New Studies and a Review*, Journ. Roman Archaeology Suppl. Ser. 36, 191–6.

Milne, G. (ed.), 1985, *The Port of Roman London*, London.

—— 1992, *From Roman Basilica to Medieval Market*, London.

Milne, G., Bateman, N. and Milne, C., 1984, 'Bank Deposits with Interest', *London Archaeol.* 4.15, 395–400.

Milne, G. and Wardle, A., 1995, 'Early Roman Development at Leadenhall Court, London and Related Research', *Trans. London and Middlesex Archaeol. Soc.* 44, 23–169.

Mitchelson, N., 1964, 'Roman Malton: The Civilian Settlement. Excavations in Orchard Field 1949–52', *Yorkshire Archaeol. Journ.* 41, 209–61.

Morris, P., 1979, *Agricultural Buildings in Roman Britain*, BAR, Brit. Ser. 70, Oxford.

Museum of London, DUA, 1988, *Digging in the City. The Annual Review 1988*, London.

Nappo, S.C., 1997, 'Urban Transformation at Pompeii, Late 3rd and Early 2nd c. BC', in R. Laurence and A. Wallace-Hadrill (eds), *Domestic Space in the Roman World: Pompeii and Beyond*, Journ. Roman Archaeology Suppl. Ser. 22, Michigan, 91–120.

Nash-Williams, V.E., 1951, 'The Roman Villa at Llantwit Major, Glamorgan', *Arch. Camb.* 101, 89–159.

Neal, D.S., 1970, 'The Roman Villa at Boxmoor: Interim Report', *Britannia* 1, 156–62.

—— 1974, *The Excavation of the Roman Villa in Gadebridge Park, Hemel Hempstead 1963–8*, Soc. of Antiqs Res. Rep. 31, London.

—— 1974–6, 'Northchurch, Boxmoor and Hemel Hempstead Station: The Excavation of Three Roman Buildings in the Bulborne Valley', *Hertfordshire Archaeol.* 4, 1–135.

—— 1977, 'Witcombe Roman Villa', in M.R. Apted, R. Gilyard-Beer and A.D. Saunders (eds), *Ancient Monuments and their Interpretation*, London, 27–40.

—— 1982, 'Romano-British Villas – One or Two Storied?', in P.J. Drury (ed.), *Structural Reconstruction: Approaches to the Interpretation of the Excavated Remains of the Buildings*, BAR Brit. Ser. 110, Oxford, 154–6.

—— 1996, *Excavations on the Roman Villa at Beadlam, Yorkshire*, Yorkshire Archaeol. Rep. 2.

Neal, D.S. and Walker, B., 1988, 'A Mosaic from Boughspring Roman Villa, Tidenham, Gloucestershire', *Britannia* 19, 191–7.

Neal, D.S., Wardle, A., and Hunn, J., 1990, *Excavations of the Iron Age, Roman and Medieval Settlement at Gorhambury, St. Albans*, English Heritage Archaeol. Rep.14, London.

Nevett, L., 1994,'Separation or Seclusion? Towards an Archaeological Approach to Investigating Women in the Greek Household in the Fifth to Third Centuries BC', in M. Parker Pearson and C. Richards (eds), *Architecture and Order. Approaches to Social Space*, London and New York, 98–112.

Niblett, R., 1993, 'Verulamium since the Wheelers', in S.J. Greep (ed.), *Roman Towns: The Wheeler Inheritance*, CBA Res. Rep. 93, York, 78–92.

Nicolet, C., 1980, *The World of the Citizen in Republican Rome*, London.

Odouze, J.L., 1985, 'La Gaule Intérieure: Le Centre', in J. Lasfargues (ed.), *Architectures de terre et de bois*, Documents D'Archéologie Française 2, Paris, 93–102.

Oelmann, F., 1921, 'Die villa rustica bei Stahl und Verwandtes, *Germania* 5, 64–73.

—— 1928, 'Ein galloromischer Bauernhof bei Mayen', *Bonner Jahrb.* 133, 51–140.

Oetgen, J., 1987, 'Sapperton Roman town', *Archaeology in Lincolnshire 1986–1987*, Third Annual Rep. Trust for Lincolnshire Archaeology, 13–15.

Ogilvie, R.M., 1969, *The Romans and their Gods*, London.

O'Neill, H.E. 1945, 'The Roman Villa at Park Street near St. Albans Herts', *Archaeol. Journ.*, 102, 21–110.

—— 1952, 'Whittington Court Roman Villa, Whittington, Gloucestershire', *Trans. Bristol and Glos. Arch. Soc.* 71, 13–49.

Oswald, A., 1991, A Doorway on the Past: Round-House Orientation and its Significance in Iron Age Britain', Cambridge, unpublished BA dissertation.

Packer, J.E., 1971, *The Insulae of Imperial Ostia*, Memoirs American Academy Rome 31.

Pagels, E., 1979, *The Gnostic Gospels*, London.

Pallarés, F., 1986, 'Le techniche murarie di Albintimilium', *Rivista di Studi Liguri* 52.

Partridge, C., 1981, *Skeleton Green*, Britannia Monograph 2, London.

Payne, G., 1897, 'The Roman Villa at Darenth', *Archaeol. Cantiana* 22, 49–84.

Percival, J., 1976, *The Roman Villa. An Historical Introduction*, London.

Perring, D., 1989, 'Cellars and Cults in Roman Britain', *Archaeol. Journ.* 146, 279–301.

—— 1991a, 'Lo scavo di piazza Duomo: eta romana e altomedioevale' and 'Lo scavo di via Tomasso Grossi', in D. Caporusso (ed.), *Scavi MM3. Ricerche di archeologia urban a Milano durante la costruzione della linea 3 della metropolitana 1982–1990. 1. Gli Scavi*, Milan, 105–61 and 212–28.

—— 1991b, *Roman London*, London.

—— 1991c, 'Spatial Organization and Social Change in Roman Towns', in J. Rich and A. Wallace-Haddrill (eds), *City and Country in the Ancient World*, London, 273–93.

—— 1999a, 'Excavations in the Souks of Beirut: An Introduction to the Work of the British-Lebanese Team and Summary Report', *Berytus* 44, 9–34.

—— (1999b), 'Houses in Roman Britain: A Study in Architecture and Urban Society', unpublished D. Phil. thesis, University of Leicester.

Perring, D. and Roskams, S.P. with Allen, P., 1991, *The Early Development of Roman London to the West of the Walbrook*, Archaeol. of Roman London 2, CBA Res. Rep. 70, London.

Phillips, C.W. (ed.), 1970, *The Fenland in Roman Times*, London.

Philp, B.J., 1977, 'The Forum of Roman London', *Britannia* 8, 1–64.

—— 1989, *The Roman House with the Bacchic Murals at Dover*, Kent Monograph Ser. Res. Rep. 5, Dover.

Pitts, L.F. and St Joseph, J.K., 1985, *Inchtuthil. The Roman Legionary Fortress Excavations 1952–65*, Soc. for the Promotion of Roman Studies Monograph Ser., Gloucester.

Poulsen, V.H., 1960, *San Giovenale*, Malmo.

Poulter, A., 1987, 'Townships and Villages', in J.S. Wacher (ed.), *The Roman World: 1*, London, 388–421.

Price, J.E. and Hilton Price, F.G., 1881, *A Description of the Remains of Roman Buildings at Morton, near Brading, Isle of Wight*, London.

Pritchard, F.A., 1986, 'Ornamental Stonework from Roman London', *Britannia* 17, 169–89.

Puglisi, S.M., 1951, *Gli abitatori primitivi del Palatino*, Monumenti Antichi 41, Rome.

Purcell, N., 1987, 'Town in Country and Country in Town', in E. MacDougal (ed.), *Ancient Roman Villa Gardens*, Washington DC, 185ff.

—— 1995, 'The Roman Villa and the Landscape of Production', in T.J Cornell and K. Lomas (eds), *Urban Society in Roman Italy*, London, 151–80.

Putnam, W.G. and Rainey, A., 1975, 'Seventh Interim Report on Excavations at Dewlish Roman Villa 1975', *Procs Dorset Nat. Hist. and Arch. Soc.* 97, 54–7.

Radford, C.A.R., 1936, 'The Roman Villa at Ditchley, Oxon', *Oxoniensia* 1, 24–69.

Rahtz, P., 1963, 'A Roman Villa at Downton', *The Wiltshire Archaeol. and Nat. Hist. Mag.* 58, 303–41.

Rankov, N.B., 1982, 'Roman Britain in 1981. I: Sites Explored', *Britannia* 13, 328–95.

RCHM(E), 1983: Royal Commission on Historical Monuments (England), 'West Park Roman Villa, Rockbourne, Hampshire', *Archaeol. Journ.* 140, 129–50.

Rebuffat, 1969, 'Maisons a peristyle d'Afrique du repertoire de plans publies', *Melanges de l'Ecole Francaise de Rome* 81, 659–724.

Reece, R., 1980, 'Town and Country: The End of Roman Britain', *World Arch.* 12,1, 77–92.

—— 1988, *My Roman Britain*, Cirencester.

—— 1990, 'Romanization: A Point of View', in T.F.C. Blagg and M. Millett (eds), *The Early Roman Empire in the West*, Oxford, 30–4.

Rennie, M., 1986, 'Excavations in the Bingham Hall Gardens, 1958', in A.D. McWhirr, *Houses in Roman Cirencester*, Cirencester Excavations 3, Gloucester, 194–201.

Revault, J., 1967, *Palais et Demeures de Tunis (18e et 19e siècles)*, Editions du Centre National de Recherches Scientifique, Paris.

Rhodes, M., 1987, 'Wall-Paintings from Fenchurch Street, City of London', *Britannia* 18, 169–72.

RIB: Collingwood, R.G. and Wright, R.P. (eds), 1965, *The Roman Inscriptions of Britain, Vol. I, Inscriptions on Stone*, Oxford.

RIB: Frere, S.S. and Tomlin, R.S.O. (eds), 1992, *The Roman Inscriptions of Britain, Vol. 2, Fascicule 4* (Collingwood and Wright, eds), Stroud.

Richardson, B., 1988, 'Excavation Round-up 1987', *London Archaeol.* 5.14, 382–7.

Richmond, I.A., 1959, 'The Roman Villa at Chedworth, 1958–59', *Trans. Bristol and Glos. Archaeol. Soc*, 78 (1959), 5–31.

—— 1969, 'The Plans of Roman Villas in Britain', in A.L.F. Rivet (ed.), *The Roman Villa in Britain*, London, 49–70

Richmond, I.A. and Gillam, J.P., 1953, 'Buildings of the First and Second Centuries North of the Granaries at Corbridge', *Arch. Ael.* ser 4. 31, 205–53.

Riggsby, A.M., 1997, ' "Private" and "Public" in Roman Culture: The Case of the Cubiculum', *Journ. Roman Archaeol.* 10, 37–56.

Rippengal, R., 1993, 'Villas as a Key to Social Structure? Some Comments on Recent Approaches to the Romano-British Villa and some Suggestions towards an Alternative', in E. Scott (ed.), *Theoretical Roman Archaeology: First Conference Proceedings*, 79–101.

Rivet, A.L.F., 1964, *Town and Country in Roman Britain* (2nd edn), London.

—— 1969, *The Roman Villa in Britain*, London.

Roach Smith, C., 1876, 'On a Roman Villa near Maidstone', *Arch. Cant.* 10, 163ff.

Roberti, M.M., 1984, *Milano Romana*, Milan.

Robinson, D.M., 1946, *Excavations at Olynthus* 11, Baltimore.

Rodriguez-Almeida, E., 1981, *Forma urbis marmorae: aggiornamento generale 1980*, Rome.

Rodwell, W.J., 1980, 'Temple Archaeology: Problems of the Present and Portents for the Future', in W. J. Rodwell (ed.), *Temples, Churches and Religion in Roman Britain*, BAR Brit. Ser. 77, Oxford, 211–41.

Rodwell, W. J. and Rodwell, K.A., 1985, *Rivenhall: Investigations of a Villa, Church, and Village, 1950–1977*, Chelmsford Archaeol. Trust Rep. 4, CBA, Res. Rep. 55, London.

Rondelet, J., 1814, *Traité théorique et pratique de l'Art de bâtir: Vol. 3*, Paris.

Rossiter, J.J., 1989, 'Roman Villas of the Greek East', *Journ. Roman Archaeol.* 2, 101–10.

Rostovtzeff, M., 1957, *The Social and Economic History of the Roman Empire* (2nd edn, revised P.M. Fraser), Oxford.

Rowley, T. and Brown, L., 1981, 'Excavations at Beech House Hotel, Dorchester-on-Thames 1972', *Oxoniensia* 46, 1ff.

Rowsome, P., 2000, *Heart of the City: Roman, Medieval and Modern London Revealed by Archaeology at 1 Poultry*, London.

Roymans, N., 1995, 'Romanization, Cultural Identity and the Ethnic Discussion. The Integration of Lower Rhine Populations in the Roman Empire', in J. Metzler, M. Millett, N. Roymans and J. Slofstra (eds), *Integration in the Early Roman West*, Dossier d'Archéologie du Musée National d'Histoire et d'Art 4, Luxembourg, 47–64.

Rudolph, K., 1983, *Gnosis: The Nature and History of Gnosticism* (transl. R. Wilson), Edinburgh.

Rykwert, J., 1976, *The Idea of a Town: The Anthropology of Urban Form in Rome, Italy and the Ancient World*, London.

Saliou, C., 1994, *Les lois des bâtiments*, IFAPO Bibliothèque archéologique et historique 116, Beirut.

Saller, R.P. and Shaw, B.D., 1984, 'Tombstones and Roman Family Relations in the Principate: Civilians, Soldiers and Slaves', *Journ. Roman Studies* 74, 124–56.

Sarnowski, T., 1978, *Les représentations de villas sur les mosaïques africaines tardives*, Warsaw.

Schaff, P., 1889, *History of the Christian Church: Ante-Nicene Christianity: AD 100–325*, Edinburgh.

Schlefen, A.E., 1976, 'Some Territorial Layouts in the United States', in A. Rapoport (ed.), *The Mutual Interaction of People and Their Built Environment*, The Hague.

Scott, E., 1990, 'Romano-British Villas and the Social Construction of Space', in R. Samson (ed.), *The Social Archaeology of Houses*, Edinburgh, 149–72.

—— 1991, 'Animal and Infant burials in Romano-British Villas: A Revitalization Movement', in P. Garwood, D. Jennings, R. Skeates and J. Toms (eds), *Sacred and Profane*, Oxford University Committee for Archaeology Monograph 32, Oxford, 115–20.

—— 1993, *A Gazetteer of Roman Villas in Britain*, Leicester Archaeology Monographs 1, Leicester.

Scott, L., 1938, 'The Roman Villa at Angmering', *Sussex Archaeol. Coll.* 79, 3–44.

Scott, S., 1994, 'Patterns of Movement: Architectural Design and Visual Planning in the Romano-British Villa', in G. Locock (ed.), *Meaningful Architecture: Social Interpretations of Buildings*, Avebury, 86–98.

—— 2000, *Art and Society in Fourth-Century Britain: Villa Mosaics in Context*, Oxford University School of Archaeology Monograph 53, Oxford.

Sear, F., 1982, *Roman Architecture*, London.

Selkirk, A. and Selkirk, W., 1978, 'The Cambridge Shrine', *Current Archaeol.* 61, 57–60.

—— 1996, 'Piddington', *Current Archaeol.* 146, 57–64

Sheldon, H.L., Corti, G., Green, G. and Tyers, P., 1993, 'The Distribution of Villas in Kent, Surrey and Sussex: Some Preliminary Findings from a Survey', *London Archaeol.* 7, 40–5.

Shepherd, J.D., 1986, 'The Roman Features at Gateway House and Watling House, Watling Street, City of London (1954)', *Trans. London and Middx Archaeol. Soc.* 37, 125–44.

Shirley, E.M., 2000, *The Construction of the Roman Legionary Fortress at Inchtuthil*, BAR Brit. Ser. 298, Oxford.

Simmons, B.B., 1985, 'Sapperton', *Archaeology in Lincolnshire 1984–1985*, 1st Ann. Rep. Trust for Lincolnshire Archaeol., 16–20.

Slofstra, J., 1983, 'An Anthropological Approach to the Study of Romanization Processes', in R. Brandt and J. Slofstra (eds), *Roman and Native in the Low Countries. Spheres of Interaction*, BAR Int. Ser. 184, Oxford, 71–104.

—— 1995, 'The Villa in the Roman West: Space Decoration and Ideology', in J. Metzler, M. Millett, N. Roymans and J. Slofstra (eds), *Integration in the Early Roman West*, Dossier d'Archéologie du Musée National d'Histoire et d'Art 4, Luxembourg, 77–90.

Smith, D.J., 1969, 'The Mosaic Pavements', in A.L.F. Rivet (ed.), *The Roman Villa in Britain*, London, 71–125.

—— 1977, 'Mythological Figures and Scenes in Romano-British Mosaics', in J. Munby and M. Henig (eds), *Roman Life and Art in Britain*, BAR, Brit. Ser. 41.1, Oxford, 105–94.

—— 1978, 'Regional Aspects of the Winged Corridor Villa in Britain', in M. Todd (ed.), *Studies in the Romano-British Villa*, Leicester, 117–47.

Smith, J.T., 1964, 'Romano-British Aisled Houses', *Archaeol. Journ* 120 (for 1963), 1–30.

—— 1978, 'Villas as a Key to Social Structure', in M. Todd (ed.), *Studies in the Romano-British Villa*, Leicester, 149–86.

—— 1982, 'The Validity of Inference from Archaeological Evidence', in P.J. Drury (ed.), *Structural Reconstruction: Approaches to the Interpretation of the Excavated Remains of the Buildings*, BAR Brit. Ser. 110, Oxford, 7–20.

—— 1985, 'Barnsley Park Villa: Its Interpretation and Implications', *Oxford Journ. Archaeol.* 4.3, 341–51.

—— 1997, *Roman Villas: A Study in Social Structure*, London and New York.

Smith, R.F., 1987, *Roadside Settlements in Lowland Roman Britain*, BAR 157, Oxford.

Soja E.W., 1996, *Thirdspace. Journeys to Los Angeles and Other Real-and-Imagined Places*, Oxford.

Spinazzola, V., 1953, *Pompeii alla luce degli nuovi scavi di Via dell'abbondanza (1910–1923)*, Roma.

St John Hope, W.H., 1897, 'Excavations on the Site of the Roman City at Silchester, Hants, in 1896', *Archaeologia* 55.2, 431–50.

—— 1902, 'Excavations on the Site of the Roman City at Silchester, Hants, in 1901', *Archaeologia* 58.1, 17ff.

—— 1903, 'Excavations on the Site of the Roman City at Silchester, Hants, in 1902', *Archaeologia* 58.2, 413ff.

—— 1906, 'Excavations on the Site of the Roman City at Silchester, Hants, in 1905', *Archaeologia* 60.1, 149ff.

—— 1907, 'Excavations on the Site of the Roman City at Silchester, Hants, in 1906', *Archaeologia* 60.2, 431ff.

Stahl, A. and Stahl, P.H., 1976, 'Peasant House Building and its Relation to Church Building: The Roumanian Case', in A. Rapoport (ed.), *The Mutual Interaction of People and Their Built Environment*, The Hague.

Stambaugh, J.E., 1988, *The Ancient Roman City*, London and Baltimore, MD.

Stead, I.M., 1976, *Excavations at Winterton Roman Villa and other Roman Sites in North Lincolnshire*, London.

Stevens, C.E., 1947, 'A Possible Conflict of Laws in Roman Britain', *Journ. Roman Studies* 37, 132–4.

—— 1966, 'The Social and Economic Aspects of Rural Settlement', in C. Thomas (ed.), *Rural Settlement in Roman Britain*, CBA Res. Rep. 7, London, 108–28.

Stone, P.G., 1929, 'A Roman Villa at Newport, Isle of Wight', *Antiqs Journ.* 9, 141–51.

Stupperich, R., 1980, 'A Reconsideration of Some Fourth-century British Mosaics, *Britannia* 11, 289–301.

Sumpter, A., 1988, 'Iron Age and Roman at Dalton Parlours', in J. Price and P.R. Wilson (eds), *Recent Research in Roman Yorkshire. Studies in Honour of Mary Kitson Clark*, BAR Brit. Ser. 193, Oxford, 171–99.

Swain, E.J. and Ling, R.J., 1981, 'The Kingscote Wall-Paintings', *Britannia* 12, 167–76.

Swoboda, K., 1918, *Römische und romanische Paläste*, Vienna.

Sykes, C.M. and Brown, G.A., 1961, 'The Wraxall Villa', *Procs Somersetshire Archaeol. and Nat. Hist. Soc.* 105, 37–48.

Taylor, M.V., 1932, 'Romano-British Kent: 4 Country Houses and Other Buildings', in W. Page (ed.), *The Victoria History of the Counties of England. A History of Kent 3*, 102–26.

—— 1939, 'Romano-British Remains: Country Houses', in W. Page (ed.), *The Victoria History of the Counties of England. A History of Oxfordshire 1*, 306–23.

—— 1962, 'Roman Britain in 1961. I Sites Explored', *Journ. Roman Studies* 52, 160–90.

Tester, P.J., 1961, 'The Roman Villa in Cobham Park, near Rochester', *Arch. Cant.* 76, 88–109.

Thébert, Y., 1987, 'Private Life and Domestic Architecture in Roman Africa', in P. Veyne (ed.), *A History of Private Life. I From Pagan Rome to Byzantium* (transl. A. Goldhammer), Cambridge, MA and London, 313–409.

Thomas, C., 1981, *Christianity in Roman Britain to AD 500*, London.

Todd, M., 1973, *The Coritani*, London.

—— 1978, 'Villas and Romano-British Society', in M. Todd (ed.), *Studies in the Romano-British Villa*, Leicester, 197–208.

—— 1989, 'The Early Cities', in M. Todd (ed.), *Research on Roman Britain: 1960–89*, Britannia Monograph 11, London, 75–90.

Toynbee, J.M.C., 1964, *Art in Britain under the Romans*, Oxford.

Tram Tanh Tin, V., 1988, *La Casa dei Cervi a Herculanum*, Roma.

Treggiari, S., 1975, 'Family Life among the Staff of the Volusii', *Trans. of the American Philological Assoc.* 105, 48–77.

Trier, B., 1969, *Das Haus in Nord-West Europa*, Munster.

Trow, S.D., 1990, 'By the Northern Shores of Ocean: Some Observations on Acculturation

Process at the Edge of the Roman World', in T.F.C. Blagg and M. Millett (eds), *The Early Roman Empire in the West*, Oxford, 103–18.

Turner, E.G., 1956, 'A Roman Writing Tablet from Somerset', *Journ. Roman Studies* 46, 115–18.

van der Veen, M., 1989, 'Charred Grain Assemblages from Roman-Period Corn Driers in Britain', *Archaeol. Journ.* 146, 302–19.

van Es, W.A., 1967, *Wijster, a Native Village beyond the Imperial Frontier*, Palaeohistoria 11, Gronigen.

Van Ossel, P., 1992, *Etablissments ruraux de l'antiquité tardive dans le nord de la Gaule*, Gallia Suppl. 51, Paris.

Vermaseren, M. J., 1977, *Cybele and Attis, the Myth and the Cult*, London.

Wacher, J.S., 1962, 'Cirencester 1961. Second Interim Report', *Antiqs Journ.* 42, 1–14.

—— 1963, 'Cirencester 1962. Third Interim Report' *Antiqs Journ.* 43, 15–26.

—— 1971, 'Roman Iron Beams', *Britannia* 2, 200–2.

—— 1995, *The Towns of Roman Britain* (2nd edn), London.

Wait, G.A., 1985, *Ritual and Religion in Iron Age Britain*, BAR Brit. Ser. 149, Oxford.

Walford, T., 1803, 'An Account of a Roman Military Way in Essex, and of Roman Antiquities, found near it', *Archaeologia* 14, 61ff.

Wallace-Hadrill, A., 1988, 'The Social Structure of the Roman House', *Papers British School at Rome* 56, 43–97.

—— 1994, *Houses and Society in Pompeii and Herculaneum*, Princeton.

—— 1997, 'Rethinking the Roman Atrium', in R. Laurence and A. Wallace-Hadrill (eds), *Domestic Space in the Roman World: Pompeii and Beyond*, Journ. Roman Archaeol. Suppl. Ser. 22, Michigan, 219–40.

Walters, B., 1984, 'The Orpheus Mosaic in Littlecote Park England', *Mosaico Ravenna* 433–42.

—— 1996, 'Exotic Structures in 4th-century Britain', in P. Johnson with I. Hayes (eds), *Architecture in Roman Britain*, CBA Res. Rep. 94, York, 152–62.

Walthew, C.V., 1975, 'The Town House and the Villa House in Roman Britain', *Britannia* 6, 189–205.

Ward-Perkins, J.B., 1938, 'The Roman Villa at Lockleys, Welwyn', *Antiqs Journ*, 18, 339–73.

—— 1959, 'Excavations beside the North-West Gate of Veii, 1957–8', *Papers British School at Rome* 29, 1–123.

——1981, *Roman Imperial Architecture*, Pelican History of Art Ser., Harmondsworth.

Weber, M., 1958, *The City* (transl. D. Martindale and G. Neuwirth), Glencoe, Il.

Webster, G., 1959, 'Roman Windows and Grilles', *Antiquity* 33, 10–14.

—— 1981, 'The Excavation of a Romano-British Rural Establishment at Barnsley Park, Gloucestershire, 1961–1979. Part I *c.* AD 140–360', *Trans. Bristol and Glos. Archaeol. Soc.* 99, 21ff.

—— 1988, 'Wroxeter. Virconium', in G. Webster (ed), *Fortress into City. The Consolidation of Roman Britain, First Century AD.* London, 120–144.

Webster, G. and Smith, L., 1983, 'The Excavation of a Romano-British Rural Establishment at Barnsley Park, Gloucestershire, 1961–1979. Part II *c.* AD 360–400+', *Trans. Bristol and Glos. Archaeol. Soc.* 100, 65ff.

—— 1987, 'Reply to J.T. Smith's Suggested Reinterpretation of Barnsley Park Villa', *Oxford Journ. Archaeol.* 6, 69–89.

Weeks, J., 1982, 'Roman Carpentry Joints: Adoption and Adaption', in S. McGrail (ed.), *Woodworking Techniques before AD 1500*, BAR Int. Ser. 129, Oxford, 157–68.

Wheeler, R.E.M., 1921, 'A Roman Fortified House near Cardiff', *Journ. Roman Studies* 11, 67–85.

Wheeler, R.E.M. and Wheeler, T.V., 1936, *Verulamium. A Belgic and Two Roman Cities*, Soc. of Antiqs Res. Rep. 11, Oxford.

Whittaker, C.R., 1997, 'Imperialism and Culture: The Roman Initiative', in D.J. Mattingly, (ed.), *Dialogues in Roman Imperialism. Power, Discourse, and Discrepant Experience in the Roman Empire*, Journ. Roman Studies Suppl. 23, Portsmouth, Rhode Island, 143–64.

Wightman, E.M., 1985, *Gallia Belgica*, London.

Wild, J.P., 1974, 'Roman Settlement in the Lower Nene Valley', *Archaeol. Journ.* 131, 140–70.

Wild, R.A., 1981, *Water in the Cultic worship of Isis and Serapis*, Etudes Preliminaire aux religiones orientales dans l'empire Romain 87, Leiden.

Williams, A.M., 1908, 'The Stroud Roman Villa, Petersfield, Hants. Report on 1st Season's Excavation, 1907', *Archaeol. Journ.* 65, 33–52.

Williams, J.H., 1971a, 'Roman Building Materials in South-East England', *Britannia* 2, 166–95.

—— 1971b, 'Roman Building Materials in the South-West'. *Trans. Bristol and Glos. Archaeol. Soc.* 90, 95–119.

Williams, T.D., in preparation, *The Development of Roman London East of the Walbrook*, CBA, Res. Rep., Archaeol.of Roman London 4. London.

Wilson, D.R., 1970, 'Roman Britain in 1969: I Sites Explored', *Britannia* 1, 269–305.

—— 1972, 'Roman Britain in 1971: I Sites Explored', *Britannia* 3, 299–351.

—— 1984, 'The Plan of Viroconium Cornoviorum', *Antiquity* 58, 117–20.

Wilson, R.J.A., 1983, *Piazza Armerina*, London.

Winbolt, S.E., 1925, *Roman Folkestone*, London.

—— 1932, 'Roman Villa at Southwick', *Sussex Archaeol. Collections* 73, 12–32.

Wiseman, J., 1973, *Stobi: A Guide to the Antiquities*, Belgrade.

Witts, P., 1994, 'Interpreting the Brading "Abraxas" Mosaic', *Britannia* 25, 111–18.

—— 2000, 'Mosaics and Room Function: The Evidence from Some Fourth-century Romano-British Villas', *Britannia* 31, 291–324.

Woodward, A.M., 1935, 'The Roman Villa at Rudston (E. Yorks). Interim Excavation Report', *Yorkshire Archaeol. Journ.* 31, 365–76.

Woodward, P.J., Davies, S.M. and Graham, A.H., 1993, *Excavations at the Old Methodist Chapel and Greyhound Yard. Dorchester, 1981–1984*, Dorset Nat. Hist. and Archaeol. Soc. Monograph Ser. 12.

Woolf, A., 1998, 'Romancing the Celts. A Segmentary Approach to Acculturation', in R. Laurence and J. Berry (eds), *Cultural Identity in the Roman Empire*, London and New York, 111–24.

Woolf, G., 1995, 'Romans as Civilizers. The Ideological Pre-conditions of Romanization', in J. Metzler, M. Millett, N. Roymans and J. Slofstra (eds), *Integration in the Early Roman West. The Role of Culture and Ideology*, Luxembourg, 9–18.

—— 1998, *Becoming Roman: The Origins of Provincial Civilization in Gaul*, Cambridge.

Yegul, F., 1995, *Baths and Bathing in Classical Antiquity*, New York.

Yule, B., 1989, 'Excavations at Winchester Palace, Southwark', *London Archaeol.* 6.2, 31–9.

Zanker, P., 1979, 'Die Villa als Vorbild des spaten pompejanischen Wohengeschmacks', *Jahrbuch des deutschen archaeologischen Instituts* 94, 460–523.

Zant, J.M., 1993, *The Brooks, Winchester, 1987–88. The Roman Structural Remains*, Winchester Museums Service Archaeol. Rep. 2, Winchester.

Zienkiewicz, J.D., 1993, 'Excavations in the *Scamnum Tribunorium* at Caerleon: The Legionary Museum Site 1983–5', *Britannia* 24, 27–140.

INDEX OF SITES

GENERAL INDEX

Lightning Source UK Ltd.
Milton Keynes UK
09 July 2010

156735UK00001B/32/P

9 780415 488785